ON-THE-JOB
LEARNING IN THE
SOFTWARE INDUSTRY

ON-THE-JOB LEARNING IN THE SOFTWARE INDUSTRY

Corporate Culture and the Acquisition of Knowledge

Marc Sacks

QUORUM BOOKS
Westport, Connecticut • London

Library of Congress Cataloging-in-Publication Data

Sacks, Marc.
    On-the-job learning in the software industry : corporate culture
and the acquisition of knowledge / Marc Sacks.
        p.   cm.
    Includes bibliographical references and index.
    ISBN 0–89930–865–1 (alk. paper)
    1. Computer software industry—Employees—Training of—United
States. 2. Learning. 3. Cognitive styles—United States.
I. Title.
HD5716.C65222U67   1994
005.3′068′3—dc20   93–37026

British Library Cataloguing in Publication Data is available.

Library of Congress Catalog Card Number: 93–37026
ISBN: 0–89930–865–1

First published in 1994

Quorum Books, 88 Post Road West, Westport, CT 06881
An imprint of Greenwood Publishing Group, Inc.

Printed in the United States of America

The paper used in this book complies with the
Permanent Paper Standard issued by the National
Information Standards Organization (Z39.48–1984).

10 9 8 7 6 5 4 3 2 1

Contents

Acknowledgments

I wish to thank Professors Tim Weaver, Gaylen Kelley, and George Psathas of Boston University for their comments and insights, and for their general encouragement and support throughout this project, both in developing the ideas as a dissertation and encouraging me to publish. Professors Alan Gaynor and Mary Shann were also helpful as sounding boards during the early stages. I also owe Professor Ronald Ray Schmeck of Southern Illinois University a debt of thanks for furnishing me with several of his papers.

In addition, I must thank all my study participants for their time and interest, and those at "Cellsoft" who gave me permission to conduct the study.

I also extend thanks to others who showed interest, gave support, suggested references, read and commented on early drafts, or just listened and nodded approvingly. These include, but are not limited to, Robin Bergman, Dave Glass, Mary Hébert, Judith Hurwitz, Judith Katz, Paul Krugman, Judith Lebow, Craig Murphy, Andrew Oram, Mark Rosenthal, David C. Smith, Tom Smith, Dean Solomon, Richard Stallman, Jan Stetson, JoAnne Yates, and Roy Zito-Wolf.

Finally, and most important, to my wife, Naomi, more thanks than words can express for standing by me through the years of research and writing; to her, and to Deborah, Daniel, and Susanna, this work is lovingly dedicated.

1

Background

This book is an analysis of the skills that workers in one field, namely, programmers and other professionals in the computer-software industry, have used to learn the systems on which they work. These people spend their working hours analyzing, designing, enhancing, correcting, testing, and maintaining software systems. How do they know what they are working on? How do they know the effect that a change in one part of a complex system will have on another part? How do they know where to go for help? How much is their learning specific to the field (available, perhaps, by specialized academic training or through initiation into an informal guild), and how much is really the same sort of activity by which they learned how to drive in traffic (as opposed to learning how to drive)?

Another interesting question is that of individual differences in learning versus situational differences. Learning theorists have spent decades developing models of "cognitive style" or "learning style." Based on laboratory models or classroom behavior, these theories have tried to identify individual differences in learners, consistencies within people that they carry from place to place, from one learning situation to another, like a pillow that makes them comfortable at the opera, the beach, or the bus stop. (We shall examine and attempt to apply some of these models in chapter 10.) Researchers have paid much less attention to situational consistencies. How similar do people become just by virtue of doing the same thing in the same place at the same time for the same boss? Perhaps the pillows people carry with them mold so well to their surroundings as to be irrelevant. Maybe what is important in learners is their ability to adapt, rather than a set of fixed traits (learning style, then, rather like skin color or left- or right-handedness, is nothing to be prejudiced about, but it doesn't tell us anything useful, either). As with most false dichotomies, the answer, of course, is somewhere in between. I do not pretend to say exactly where, but in this work I present some real people doing what they do and describing what they do. I make no case for one theory or the other except as these people understand their own work in their own lives.

The material for this book comes mainly from interviews conducted at a small company that produces software for the cellular communications industry. I spoke with sixteen employees at that company, as well as twelve employed elsewhere, in an effort to draw on the knowledge of computer professionals in a variety of roles in the software industry. In these interviews I sought answers to the following questions:

- What are the techniques programmers use in learning systems? Are these techniques employed systematically or randomly? How wide a range of activities do individuals engage in when they are learning systems on the job?
- Are some techniques more useful than others? If so, are those techniques more commonly employed? Does usefulness vary with the individual?
- What are the variables that determine which techniques are used, in what order, and in what organizations?
- Is there any relation between learning style and organizational culture?
- Is there any relation between learning style and workplace design?

The study was based on a number of assumptions, some of which were borne out by the research while others were not (see chapter 11). These were:

- *People differ in how they learn.* This should be beyond dispute. Any teacher knows that students have different levels of ability, and learning-style and cognitive-style research has focused on specific kinds of attributes contributing to learning (for example, field dependence versus field independence) and specific strategies different students use in learning.
- *People who study for and pursue careers in the same profession can be expected to have similar learning styles.* Any professional field (such as law, medicine, or engineering) embodies particular types of knowledge and particular ways that knowledge is applied. Each field requires its members to acquire a range of skills and information about a number of topics. Since people differ in their aptitudes and interests, individuals are likely to be drawn to fields whose requirements are congenial to them; for example, someone with poor spatial relations is unlikely to become a sculptor. Cognitive style is an important aspect of personality and can be expected to have a significant impact on a student's intellectual tastes, and these in turn should have a great deal to do with his or her choice of profession.

- *Learning style is a significant factor in how well people learn.* There are differences in achievement that have been linked to learning style. Learning styles well suited to one type of learning may be less helpful or even harmful to other types. There may also be a connection between learning style and intelligence: People below a certain level of intelligence or maturity may be unlikely to develop some learning styles or to use particular learning strategies.
- *There is more than one way to learn systems.* Though theorists like to speak of a "top-down" approach to designing systems, the new programmer's job is really to synthesize extant materials, so he or she must work essentially from the bottom up. The balance between details and overview may be different for each individual, but some balance is essential in order to understand systems accurately. This parallels the distinction that learning-style theorists make between serialistic and holistic learning (Entwistle, 1983, pp. 89-92) and between abstract and concrete (Kolb, 1984).
- *Organizational cultures lead people to behave and interact in certain ways, which can be either helpful or harmful to learning and to job satisfaction.* For example, an organizational culture strongly rooted in individualism may discourage people from helping one another or may produce redundant learning. In general, organizations do not view themselves primarily as learning environments, so the effects on employees' learning are likely to be inadvertent and therefore difficult to control.

THE IMPORTANCE OF ON-THE-JOB LEARNING

All organizations need to train people quickly in specific tasks. Most of the literature on on-the-job learning focuses on the process of orienting new employees to the organization or on training them in specific job-related skills. The emphasis in this literature is on the role of the supervisor or trainer, not on the experiences of the newcomers themselves. The kinds of materials managers and personnel administrators read on the subject (and my experience has been that most managers read nothing at all about it) pay little attention to learning style or to the psychology or the experience of learning. David Kolb (1984) referred to the workplace itself as a learning environment. Certainly, for professionals in high-technology fields such as computer programming, learning is a process that continues throughout their careers, and although much has been written about techniques of formal training, surprisingly little has been written about how people actually learn their jobs.

An analysis of the jobs of professionals in computers or in the information-systems industry (that is, computers applied to business settings) would include a number of simpler skills such as programming, analysis, and system design. Programmers do receive training in these skills in academic courses, in in-house classes given by their employers, or at corporate training centers belonging to manufacturers of the products they use. However, the courses they take in such settings inculcate the skills in isolation from real problems. For example, students learn programming languages by using them to solve small problems in computation, file handling, or report writing. In courses on programming techniques such as structured programming, students learn to break a large task into smaller subsystems and these into still smaller subsystems, until one reaches the module, or smallest programmable unit, with a clearly defined input and output. The assigned task is unanalyzed at the beginning; it is the student's job to break it down into manageable pieces. Systems analysis and design is a more sophisticated version of essentially the same techniques, applied to systems too large to be encompassed in a single program. The systems approach is widely used in understanding all kinds of social and political systems as well as business or computer systems (Weinberg, 1975).

On the other end of the systems hierarchy from program modules, just as programming classes start with programs isolated from whole systems, systems analysis begins with systems that have never been analyzed before. However, neither of these conditions characterizes the environment of a computer programmer or other software professional (for example, a technical writer, quality-assurance engineer, or trainer) learning a new job or task. Most of any programmer's work, and generally all the work of people new to their jobs, does not involve designing systems or programs, but rather understanding, enhancing, or fixing those that already exist. Further, just as most cities are not designed and laid out by planners, many of what pass for systems in the world of information processing simply grow haphazardly, as they expand, change in ways not predicted at the outset, or respond to conditions that did not exist at their creation. Rather than start over, most managers and developers simply add layer upon layer to the original software, so that its original purpose or structure is often hard to determine. It is common to find thousands of lines of useless code in an operating system, code that has ceased to perform any useful purpose but that no one dares to delete. Further, many such systems are documented poorly or not at all. Programmers are often under pressure simply to have their programs working by a deadline, leaving them with insufficient time to explain their procedures or the purpose of what they have written. Also, computer professionals move a great deal, whether from one employer to another or merely from one project to another, and even if they are around to explain work they did in the past, they may no longer remember what their old code meant or why they wrote it. Given all these factors, new members of a project team may have no idea where to begin in order to understand the context of their work; and if they simply work on their own pieces of the puzzle without understanding the structure of the whole, they will inevitably generate problems in other parts of the system.

Another difficulty with learning a system relates to the way people who work with computers learn their trade. Since the first digital computers were developed in the 1940s and 1950s, computer workers have been in such demand that employers have not been able to insist on any sort of formal qualifications, such as those required for doctors and lawyers. Experience is considered an acceptable substitute for education in the field. Stories abound of high-school students developing software in their basements and of college dropouts starting multimillion-dollar companies. On a more mundane level, the computer field has provided job opportunities for many who have worked their way up from entry-level clerical or administrative jobs.

Programmers, then, come from many backgrounds: computer science and engineering, undergraduate business programs, liberal arts, community colleges, and no college at all. Philip Kraft (1977) postulated a hierarchy of schools that provide training in computers and has claimed that career advancement is largely based on this hierarchy, itself largely based on class and racial divisions; however, in attempting to provide a class-based analysis of the computer-software profession, Kraft underestimated the dynamism of the industry. He attempted to describe workers in the computer industry with language that Harry Braverman (1974) applied more successfully to the working class. (Kraft's model is discussed in more detail in chapter 2.) In fact, the computer and information-systems industries reward hard work, long hours, innovation, and creativity more than do older, more established industries.

Because computer professionals come from so many different backgrounds, project managers cannot be certain, to the extent that professionals in other fields can, that all the people working on a project share a terminology, a discipline, and a way of approaching problems. People have learned their skills in many ways. Some people simply learned by following mentors, who may themselves have had no formal training. Others learned through classes in school, by spending time at the computer center at their college without taking any courses, or by themselves from studying manuals or by talking with friends. Some people simply learn on the job. Because of this variety, it is questionable whether computer programming is a paradigm-based profession like engineering or one that, like social work, has yet to define itself completely as a profession. (For more information on the definition of professions, see Kraft, 1977; Joffe, 1977; and Kolb and Wolfe, 1981.)

However, few managers whom I have known show a recognition of individual differences and the ways that those differences can affect people's abilities to master their jobs. Most people assume that others think, learn, and work the way they themselves do and see others' differences as deficiencies; this assumption can become embedded in an organizational or professional culture. For example, though few managers will ever articulate this, organizations differ on how acceptable it is for someone to ask questions and to draw on other people for advice or for emotional support. In this context, a knowledge of learning styles and of individual differences can be valuable in building understanding within a group and in orienting new members and teaching them their jobs. The theory of styles is especially valuable in its insistence that anything defined as a style be value-free: that is, any manner of learning has both strengths and weaknesses and can be adaptive or maladaptive in particular settings. As Kolb (1984), following Jung, has stressed that it is important for people to develop nondominant aspects of themselves, so should those whose task includes training and developing others be sensitive to the variety of ways in which people learn and work, and recognize that there are many ways to produce skilled, productive, and satisfied employees and team members.

THE SETTING

This book focuses on a single company (which I have given the name "Cellsoft"), the industry in which it functions, and the people who create the software. In order to explain what Cellsoft is and the world in which it operates, I begin with a discussion of the cellular telephone industry and then describe the company and how its software workers are organized.

The Industry

The cellular telephone industry is one of the most dynamic segments of the world economy. In less than a decade, it has averaged annual growth of over 60 percent, prompting the authors of one financial report on the industry to call cellular "the most important event in the telephone industry in 100 years" (Leibowitz, Gross, and Buck, 1991, p. 29). As such, it was a natural candidate for entrepreneurs looking for clients for a new software business.

According to a document prepared for people attending an industry conference in 1991 (Cook and Roach), the earliest form of mobile communications was the two-way radio, first used by the Detroit police department in 1921. The first commercial mobile telephone dialing system was developed in 1948 but was not used until 1963. The early systems had a very limited calling range. The Improved Mobile Telephone System (IMTS), developed in 1969, had a radius of twenty to twenty-five miles, operated at 250 watts of power, and had only twelve available channels. If a caller left the transmission area, the call would be disconnected, and if all twelve channels were in use, no call could go through; the caller would hear a busy signal. Because of these limitations, mobile phones were not generally useful.

It was the transformation from mere mobile communication to *cellular* communication that made expansion of the industry possible. In a cellular communication network, a geographical area is divided into small, overlapping *cells*, each just a few miles across. As a caller moves from one cell to another, the system hands off calls between them, so that the range of communication is expanded and so that callers do not lose their connections when they pass from one cell to another. At the center of each cell is the *cell site*, containing the radio receiver and transmitter; the cell sites are linked by a mobile telephone switching office, or MTSO. Under this system there can be a maximum of forty-five channels instead of just twelve, and carriers have the ability to split cells into smaller areas should the channels be frequently saturated. This flexibility makes it possible for a carrier to expand the subscriber base. A further development, the IS-41 switching standard, allows handoff of calls between carriers as well as between adjoining cell sites belonging to the same carrier.

As technology improved, the industry expanded. In 1968 the Federal Communications Commission designated the 800-megahertz frequency range for all land-based mobile telephones in the United States. In 1974 the FCC began regulating the new industry, restricting its operations to subsidiaries of the wireline carriers—that is, of the preexisting telephone companies. In 1975 it allowed nonwireline companies to enter the market. In 1977 the first two experimental cellular systems were launched, one by Illinois Bell in Chicago and the other by American Radio Telephone Service in the Baltimore/Washington area. In 1980 the FCC proposed a scheme, still in effect in the industry, in which each area would have two competing cellular carriers: One would would be the local telephone company (the wireline or *A-band* carrier), the other any other company (the nonwireline or *B-band* carrier).

Once the system started, growth was dramatic. By the end of 1988 there were 2.2 million cellular subscribers in the United States and 1.2 million in Europe, where the first cellular system had been installed in Sweden in 1981 (Ross, 1989). The industry has grown to such a degree that according to Malcolm Ross, an analyst at Arthur D. Little, between one-sixth and one-third of all telecommunications infrastructure installed today is used to support mobile phones. Ross predicted (p. 2-4) that "when the price of a cellular phone does come down to that of a VCR (predicted for 1992), market penetration will occur at roughly the same rate as the VCR, or 50% penetration in the first eight years. Market penetration at this rate implies that about 20 million personal communications terminals will be sold in the first five years after introduction in the United States, and 25 million in Europe."

Ross continued:

In the first four years in the United States [1984-1988], sales of cellular telephones grew faster in dollars than sales of VCRs, color video cameras, and projection televisions—three fast-take-off consumer products—in a comparable period. Impressively, cellular is already behaving like a consumer product, although it is still too expensive for most consumers.

It was within this industry that the founders of Cellsoft believed—accurately—that they could find an important market niche.

The Company

Cellsoft was started late in 1986 by two graduates of MIT (one with a bachelor's degree in electrical engineering, the other with a doctorate in business) who had been working together for several years at another company, designing manufacturing software. When that company started to fail, they founded Cellsoft, seeing a new business opportunity in the growing cellular communications industry. They recruited four other employees within the first two months and began developing software, setting up their office in a garage lent to them by a cellular telephone company that was to be their first customer.

This particular industry was exciting to them because it was new—the FCC had awarded the first cellular license in 1984—and because it was rich. Cellular companies had been spending millions of dollars on switches and other equipment, and the founders of Cellsoft reasoned that these companies would also be willing to invest large amounts of money in management-information systems (MIS). Unlike manufacturing systems, where the market was already saturated with software vendors and where the clients, many of them financially constrained, had little money to invest in software development, the cellular industry had the capital needed to create new systems.

It also badly needed these systems. The first cellular carriers were originally cable television franchises, whose MIS requirements were quite small and whose systems could be run from a personal computer. With the rise of cellular telephone systems, whose subscriber base has been growing astronomically since the start of the industry (Leibowitz, Gross, and Buck, 1991; Ross, 1989), there would clearly be a need for much larger and more sophisticated customer-tracking and billing systems.

The founders of Cellsoft recognized two aspects of this business that motivated the nature and pace of their development efforts. First of all, while there are thousands of manufacturing companies, there were and would always be only a limited number of cellular carriers, so there would be only a finite number of sales of the new product. Second, time to market was critical; the new company was not the only one interested in this exciting new industry, and only someone who brought out a new product quickly would have much chance of success. With this in mind, the fledgling company was able to release its initial product to its first customer (the one that had lent it garage space) by October 1985. Once Cellsoft created the initial customer-tracking system, it gradually added billing, rating, and user-verification functionality.

The company grew rapidly. By 1988 Cellsoft employed roughly 60 people; by 1990, at the conclusion of the research for this study, there were about 125. By early 1991, when Cellsoft was acquired by another company, it had well over 200 employees.

Once the company was out of the garage, it rented space on the first floor of a small office building, space that it quickly outgrew. Programmers and others worked in small cubicles in narrow rows. Some weren't even this lucky: For a time, some people had desks in the reception area or in the hall of the office building. The company expanded its space twice in 1989, first taking over space on the third floor of the same building and then expanding into the space adjoining the original first-floor office. Other areas in the building housed the computers and data-communications equipment.

By the beginning of 1988 the company had split into two major functional areas. One group, which was to become known as the Information Systems (IS) department, continued the original work of customer tracking, billing, and rating, while the other, Intercarrier Settlement Services (ISS), concentrated on user verification, networking, and the settlement of roaming charges between cellular carriers. (A third area of the company, involved in automated credit-decision software, became an independent entity in 1989.)

By late 1988 ISS generated approximately two-thirds of the company's business. At that time IS included a dozen or so people, of whom six were programmers and half (some of them the same people) were managers of one sort or another, as the group braced for rapid growth. At the beginning of 1990 IS moved out of the company's main office to the smaller one on the third floor. Where previously programmers had worked in small cubicles, now they were seated at desks in small offices, with two managers sharing an office, six programmers in a large central office (formerly a conference room), and three support people in a smaller room next to the programmers' office. This arrangement led to feelings that IS was isolated from the main work of the company and was not recognized and respected by upper management. The fact that this organization was still growing, had few customers, and for some time was not profitable also contributed to this feeling.

Within the group, however, a certain solidarity began to form. There was a great deal of interaction among the programmers sharing a common area. For a while there were two Mandarin-speaking Chinese programmers in the same area, with one, both more senior in the organization and more acculturated to America than the other, serving as mentor (and later as formal supervisor as well). Although the staff complained of lack of privacy due to the lack of cubicle walls, the amount of conversation about business and other subjects declined when partitions were introduced after several months.

The walls within the overall area served as informal barriers. People would confer easily with those in the same room, but crossing between rooms was limited to deliberate, though not necessarily formal, occasions. A programmer might enter a manager's office to ask a question or to discuss problems, and the office doors were almost always open, but in practice people did not go where they did not have reason to be. Because I was hired to be quality-assurance manager, I worked in a two-person office, and while I appreciated the relative privacy, I lost the ease of access to the programmers: I could certainly enter their room and speak with them, but it became very difficult to spend time casually observing what was going on unless I had other business there.

In January 1990, in response to still-uncontained expansion (within a year the company had grown in size to over 100 employees), the entire company was moved to a larger space in a much bigger building. In this building there were very few offices (reserved for directors, sales and marketing, and upper management), and all staff people and first-line managers were assigned to small cubicles, perhaps slightly larger than the space where programmers were working when I started with the company in late 1988. In this setting the cubicles were arranged in corridors, with five-foot-high partitions separating the cubicles but only four-foot partitions between the work spaces and the corridors. Thus all employees were visible and accessible to anyone passing by. Because all corridors provided through access (that is, there were no dead ends), the effect of this was virtually to eliminate any sense of enclosure or privacy, and the whole organization became relatively porous.

For IS programmers who had worked in a small but unpartitioned office, this environment was a shock. Dubbed "the bull pen" by one employee, the new work space, in long, even rows, with the partitions decorated in a dark blue often described as "drab" or "funereal," afforded little sense of privacy or comfort. The short walls separating cubicles from corridors gave employees a constant sense of being watched and in fact provided management with opportunities for seeing at any moment what the staff was up to. At the same time, the lack of doors or concealing walls gave employees a feeling of informality. Unlike the situation where entering someone's office seemed to require a reason, in the new environment people approached each other constantly with questions, requests, or simply a desire for conversation. Also, informal meetings tended to spring up in corridors, as people passing by would be drawn into conversations. While this sort of workplace design was clearly advantageous for fostering communication between employees, and in some ways for strengthening informal contacts, it also had the effect of making it more difficult for people to concentrate on their own work.

Early in 1991, after acquisition, further expansion led Cellsoft to take over additional office space adjacent to what it was already using. This space was also partitioned into cubicles but was designed differently in two important respects. First, the walls were higher: partitions were six feet high on all sides. Second, most paths between rows of cubicles were dead ends, so no one would pass through a row without having business there. (Other aspects of the design of this area were that the cubicles were smaller but better equipped with shelving and file space, and that the rows were narrower.)

Again, there were advantages and disadvantages to the new arrangement. What the staff moved to the new space gained in privacy from the higher walls and the relative lack of disturbance, they lost in greater isolation and a smaller, more cramped work space. At one time employees had been asked for suggestions on a redesigned work area, but few if any of them were ever implemented. The company was motivated more by cost than by anything else in designing the new work area.

CELLSOFT AS A LEARNING ENVIRONMENT

Before discussing how workers at Cellsoft use resources to learn the systems they work on, it is necessary to consider the layout of those resources, including people (already discussed), documentation, computer hardware, and training materials.

Documentation

Documentation falls into two categories: manuals dealing with the software that programmers need to use on the job (for example, the Digital Equipment Corporation's manuals for VMS operating-system commands, programming languages, and database utilities) and reference materials describing and explaining how to use Cellsoft's products, such as the customer-information and billing systems. Programmers at Cellsoft did not use documentation extensively for a number of reasons.

First of all, system software reference manuals were never plentiful. There were typically one or two copies of Digital's reference manuals for the entire company. There were periodic attempts to order more materials, but until mid-1991 there was no central library space, and the few attempts made to keep track of materials were not well maintained. As a result, manuals often, to use the programmers' words, "grew legs" or "walked," ending up in one or another person's cubicle. This was the case even when the manuals were the personal property of individuals; electronic mail messages would often appear throughout the system, asking people to return borrowed materials. The greatest problem with this was the sheer inconvenience of searching potentially every cubicle in the company until one could find the proper manual. On occasion the company would order a complete new set of manuals from Digital, but many of these would be gone from the shelves within a few weeks. The result of this difficulty in obtaining software manuals was that programmers at Cellsoft tended to use them as little as possible.

They also tended to avoid using Cellsoft's own product documentation for these and other reasons. Due to the expense of printing manuals, the company made very few sets, primarily for sale to customers. Programmers seeking to learn the system from its own reference manuals would have a hard time finding them. Also, the manuals were often inaccurate, and there were no technical descriptions of the system, only functional descriptions primarily useful to managers and operators of the software but only minimally helpful to those developing or maintaining it.

Computer Hardware

Unlike manuals, a computer terminal is on each programmer's desk. This has always been programmers' primary resource for learning, as it is readily available (see chapter 8). The computers themselves are kept in locked rooms and are usually inaccessible to programmers. They are also not needed, as the programmers' work requires little or no direct contact with the machine. The terminal as a learning resource gives programmers access to the following resources:

- The commands of the operating system, programming languages, and utilities; that is, the actual software with which the programmers work
- *On-line help,* instructions for every command
- *Computer-based training* on a variety of topics, purchased by the training department and available to any employee who requests it
- *Electronic mail,* used as a way of broadcasting questions to a large number of people in the company

Having all this material at their fingertips through the terminal keyboard, the programmers at Cellsoft use their terminals extensively as their main learning resource, rather than undertake a difficult and often fruitless search for printed documentation (which, in the case of Cellsoft's product manuals, was often inaccurate anyway).

METHOD

I was hired as quality-assurance manager into the Information Systems group at Cellsoft in November 1988. This study grew out of my initial interview for that job. At that interview I met with the vice president of IS and also with one of the founders of the company. They explained the rapid growth of both the cellular industry and the company and mentioned in passing that they had recently hired several programmers and were planning to hire many more in the near future.

I had originally intended to study the learning styles of engineers, because I had been employed at a company specializing in mechanical-engineering design software. However, the impending failure of that company had led me to look for work elsewhere. At my job interview I described the research in learning styles that I had done up to that time, and one of the people interviewing me suggested that I apply it to programmers. He indicated that it would be important to bring large numbers of new employees up to speed in a fairly short time and thought that a study of the learning styles of programmers could contribute to this effort (little realizing that it would take over two years to complete).

My own background had prepared me for a study of this nature. By 1988 I had been working in the computer industry for more than twelve years as business programmer, trainer in systems programming, and technical writer. I was therefore well acquainted with the work of programmers, the language they used in discussing both the organizational and the technical aspects of their work, and the corporate structures in which the work took place. I would therefore not suffer the difficulties of many participant-observers in coming to understand the language of my informants.

The problem of how involved a participant-observer can be in the environment he or she studies, and how much a stranger to a world can understand the work that members do in constructing and maintaining that world, is a familiar one in anthropology and in ethnographic inquiry generally. Robert Emerson (1983, p. 105) briefly described the problem when he cited Egon Bittner's insistence

> that the ethnographer can never completely adopt the actor's perspective and attitude, but can only approximate it. In part this results from the limitation that the ethnographer's experience can never exactly duplicate that of a member. In some cases, for example, the member has grown up in that culture, whereas the fieldworker comes upon that culture as a "second culture" apprehended in light of his or her first culture.

In my case this problem was easily solved. As a computer professional, I was no stranger to the language of my co-worker informants. The culture of the programmers had been my own for many years. Along with that familiarity, however, I brought to the work my training in educational research and the sociological perspective that comes with an original strangeness to the field. That is, my early life and interests and my academic background had prepared me for a career as a musician or as a medievalist; I had no inclination to enter the business world or to learn about computers until I actually needed to find a job in the "real world." Therefore, the language of programmers was originally a foreign one for me, and when I learned it I was always conscious of it in this way. Although I am now fluent in the technical jargon of the trade, I have managed to preserve this sense of the strangeness of it all and the feeling common to anthropologists of being a "marginal native," never quite at home in the culture even though it is my own. I hope that this perspective has enabled me to keep my distance despite my participation in the study as an employee as well as a researcher.

Also, as an employee of the company I was to study, I could surmount the problem of dealing with a "gatekeeper": having the department vice president for a boss meant that I only needed his permission, which was granted provided the work did not interfere with my official duties or unduly take up others' time. I also hoped to have little difficulty gaining the confidence of my co-workers. Early on in the research I explained to them my dual role as employee and researcher, and in fact most of them have always been very cooperative with me in both of these capacities.

In spite of this, there were difficulties with the process. It was often hard to arrange meeting times because everyone, including me, had a heavy work load. I had to take advantage of any chance to observe, talk, or ask questions. As Buchanan, Boddy, and McCalman (1988, pp. 53-54) pointed out, organizational research is an opportunistic activity:

> Fieldwork is permeated with the conflict between what is theoretically desirable on the one hand and what is practically possible on the other. It is desirable to ensure representativeness in the sample, uniformity of interview procedures, adequate data collection across the range of topics to be explored, and so on. But the members of organizations block access to information, constrain the time allowed for interviews, lose your questionnaires, go on holiday, and join other organizations in the middle of your unfinished study. In the conflict between the desirable and the possible, the possible always wins. So whatever carefully constructed views the researcher has of the nature of social science research, of the process of theory development, of data collection methods, or of the status of different types of data, those views are constantly compromised by the practical realities, opportunities and constraints presented by organizational research.

It is also necessary to consider problems that can arise from studying one's organization. Bogdan and Biklen (1982, p. 85) stated that "people who are intimately involved in a setting find it difficult to distance themselves both from personal concerns and from their common-sense understandings of what is going on. For them, more often than not, their opinions are more than 'definitions of the situation'; they are *the* truth."

Bogdan and Biklen also raised the objection that "others in the setting in which you are doing your research, if they know you well, are not used to relating to you as a neutral observer. . . . They may not feel free to relate to you as a researcher to whom they can speak freely." This problem arises if the researcher and his subjects have worked together for a long time. This was not the case at Cellsoft, as none of us had worked there for more than a few months when my study began, and most had just begun working there within days or weeks when I first approached them for interviews.

The bulk of the data for the study came from thirty-three audiotaped interviews carried out between May 1989 and May 1990 and several others on which I took notes but that at the informants' request were not taped. Of these, thirty were transcribed during the second half of 1990. In addition to the tapes and transcripts, I had countless informal conversations with my co-workers at Cellsoft and also kept and studied written materials, such as program specifications, notes from courses programmers had taken, and copies of people's day-to-day notes.

My informants included twenty-eight people, of whom sixteen were Cellsoft employees, four were consultants hired by Cellsoft for one project, and eight were computer professionals employed elsewhere. The group not affiliated with Cellsoft was chosen as a potential contrast to the Cellsoft people, because they were involved with systems rather than applications programming, and most of them were graduates of MIT or other elite technical universities. The informants can be grouped as shown in Table 1.

Company	Job Category	# Men	# Women
Cellsoft	Client-services Representative	0	1
	QA Analyst	0	1
	Programmer	8	4
	Technical Writer	0	1
	Trainer	0	1
Consulting Firm	Programmer	3	1
Other	Instructor	1	0
	Programmer	5	2
Total		17	11

Table 1: Participants Categorized by Job Category and Sex

After transcribing as many tapes as time permitted, I analyzed the transcripts and drew coding categories from the material. Rather than base these categories on any preconceived theory, I drew them from topics the programmers themselves brought up repeatedly, creating what Goetz and LeCompte (1981, p. 59) have called a "mundane analytic system." This method of categorization derives loosely from Glaser and Strauss's ideas of grounded theory (Glaser and Strauss, 1967; Glaser, 1978; Charmaz, 1983). As in grounded theory, my work derived its insights from the data themselves and was refined as more interviews fleshed out a model or disconfirmed early hypotheses. However, I made no attempt to account for the totality of all experience involved in learning. In this work I can only take the data as far as they apply to a limited sample of computer professionals and must leave broader generalization to future research.

After my initial analysis of the interviews, I made extracts from the transcripts, one for each coding category; these varied in length from less than one page to over ninety. All of this was done manually; I used no formal statistical analyses, gauging the importance of categories by the size of the material that fell into them. The categories themselves could be arranged into larger ones, which form the basis for the arrangement of topics in Chapters 3 through 9.

In general, I took people at their word when they described how they learn and what is important to them. Everyone I interviewed was open and enthusiastic on the subject of learning; this is not an issue (such as, for example, drug use) that induces secrecy or deception. The worst problem with this topic is that many of my informants simply never thought about it, and it was necessary to flesh out their responses with probing questions or to assemble their thoughts into broader categories than they themselves were aware of.

OVERVIEW

In this book I explore the world of programmers as a corporate environment and as the setting for continual learning. Chapter 2 describes the work of programming, especially that of professional programmers in business, which is different in important respects from what is taught in academic programs in computer science and information systems. The results of the interviews, which form the nearest equivalent in this study to the tables that make up the bulk of statistical research, are presented in chapters 3 through 9.

One of the underlying beliefs informing qualitative methodology is that theory should flow from the data rather than providing a hypothesis for confirmation or disconfirmation. When one begins with a theoretical base, it is too easy to see it in one's surroundings even if it is not really there. For this reason, although I spent several months researching the literature on learning styles before beginning to interview programmers, during the interview period I read as little as possible and tried to keep this theoretical knowledge as far from the live subjects as I could, though it would creep into interviews from time to time. For the same reason I delay presenting the review of the literature until chapter 10. That chapter concentrates on three of the most important theories of learning style—field independence/dependence, depth of processing, and experiential learning—and attempts to relate them to the learning world of programmers.

The attempt, I believe, must meet with only limited success. There are two reasons for this. The first is that nearly all of these theories stem from populations of college students rather than of adult workers, and that extensions to adult populations may be inapplicable or at best limited. The one that has been used most extensively with adults, David Kolb's experiential-learning model, is also the one that describes on-the-job learning most accurately, and that proved the best fit with the interview data. The second reason is that all the theories are verified with measuring instruments of some sort, which ultimately provide no more than statistical demonstrations of their own validity, and at best can only touch a small part of the real activity of learning. For this reason I did not administer any sort of questionnaire or apply any statistical reasoning to my research; my interest was in capturing and understanding what people do, not in measuring any predefined subset of criteria one or two removes from actual learning and actual life.

Instead of applying a predetermined model, as many theorists do, I drew on the life and work experiences of my study participants. The model I derive in the final chapter, and in the summaries in chapters 3 through 8, is entirely a compendium of themes inherent in people's own understanding of what they do. In this respect I have followed (though unwittingly at times, rather like speaking prose all my life) the sociological method known as ethnomethodology, a method often used to analyze the mundane activities of everyday life. Although this method has on occasion (Garfinkel, 1986; Suchman, 1987) been applied to the workplace and even to computer programming (Button and Sharrock, 1994), I believe that this is the first full-scale study of the work of programmers to employ this approach.

Finally, in chapter 11 I review the data detailed in the preceding chapters in order to answer the questions and to validate or refute the expectations described earlier. I conclude with recommendations both for further research and for utilizing the findings of this book in enhancing learning in the workplace.

2

The Programmer's World

Before describing how programmers learn the systems they work on, it is necessary to discuss what programmers do and where they do it. In this chapter I describe the work of programmers and other professionals involved with computer software. Although roles and structures vary somewhat from one company to another, the basic functions of computer workers are fairly consistent in a variety of industries and organizations.

This chapter is directed at readers who may not be familiar with computers in any detail. As this book is a study of people, not of computers or of software, this discussion is no more technical than necessary to explain programmers' work and the machines that they use, and to introduce the roles that computer professionals play within their organizations. Here, then, I present only as much technical background as is needed to understand the discussion with the programmers themselves starting in chapter 3.

In order to understand what it means to learn a system, it is necessary to use the term as programmers use it. I shall describe the kinds of systems that programmers speak of. Also, programmers have long maintained a division between "systems" and "applications" programming, and this will be described as well, with a brief general discussion of types of applications. I shall also discuss the types of work necessary to build and to maintain computer systems, and the roles people play in computer organizations within companies.

WHAT IS A SYSTEM?

The *American Heritage Dictionary*'s (1969) first definition of system is "a group of interacting, interrelated, or interdependent elements forming or regarded as forming a collective entity." In this sense of the word, what are the elements of a computer system? The answer is not as easy as it seems at first.

We can view a computer system, first of all, as consisting of the machines that do the computing (the computer itself along with its peripheral devices, such as disks, tapes, and terminals, known collectively as *hardware*) and the coded instructions (programs, or *software*) that tell the hardware what to do. (There is also an intermediate layer, known as *firmware* or *microcode*, consisting of instructions that are built into the electronic circuitry of the machines.) However, other than the builders of the machines themselves, most people who think about "systems" are not working at this level. In fact, there is a hierarchy of entities approached by different levels of users, any of which can be thought of as a system.

The most basic of these entities is the hardware-(firmware-)software configuration just described. In general, there are two categories of people at opposite ends of the spectrum of technical knowledge who mean this when they refer to "the system." At one end are those, generally engineers or "systems programmers," who design, build, and package the machines themselves; their work will be described in more detail shortly. At the other are those who buy entire packaged machines (typically microcomputers such as the IBM PC or the Apple Macintosh), for whom "learning the system" means figuring out how to turn the computer on, connect the monitor and the printer, insert diskettes into a drive, use a spreadsheet or a word processor, and display or print the results. It is between these two levels that most computer professionals work and relate to their machines, and for most of these people the term system has a somewhat different connotation. The systems with which most computer workers are concerned are not physical but sociotechnical. The interrelated elements are not primarily hardware, software, and peripheral devices (though these are certainly important), but rather people, the activities they perform, other people for whom the activities are performed, and the means of carrying out the activities. Only the last of these is the computer as such, but the "system" must include all of them. As it happens, the language and the work of programmers situates them at an intermediate point between the developers of the machine and the people whose activities the machine is designed to aid and in some way to model. Although programmers and other people closely involved with computer systems often appear, and believe themselves, to view their systems as mechanical rather than as sociotechnical, in fact they cannot long forget the human and extratechnical dimensions of their work.

Growing outward from the basic functions of computer work (creating the machine, connecting the devices, and so on) is the hierarchy of activities that computer programs model. The most basic of these activities (in computer parlance, the "lowest-level" activities) are those that the computer itself performs. These in turn correspond to the most elementary operations of mathematics and logic (addition, multiplication, Boolean algebra) as these are mapped into the memory and logical structures of the computer hardware (what are known as its *architecture*). At this level, describing the addition of two numbers takes this form: "Take the numerical value, expressed as a group of ones and zeroes, or 'bits,' stored in one location in computer memory and copy it to an arithmetic register. Then take the numerical value stored in a second location and add it to the arithmetic register. Finally, move the contents of the arithmetic register to a third memory location." In the lowest-level programming language, called an *assembly language*, this addition operation might be written like this:

```
LOAD            1, LOC1
ADD             1, LOC2
STORE           1, LOC3
```

Languages of this sort are generally used to perform the most basic functions a computer needs to do. The most important of these is to keep track of the computer itself, to enable the people working with it to do their jobs. The program that does this tracking is called an *operating system*, and people who work at this level of computer operation are called *systems programmers*. The "system," to this group, is the programs that regulate the overall working of the computer.

Systems programmers are concerned with the machine itself, with its operation and maintenance. Their work involves such programs as the following:

- *Operating systems*, programs (such as Microsoft's MS-DOS for IBM and compatible personal computers, Digital's VMS, or Novell's Unix) that control the computer's operations; Functions of operating systems include process control and scheduling, memory management, and device management, among others.
- *Utilities*, such as text editors, sorters, compilers (programs that translate programming languages into machine-readable code), and linkers (programs that take compiler output and turn it into the actual data the computer loads into its memory and runs).
- *Device drivers*, which control the operation of peripheral devices such as disk drives, tape drives, and terminals.
- *File servers and database-management systems*, programs designed to store and retrieve data in the most efficient ways.

Systems programmers are the users of the most elementary structures of computers. The term *user* simply refers to anyone who uses other people's work on a computer. The creators at each level of the hierarchy are the users of the work of the lower levels and as such define the needs that the lower-level work addresses. For example, an operating-system programmer may be concerned with allocating enough memory in the computer's hardware and with scheduling its central processing unit so as to optimize the concurrent work of twenty-five programmers, ten managers, and sixty-two data-entry clerks, most of whom may be quite unaware of what is necessary to sustain this activity.

The needs of programmers at the next level of the computer hierarchy (I am referring here to closeness to the structure and functions of the actual machine, not to status in an organization) relate to questions like these: "How can I enter the text of the program into the machine? How can I read the data I have entered? How can I find out what programs are available?" Systems programmers translate these questions into issues such as compiler optimization, sorting algorithms, directory-tree structures, and database design principles; the users do not need to think at that level at all, any more than most people think about the structure of language when they are asking questions and listening to the answers.

One level above the systems programmers, the people asking the questions just described are answering another set of questions for *their* users: "What is the fastest way to get my company's paychecks processed every week? How can I see all the bills we paid yesterday? What happens if I alter one dimension in this drawing, keeping all others unchanged? How can I monitor a patient's heartbeat most accurately?" People whose programming answers questions of these types—closer to human and business needs, further from completely technological ones—are known as *applications programmers*, and the programs they write, designed to answer questions that are not really about the computer itself, are called *applications*. Typical applications in industry include medical monitoring systems, billing and payroll systems, and statistical packages such as SPSS, used by students and social scientists. The word has also passed into the personal computing realm to be practically a synonym for "program"; thus a word processor like Microsoft Word is considered an application.

Unlike assembly language, programming languages at this level (called *higher-level languages*) do not directly address machine architecture, but rather express formulations that application users, such as scientists or business programmers, would employ. For example, in FORTRAN, a language often used in mathematical and scientific applications, the addition described earlier in assembly language might be represented as

$$C = B + A,$$

while in the business language COBOL, a programmer might write

ADD OLD-BALANCE, NEW-CHARGES GIVING NEW-BALANCE.

Thus the hierarchy of system tasks proceeds outward from the computer itself (hardware and microcode architects) through systems programmers and applications programmers to the nonprogramming "end users," with those at each level being users of the work of (or posers of the questions answered by) those at the lower level.

At each level, the meaning of "system" is a bit different. For the end users, the system is the totality of their work. It could be the machine they use ("I bought a new system for my office at home") or the particular application they run, such as the patient-tracking system a hospital receptionist uses. For applications programmers, the system is one application, or a connected group of applications, such as a billing system, while for systems programmers, it is the hardware, microcode, and operating system of the computer. It is important to keep these different concepts of "system" in mind when discussing how programmers learn systems, for they are learning different things.

Beyond this, as stated earlier, computer systems are sociotechnical systems. That is, it is also possible to describe the users of the system as themselves part of it, for if they did not ask the questions, there would be no answers (that is, programs); and how they approach the machine must inevitably affect how it is programmed as well. If one asks a question in English and is answered in German, one may understand the answer well, vaguely, incorrectly, or not at all; and part of creating computer systems is knowing how to answer the questions so that the askers understand the responses. Whether this is posed as a training issue (teach German), a user-interface issue (speak English), or something in between (speak pidgin and provide a phrasebook), this is another question whose answer provides important understanding of what a "system" is for those who work with it.

WHAT PROGRAMMERS DO

The activities programmers engage in fall into three general areas. The first of these is analytical: analysis, design, and problem solving. The second is mechanical and technical: the physical acts of coding, running programs, and interacting with the computer and its associated devices. The third is interpersonal (though actual people may not be around for all of it). This aspect, which includes such activities as documenting one's work, helping customers or fellow workers, asking questions, attending meetings, and training users, may form a large part of a programmer's workday, but many programmers are barely conscious of this activity as an important facet of their work.

The analytical pieces of the programmer's job, primarily intellectual in nature, include the following activities:

- *Systems analysis*: the breakdown of a technical or business problem into component parts and translation of those components into the technical language and concepts of computers
- *System and program design*: the conception of a computer system whose purpose is the solution or automation of the analyzed problem
- *Technical problem solving*: addressing failures within functioning programs (an activity commonly called *debugging*) or identifying and overcoming limitations in the underlying computer hardware

and software when those limitations interfere with the
implementation of program design

These analytical activities form a hierarchy in which solving technical
problems is subordinate to systems design, and in which design must follow
from analysis. However, technical analysis and design feed back on one
another, because it is sometimes necessary to redesign a system in order to
overcome technical limitations. The highest level of analysis, however, really
addresses the answering of questions and as such is interpersonal in nature:
The feedback must be, if only at some remove, between analyst and user; the
analyst poses another layer of question to the designer, as the designer does to
the technical expert. (Of course, this distinction, like others to be discussed
later, is somewhat artificial, as these are often the same person.)

The technical aspects involve direct interaction with the computer. These
include the following:

- *Typing text into the computer through a terminal,* including
  editing programs and other text files
- *Querying the computer*: asking for information about files,
  programs, or the status of one or another aspect of the machine or
  the operating system
- *Testing*: running programs to validate their correctness
- *Learning*: using the computer as a learning tool; experimenting by
  running programs with different inputs; using the terminal in
  conjunction with a manual to learn how different commands and
  programs work
- *Playing*: trying things out for fun
- *Frittering, or "working at working"*: doing any number of
  activities to "set up" for work without contributing anything useful
  to the work itself (Nash, 1990)

These technologically oriented activities usually occur in conjunction with
more analytical tasks. Although the analysis and programming functions can
be separated and in some companies are performed by completely different
people, most computer workers like the combination of mind and machine
tasks. For many, the terminal serves as a reference, whether as an on-line
dictionary, a source of validation for insights, or a medium for communication
with other people through electronic mail. We shall look at examples of this
use of the computer in chapter 8.

Interpersonal activities programmers engage in include the following:

- *Documenting* the results of analyses in the form of memos and
  specifications, and documenting the flow of program code within
  the programs

- *Conversing* with peers, users, and managers about the work (talk as an educational activity) and about life in general (work as a social activity)
- *Training*, both as students and as teachers, either formally or informally
- *Presenting* the results of their work at formal meetings with fellow workers or with customers
- *Demonstrating* problems or successful programs

These social activities consume a large part of programmers' time and play an important role in determining job satisfaction, contradicting the myth that programming is largely a solitary activity and that most programmers spend the bulk of their time working in isolation (Weinberg, 1971).

COMPUTER JOBS AND THE COMPUTING WORLD

The activities of programmers form a part of what Kling and Gerson (1977) have referred to as the "computing world." These authors described the social world of activities revolving around computers and the ways that people who work with computers appear in work organizations that are not oriented toward computing. According to Kling and Gerson (1977, p. 133), "There are fourteen major orientations that people or groups may adopt within the computing world," identified as follows:

- *Technology stimulators*, or funders of basic research and technology development
- *Innovators*, the creators of new technologies
- *Diffusers*, adapters of the technologies for use by others
- *Vendors*, those who produce and market computer hardware and software
- *Service providers*, who provide computer time or specific computerized services such as billing
- *Educators*, who train others in computers and their use
- *Systems architects*, who design or create general-purpose hardware or software (the systems programmers and hardware engineers described earlier)
- *Applications architects*, who design or create programs built upon more general ones for more specific purposes (applications programmers, as described earlier)
- *Users*, a term that Kling and Gerson used differently from my definition above, and that I shall discuss later
- *Feeders*, who enter data into computers
- *Tenders*, who operate computer equipment

- *Sustainers*, who maintain the equipment
- *Hobbyists*, who use computers for fun
- *Consumers*, who use computer outputs but do not use the computers themselves

Kling and Gerson's computing-world model is far larger than merely that of programmers described earlier, but there is some overlap. Most programmers fall into Kling and Gerson's categories of "systems architects" and "applications architects," with classification varying by how specific the application is defined to be.

Kling and Gerson (1977, p. 133) defined users in a somewhat unusual way as

> people (or groups) who specify the way data should be manipulated so that it can be used in other work settings in which computer support is largely a means to some other ends. Since a computer system can be viewed as a hierarchy of data-manipulation schemes, we also add the condition that a "user" specifies his manipulation, in large part, using labels meaningful to other people who use that computer system purely as an instrument for other work.

This broad definition of users, which really encompasses the category of systems analysts, is a somewhat curious one. It is the last part of the definition, "people who use [a] computer system purely as an instrument for other work," that most people who speak of users really mean. More accurately, although people at each degree of distance from the central computer system are users of all products closer to it, it is not at all the case that most of them define the "labels" by which they may reference those products. It is a common source of tension for users and developers "not to be speaking the same language," and the common language, or *user interface*, between the two, must be carefully defined, either in direct collaboration with users or with a great deal of understanding on the part of developers.

It is also worth noting that Kling and Gerson's schema, broad as it is, leaves out a number of functions within the computing world. The following are only four of these:

- *Documenters*, who write reference materials for computer users
- *Implementers*, who install computer systems for clients
- *Supporters*, who help users solve problems;
- *Testers*, who make sure programs work as specified before releasing them to clients

It is necessary to distinguish *jobs*, or professional categories, from *activities* that individuals perform. Thus we have, for example, programmers, technical writers, and testers; and it is easy to overlook the fact that programmers document and test their own code, that writers of manuals may develop their own sample programs and test their accuracy, and that testers write programs to automate their own activities and also document their results. Thus in many cases the functions people perform overlap and transcend their job categories.

Within programming itself as an activity (as distinct from other computer-related activities such as documentation, training, or operations), there are a number of subactivities that again may be grouped hierarchically. The hierarchy here relates not to distance from the machine, as described earlier, but to the degree of skill required, and to some extent to positions within formal organizations. These may be arranged as follows, in ascending order of skill and associated status, both of the activities and of those who perform them, at least as computer workers perceive this order:

1. *Debugging*: finding and correcting problems within programs
2. *Enhancement*: adding features to existing programs
3. *Development*: creating new programs
4. *Analysis and design*: laying the foundation for the creation of new programs
5. *Project leadership*: serving as *primus inter pares* and formal or informal supervisor for a group of people engaged in the previous four tasks
6. *Management*: formally supervising programming projects and subordinate employees. Unlike the other activities in this hierarchy, the management role is often ascribed rather than achieved and need not reflect technical expertise.

Some theorists — and many workers in the field as well — draw formal distinctions among these tasks. These distinctions are often reflected in job titles: "programmer," "programmer/analyst," "systems analyst," "project leader," "manager," or "director" (typically a manager of other managers). They are reified in some theoretical models to the status of virtual castes.

Philip Kraft is the most thorough exponent of the theory of social stratification as applied to programming tasks. His major work on the subject (Kraft, 1977) grew out of Harry Braverman's work on the "de-skilling" of industrial work (Braverman, 1974). Braverman traced the development of systematic management theory from the days of Frederick Taylor and "scientific management" to the present in the direction of separating the conception of work tasks from their execution. The purpose of managers is to define all the tasks in an industrial process that traditionally a single craftsman would perform, then to divide them into subtasks requiring minimal amounts of skill. The final act in this process is to assign the subtasks to workers far less skilled than a true craftsman, workers who are less expensive than traditional craftsmen and also far more amenable to hierarchical control. This analytic process results in a small cadre of managers and a large army of docile, alienated, easily replaceable, unskilled, or, to use Braverman's term, "de-skilled," workers.

Braverman traced this process both in industrial and in clerical occupations. Kraft, in turn, applied Braverman's analysis to the work of computer programmers. The methodology of "structured programming" or "top-down design," a basic engineering method used for breaking a problem or task down into manageable, programmable components (described in programmers' own words in chapter 3), became for Kraft a management tool for reducing programming to an intellectual equivalent of assembly-line labor. To managers looking for ways to control programmers, who were traditionally highly skilled, in a manner analogous to industrial craftspeople, structured programming

> offered an entirely new way of writing programs, elegant in theory and unambiguous in principle. Indeed, the principle was simple: if managers could not yet have machines which wrote programs, at least they could have programmers who worked like machines. Until human programmers were eliminated altogether, their work would be made as machine-like—that is, as simple and limited and routine—as possible. Briefly, programmers using structured programming would be limited to a handful of logical procedures which they could use— no others were permitted. (Kraft, 1977, p. 57)

The workplace was redesigned to reflect this mechanistic model. Kraft described the layout of one "shop" as

> a large room, filled with desks occupied by coders and junior-rank programmers, surrounded on all sides by glass-walled offices, each occupied by one or two managers, analysts, or senior programmers. The hardware [i.e., the computers themselves] was out of sight in a different building. Desks were clean except for loose-leaf binders and coding manuals, an occasional portable typewriter or hand calculator, and assorted personal oddments. Phones, remote terminals, and collections of software-related publications were kept in the managers' or analysts' offices. (Kraft, 1977, pp. 69-70)

In this Dickensian setting, even a programmer's starting the day with a cup of coffee

> indicates that in spite of routinization, programming, even coding, has not yet been completely remade to look like assemblyline work. Unlike line workers, programmers are not forced to adapt their physical motions to the rhythm and speed of a machine controlled by managers. (Kraft, 1977, p. 70)

Kraft turned the task hierarchy described earlier into an occupational hierarchy with three levels: coders, analysts, and managers. In Kraft's analysis, not only are these categories fairly well separated (though he admitted of some overlap), but workers are channeled into them through their earliest training. This is done through a hierarchy of schools that at one end match the social origins of the students and at the other produce workers for the corresponding level of software work. Thus students from poor and working-class families usually attend community colleges, junior colleges, state schools, or technical colleges, which prepare them for work as technicians, coders, or lower-level engineers. Course work in these schools focuses on basic skills needed for lower-level jobs in industry. On the other hand, students from middle- and upper-class backgrounds attend more prestigious technological institutes or business schools. These schools are largely research institutions on the forefront of technology, funded by corporations and the military, and their graduates form the technical and managerial elites in business. Thus programmers from this sort of training become systems analysts, "super programmers," and managers of programming organizations.

One of the most salient features of the programmers' world according to Kraft is its lack of true career mobility. He described the training of "coders" as follows:

> The training of low-level software workers is narrowly vocational and heavily ideological, that is, coders learn not only what they are expected to do for their entire working career and to accept without question the reason for doing it, but the right of superiors to tell them what to do. They are explicitly discouraged from exploring questions or issues beyond their assigned tasks. Programmers are praised when they stick to their assigned, narrow roles. Virtue is turned into vice, however, if programmers ever question the wisdom (or competence) of their managers. Their training provides them with only a limited view of the "Big Picture," and therefore managers can claim programmers are neither capable nor entitled to make decisions beyond those specifically assigned to them. (Kraft, 1977, p. 82)

In this world programmers are sometimes promoted or given salary increases, but the promotions are largely meaningless: The same work is given a slightly different title and salary range, but the responsibility increases little or not at all. Or job titles are based on seniority and on formal credentials, not on actual skill or responsibility. Kraft gave all of this a nefarious twist:

> Indeed, it seems likely that arbitrary and artificial divisions have been manufactured by managers to provide the appearance of career opportunities just as real opportunities shrink. . . . The technique . . . is designed to allow managers to channel "acceptable" people into

"appropriate" jobs. Those considered good workers can be rewarded with "advancement" from one fragment to another essentially identical to it but with a higher rank and perhaps a carefully regulated salary increment. Those exhibiting fewer management-approved virtues can be warned to improve their attitudes and performance by holding back career and income. (Kraft, 1977, pp. 81-82)

According to Kraft, programmers are kept in this state of proletarian subservience through a spurious ethic of professionalism. As he saw it, true professionalism, as exemplified by physicians, is characterized by a high degree of independence and by the fact that the professionals themselves define the content, conditions, and standards of their work and limit entry to the profession through licensing. Thus true professionals exercise a high degree of autonomy and control in their jobs due to an independent economic and political power base.

Programmers, however, though constantly exhorted to think of themselves as "professionals" and to "behave professionally" (which for Kraft meant never to think of forming unions), are really not analogous to doctors or lawyers at all:

Professionalism for programmers as it has emerged in management literature means: the establishment of universal job descriptions and standards, formulated, of course, by managers; common training programs; and perhaps a common certification process similar to that found among traditional engineering employees. On the other hand, the managers' image of professionalism does *not* include certification by an authority controlled by the programmers' peers; it does not include, certainly, licensing, nor does it foresee under any circumstances making independent entrepreneurs out of software workers. Management's vision, in other words, is of a profession without professionals. . . . In short, the managers' notion of professional programmers is one which gives them and not the programmer the power to define what programming is. (Kraft, 1977, p. 95)

This picture of programming has undoubtedly existed in some organizations. In large insurance companies, for example, one sometimes has found long rows of programmers sitting at desks and engaged in virtually identical tasks. In fact, this model was common enough, at least when Kraft was writing, to inspire parody, but parody based on the fact that a vastly different practice was in effect elsewhere. The cultural split between Kraft's model and a more humanistic, flexible one was exemplified in the difference between IBM and the Digital Equipment Corporation (DEC). IBM, or "Big Blue," was portrayed in organizational folklore as the archetypal business company, where programmers wore suits and ties (or dresses, but women figure far less in computer folklore than in the reality of computer work), and where strict hours and a bureaucratic hierarchy were rigidly enforced, while Digital was populated by programmers in blue jeans and torn T-shirts, who were so wedded to their jobs that they didn't know or care who the boss was. (Kraft, incidentally, felt compelled to explain in a footnote that his fieldwork was *not* at IBM, so well known was the picture of IBM life.) This mythic distinction was captured in *CPU Wars*, a comic book that appeared not long after Kraft's book (Andres, 1980).

In *CPU Wars*, governments had stopped fighting wars, so the arms manufacturers started selling weapons to corporations. One corporation, the Impossible to Program Machine (IPM) company, invaded another, the Human Equipment Corporation (HEC). When one of the uniformed IPM soldiers captures a HEC employee and tells him to take them to his leader, the poor fellow doesn't even know who it is:

"All right, TALK you! Who is your superior?"

"Do you mean my supervisor, my project manager, my cost center manager, my project leader or the developers?"

The IPM people (in storm-trooper uniforms) do not understand the apparent anarchy of HEC:

"Isn't there any organization to this place at all?"

"There must be! Our surveys show they are making money and growing at an alarming rate!"

"Well, we damn well better *find* it so we can CAPTURE it and control HECland for ourselves!"

"I don't know, sir—If he WAS telling the truth, there doesn't seem to be any! ZERO! Zilch! The Null Set! None as we know it!"

"HELL! There must be some sort of central control! You couldn't run any business without a RIGID one! How do you get anyone to do any work if you don't crack the whip?" (Andres, 1980, p. 4)

Ultimately, however, the poor HECkies are captured, made to put on suits, and forced to sit at long rows of desks. They are forced to obey orders like "those of you with interactive terminals will turn them in. You will work at your desk, and then go down to the keypunch room, wait for a terminal, punch in your cards, take them to batch input, and wait three hours for the output" (Andres, 1980, p. 5). (The story does have a happy ending, after two HEC people, aided by Digital Dog, escape and foment a revolution, in which IPM soldiers are all gradually sucked into a HEC computer and get permanently lost in an adventure game.)

If *CPU Wars* portrays Kraft's world to a large extent (and if that world did not exist, at least the cartoonist felt compelled to invent it), it also portrays a very different one. HEC is clearly the paradigm for a nonbureaucratic, highly individualistic, "human" approach to industrial organization and to the work of programming. In this paradigm, programmers set their own hours, their own dress codes, and their own styles of work. This model values more idiosyncrasy in personal styles and lends itself to much more individual creativity than the bureaucratic model. This model is also the way that many programming organizations were (and still are) set up. It is closer to Peter Senge's model of the "learning organization" (Senge, 1990).

Kraft's picture, though descriptive as a picture of one segment of the industry at a particular point in history, fails in a number of points to capture the programmers' world today. It falls short in four major capacities. Kraft greatly underestimated job mobility in the computing world. He also overestimated the uniformity of background among programmers. His definition of "professional" is too narrow to characterize programmers' work and their self-image. Finally, his analysis of the fragmentation of programming tasks missed the importance, to programmers and managers, of spreading the overall knowledge of the business as broadly as possible within an organization.

Limits to Job Mobility

Kraft stressed the career limits of "mere coders," indicating that they have only artificial mobility along rigidly defined paths. In fact, if this were true, most entry-level programmers would leave the industry very quickly. However, the following factors militate against managers restricting programmers in this way even if they wanted to:

- The ever-increasing demand for programmers during economic expansion, and during recession the desire to function with as few people as possible, requiring those people to be flexible and highly trained
- The ever-changing knowledge base in the computer industry, demanding that programmers keep up with new products and services
- The value in business of general rather than specific knowledge and of skills transferable across functions within an organization
- The length of time and the cost of training new employees, as opposed to drawing on the knowledge current employees already have

- The fact that fewer higher-skilled workers cost less than many lower-skilled ones and have more long-term usefulness to their employers

Also, contrary to Kraft's assertions, most programming managers do come from the ranks of programmers. This can cause problems because the interpersonal skills needed to manage people effectively are not part of the training students receive in computer-science and engineering programs (Kolb and Wolfe, 1981), and because people whose skills and aptitudes are primarily interpersonal do not often choose to pursue careers in programming. Programmers often show contempt for managers who do not understand the technical aspects of their work, and this can result in poor attitudes toward their work and poor productivity (Kelley, 1985). On the other hand, problems of a different nature result when managers try to motivate programmers and other technically oriented employees with incentives, such as promotions or salary increases, more applicable to standard bureaucratic employees and neglect other factors that figure prominently in programmers' orientations, such as technical challenge and team spirit (Weinberg, 1971).

In any case, from the 1950s to the present, leadership in the computing world has most often come from those trained or skilled in its technical mysteries, even though it is certainly true, as Kraft and Dubnoff (1986) asserted, that a more general background is often required for movement to upper management. (However, their statement [p. 192] that "the key to financial success in software is to not specialize and not get too technical" is an exaggeration.) It is also true that programmers, like engineers and other technically trained people, find over the course of their professional lives that they need to develop aspects of themselves, chiefly in interpersonal relations, for which neither their general temperaments nor their specific training has equipped them (Kolb and Wolfe, 1981), but more opportunities exist for programmers than Kraft acknowledged.

Uniformity of Background

Kraft's notion of programmers' backgrounds was that those at a particular level (coders, programmers, analysts) differ in training from those at other levels but are largely similar to one another. Both halves of this view are incorrect. As we shall see in chapter 3, many people come to programming with no academic training in the field at all; and within an organization one's particular college affiliation has a minimal impact on one's career growth (though it may affect where and how easily one gets one's first job). Unlike some other fields, such as education, in the computing world neither hiring nor promotion requires a particular degree, level of educational attainment, or any sort of certification; conversely, no salary increases or promotions automatically follow attainment of any degrees. Lack of a college degree may be a barrier to being hired by some companies or managers but not to entering the field, and programmers' career success is largely tied to their own skills and achievements, not to formal credentials.

There is one exception to this picture, though Kraft did not mention it. Within the computing world there is a hierarchy of industries as well as of tasks. Certain specialties, such as artificial intelligence, robotics, and the creation of computer architectures themselves, require deeper training in the intricacies of computer engineering than more easily learned applications, such as those used in data processing, and therefore these areas are more likely to draw on graduates of elite technical universities; but even here, companies gladly hire experienced people with any sort of training, as long as their work has taught them to do whatever is needed.

Professionalism

Kraft defined programming as a nonprofessional activity by defining professionals in a way that excludes programmers. As stated earlier, Kraft treated medicine as the model profession. What distinguishes doctors (and lawyers and a few other such professions) is the following:

- They have their own organizations to control entry into the profession through a formal licensing procedure
- Training requirements are established, and training institutions are staffed and controlled, by the profession itself
- The professional organization has a legal monopoly on the right to offer certain categories of services
- The profession maintains and controls its own code of ethics and other standards

By this definition, there are very few "professions," most notably medicine, law, and the clergy (for some religions), some "semi-professions" (Etzioni, 1969) like nursing, and others gradually trying to establish their identity and credibility (such as child-care workers; see Joffe, 1977).

Clearly, programming does not fall into this category, except as a sort of stepchild of engineering. However, Kraft exaggerated when he viewed programmers as deluded by management into a false consciousness of themselves as professionals when they are really clerical workers. By defining professionalism as narrowly as he did, he neglected what most people mean when they speak of themselves as professionals. This is a socially constructed definition, not a formal one, but it leaves the definition in the hands of those who use it. To most people who think of themselves as professionals, professionalism includes the following characteristics:

- Making or having a say in decisions affecting their work
- Bringing intelligence, training, and experience to bear in solving problems on the job
- Not feeling obligated to accept orders from above unquestioningly (Kelley, 1985)
- Having at least some flexibility in matters of dress and schedule
- Applying internal standards to their work and their work behavior rather than just conforming to externally imposed rules

Most programmers speak with some pride about the amount of responsibility in their work and the autonomy they are allowed in performing it. Programmers also consider their work professional rather than clerical because of their training and because of the amount they use their minds in performing their tasks. In this sense programming is indeed a professional activity, and managers who know what they are doing foster this sense and encourage it genuinely, not artificially.

Task Fragmentation and the "Big Picture"

The fragmentation of work Kraft saw in programming shops belies the varied, complex nature of the work and the interdependencies involved, both of tasks and of subsystems. An individual is, at various points in a project, and sometimes within a single day, coder, analyst, debugger, tester, documenter, trainer, and student. Although different aspects of this job are emphasized at different phases in a career, all are present in the same person; it is impossible to fragment the work of programming as Kraft indicated, except in very large organizations, and even then it cannot be done over a long time. Even in large, bureaucratically organized shops, coders gradually become analysts, project leaders, and eventually managers, and in smaller companies such as Cellsoft, this process is telescoped because there are not enough people to assume fragmented roles for long.

Kraft also was precisely wrong about management's interest in insulating programmers from the "big picture." A system falls apart when those responsible for maintaining it (or even maintaining only small pieces of it) do not understand how it all fits together. Ultimately, it is impossible to assign responsibility for a whole system to a small group of designers, with the bulk of programmers kept in ignorance, for a number of reasons:

- The very fact that programmers identify themselves as professionals, and that they have trained for work in this field, drives them to learn about their work in as much detail as possible.

- System designers, like most people, seek recognition and appreciation for their work and enjoy explaining it to others, including those working on the same project.
- Contrary to Kraft's assertions, programmers are often chosen for their skills and experience, not for their lack of them; and the ability to learn complete systems is valued and rewarded, not minimized or discounted.
- The high turnover in programming projects necessitates continual retraining and cross-training of all people involved in them. Precisely because no one knows when a designer or a lead programmer will move on to another project or another company, it is critical to management to have potential replacements ready. Indeed, in one company where mobility between projects is the norm rather than the exception, anyone seeking a transfer is required to have a replacement trained.

Thus the world of programmers is much more intricate and complex than Kraft's analysis would indicate. If his picture were accurate, then a study of how programmers learn the systems they work on would be unnecessary: they would not learn them, and no one would care. But since programmers need to learn those systems, and since their understanding is vital to management in dynamic, growing corporations, studies of this nature can contribute a great deal to enhancing the computing world.

This study focuses on a small software company in which it may be more important for programmers to understand the systems in which their work is embedded than it would be in a larger firm with more people available to work on smaller problems, but learning of the sort done at Cellsoft is critical to computer workers and their managers in larger environments as well, for reasons just described. In chapters 5 through 9 we examine the specific work programmers do when they learn systems.

3

The Participants

Programmers work at the confluence of a number of domains. Their education, training, prior experience, and individual learning and cognitive styles intersect with the culture of the organization in which they work, the demands of the technology, co-workers, management, and customers or users, and the systems, programs, and other work artifacts that already exist in the programmers' and other computer professionals' workplaces. In this chapter I examine the impact of these various aspects of programmers' lives and backgrounds and show how individuals uniquely bring these elements to bear on their jobs.

HOW THEY CAME TO BE WHERE THEY ARE

Computer professionals do not come from homogeneous backgrounds. Programming does not require a license or any particular degree. Because there were a great many jobs in the computer industry in the 1970s, even during recessions, and because many of these jobs were created in the computer-manufacturing and software firms in the Boston area, always a magnet for college students and recent graduates, many young people looking for work in the area inevitably gravitated to the programming field. This included the generation that came of age in the late 1960s, an era marked by idealism in people's personal and political goals and by a strong sense of possibility. Many students were graduated during that period with no clear career goals and no reason for choosing any early in their lives. Alvin Toffler (1971) wrote of career "trajectories," in which people could expect to change work paths several times during their adult lives, rather than settle early and for good, as their parents had done.

However, the recession of the early 1970s made it difficult for many recent graduates to find work, and much of the funding for graduate study had dried up, especially after the Nixon administration cut student aid dramatically. Though defense-related employment (anathema to many younger workers, deeply antagonized by the Vietnam War) continued to be available, it was difficult for people with liberal-arts degrees and little work experience to start careers in business. Thus it was quite common to find recent recipients of bachelor's and even master's degrees doing secretarial work or serving as waiters or taxi drivers, especially in regions as overstocked with college graduates as metropolitan Boston.

This same period, however, was a time of spectacular creativity in the world of computers. Machines were growing smaller and more powerful. In software development the rise of timesharing systems in the 1960s and early 1970s, in which many people could work at terminals on the same machine at the same time, instead of having to type their programs and data onto punched cards, made it possible for more people to work on computers. The generation of programming languages developed in the 1950s and 1960s, such as FORTRAN, ALGOL, COBOL, and BASIC, were much easier to use than the ones and zeros of binary machine code or the low-level assembly languages closely tied to them. A great deal of creative work went into building the timesharing operating systems and the languages, text editors, and other utilities that made them easier to use. The new systems made computer programming a less arcane field, accessible to people who were not trained as engineers. At MIT and Harvard, at large computer manufacturers like Digital Equipment, Data General, and Prime Computer, and at software firms throughout the area, Boston and its suburbs became a center for computer development.

The computer industry itself grew in tandem with the ubiquity of computers in American life. Businesses' need for information grew as rapidly as the computers' ability to store and process it. Demand for people capable of commanding the machines seemed insatiable in the 1970s. Lack of academic credentials was no deterrent to career growth: Anyone with the intelligence, drive, and aptitude for programming was welcome in a well-paying, stimulating industry. Insurance companies, banks, and other businesses ran training programs for new employees, admitted by aptitude tests. The computer and data-processing fields provided (and still provide) steady work for a small army of poets, musicians, and folkdancers in and around Boston.

In time, starting about 1980, the supply of untrained potential programmers began to exceed demand as more people with programming knowledge and experience were being graduated from colleges and even high schools. Although specific degrees were still not required, it became more difficult for people who had never touched a computer terminal to find work in the industry. Starting about 1985, as personal computers became as common as minicomputers had become in the preceding decade, and as easier-to-use programs (such as the Visicalc and Lotus 1-2-3 spreadsheet programs and the WordPerfect and Microsoft Word word processors) became available to nonspecialists, the demand for programmers lessened. There were still jobs available, but experience and formal training became more important. Also, as minicomputers such as the Digital VAX lost out to microcomputers like the IBM PC and the Apple Macintosh for many workplace applications, the Boston-based minicomputer manufacturers reduced the work force by thousands of jobs, further restricting the opportunities for potential programmers.

By the mid-1970s many educational institutions recognized that computer programming was a burgeoning field, and computer-science programs flourished in colleges and universities. The term *computer science* covers a multitude of subjects, everything from the mathematics and design of computer algorithms, commonly found at elite institutions, technological universities, and engineering schools, to programming languages, data processing, and business uses of computers. Courses of this type are often found in less elite colleges, including publicly funded universities and community colleges. As we have seen in chapter 2, Kraft (1977) demonstrated that the schools offering majors in "computer science" form a hierarchy in terms of the courses offered, the class background and abilities of their students, and the types of jobs for which those students are prepared and that they are likely to be offered at graduation.

The participants in this study came from three general types of educational backgrounds: formal training in computer science, engineering, mathematics, or other scientific and technical fields at prestigious universities; liberal-arts backgrounds unrelated or tangentially related to computing, science, or engineering; and computer-science or business programs at state universities, state colleges, and community colleges or at private universities not noted for their technical programs. In general, members of the second group were between the ages of thirty-five and forty-five and thus represented the generation whose members came of age and began their careers in the late 1960s through the mid-1970s. Those educated at state schools (all in Massachusetts) were generally younger, having graduated in the early to mid-1980s (except for one man, fifty-two years old at the time of the study, who represented another, older type, someone who began programming even before punched cards were common). Those who studied technical courses at elite universities ranged from recent graduates to people out of school ten or more years.

One noticeable difference between the eleven women and the seventeen men interviewed for this study is that few of the women came from academic backgrounds in business, computer science, or engineering or planned to enter the field, while all but three of the men did so. All but one of the participants had a bachelor's degree, but few had any education beyond that level: two women had master's degrees in education, and two men were working on MBA degrees from local universities. Advanced degrees are not necessary for careers in the computer industry.

Among participants, the number of years of work experience ranged from zero (hired soon after graduation) to twenty-eight, with most clustering in the five-to-ten-year range. The group outside Cellsoft had somewhat more industry experience on average (75 percent had been in the field ten years or longer), but this is mainly an artifact of how they were selected for the study, not a function of their work. Also, years of industry experience is an ambiguous variable. For those who entered the field from other areas, industry experience may be the same as total experience with computers. Others have much more experience than a résumé will credit. One twenty-six-year-old man claimed twelve years' experience with computers:

> In about, I think it was eighth grade or ninth grade, one of the senior math teachers had come to me and they had just gotten in a new computer system, and [I was] part of a group of students who they took to go look at it and play with it . . . , and I started really playing with it then, this [was] in ninth grade so [I was] about fourteen, and from then started developing programs, learning what I could, reading, reading magazines.

HOW THEY GOT STARTED

A number of people were introduced to computers informally in high school or college. They may simply have found the experience fascinating or fun, rather than being motivated by any career goals. For example, here is how Ed (all names have been changed) got started:

> I know the first time I started was in eighth grade, when my school bought a little TRS-80 at Radio Shack. It was open at all free periods to any student that wanted to play around with it, and a couple of my friends got involved. We were really just playing, and there was no instruction on it and we [were] writing little games for it, and I didn't really understand how a computer worked, I didn't understand how to program, we programmed dinky little games on it. . . . So that's how I developed my interest in it, and then I pretty much taught myself through high school. I bought a BASIC Trash-80 [TRS-80 computer from Radio Shack], and got a hold of a lot of programs that were already written and tried to follow them, and just started writing my own. And then when it came time when I needed a job, I tried to get a job with my dad. My dad put me in doing data entry.

Another story is that of Jack, who entered McGill University expecting to study biology but found himself entranced by computers instead. Jack inferred a connection from one field to the other:

> I spent a weekend with a friend and he had his home PC. And he was writing something in BASIC. And he was having me read off a

program from a piece of paper so he could key it in. And I thought well, as I'm reading I'm looking at what this is doing, and after I figured out what it was doing, I said, "Why don't you do this?" And he was sort of amazed that I could see what was going on, and I said, "Wait a minute! Oh, this is great!" So then we started really playing all weekend. And it didn't seem all that bizarre to me. At that point McGill was on an IBM. JCL [Job Control Language, the set of symbols and commands used to run IBM computers] didn't seem all that bizarre to me. I think that comes from the neurobiology aspect, where, when you study how the brain works, the neurons either fire or they don't. And based on that action, you can go further. Now I had been especially involved with vision, and the entire way that [the] brain interprets the vision is, if action A happens, then this corresponds to that you're seeing this, and if action A does not happen, then this is what you're seeing. And this is how —it was kinda funny, if you understand how a bird can find out where the fly is. . . . Suddenly the symbols, BASIC or JCL was like, yeah!

Another introduction came from Bill, a student in a cooperative learning program:

The way that I got into this work was when I was in business school I cooped at Data General, and I had to learn a language. Which, [I] can't actually remember, it was Data General's own form of BASIC. And that's how I saw, I started talking to the programmers, Hey, what are you guys doing, blahblah, 'cause I was an accounting major. . . . And I saw what they were doing, and that's where I saw how they were doing it. [Then] I went back to school, and I tried a couple courses in this.

Bill changed his emphasis from accounting to computers after watching programmers. Barbara entered the field in midlife for purely utilitarian reasons. She had been working as a guidance counselor in a high school and decided to change fields:

Number one, I got burned out, and number two, I really had some doubts as to how much I was helping people. I did a lot of work with preadolescent kids, we dealt with scholastic achievement, making friends, social skills, that kind of thing, some family issues. And then I was transferred to the high school because the school was reduced in half, so I was burned out at this point and the high school, first of all it was a completely different district, so no one knew me, because at the old school I had built up a reputation and kids would come to me because their sisters and brothers had come to me and all, this was a completely new side of town, I had to build my reputation all over again and then I had to deal with pregnancies, drug abuse, runaways, and at that point I said I don't wanna do this anymore, it was a completely different world, and it was the other side of town, it wasn't the nice side of town, and so I started feeling that maybe I wanted to contribute something and started to doubt how much I was contributing, and programming appealed to me because it was very concrete, and if I had to deal with people I would give them something, I would either give them a system or I would fix a program bug, or I would give them something on paper, design a system for them. . . . There's some kind of satisfaction too in the sense that no one's gonna die. . . and I knew, when I was taking a course in programming and I would start writing a program and I would look at my watch and as if by magic it was five hours later and I said, "This is for me!" I would get so involved when the time flies and I like solving puzzles, so I'm really happy in my second career.

WHAT THEY LEARNED IN SCHOOL

Academic life has a variety of meanings for computer professionals. While a majority of people in this study spent some or all of their college life studying computer science or related topics—mathematics, engineering, and business were the most common concentrations outside of computer science itself—several people came into the field from entirely unrelated areas, of which education was the most common.

Computer work typically draws on people with a taste for practical experience. In Kolb's (1984) typology, engineers are often "convergers," people whose learning styles emphasize active experimentation over reflective observation, but who are drawn to abstract conceptualization rather than to concrete experience (see chapter 10). That is, programming and computer work involve the manipulation of symbols more than of physical objects, and "hands-on experience" to most programmers really means a chance to play with the symbolic language of computers rather than with the machinery, the "hardware," itself. Conversations with programmers in the business world often show impatience with theory and a desire to get on with work. Joyce, a quality-assurance analyst (that is, someone who tests programs written by others), left college after two and one-half years because she was anxious to acquire some real-world experience: "And this is kind of funny actually, when I think back at it, and I was very frustrated, I did want to go out and apply some of my knowledge. And that was one of the compelling reasons why I got a job: I wanted to actually work. There was really no other reason, other than [that] I wanted to go out and work and see what I liked to do."

    Given this orientation, it is not surprising that lecture courses may often
seem boring and removed from the serious business of programming. Ed,
whom we have already seen playing with his high school's Radio Shack
computer, later majored in computer science at Cornell. He was interested in
the practical side of computing and didn't care much for the theoretical approach
of many of his courses:

> I guess that from a learning standpoint I wanted hands-on things, I
> wanted the concrete, not the abstract; useful things. . . As far as
> classes and projects that I found interesting, mostly computer-science
> classes, I took a database class, and [an] operating-systems class, my
> junior and senior years, and they both involved, three credits of the
> five credits was the theory class where a professor just stood up and
> lectured on databases and operating systems and the theory behind
> them, not on a particular operating system or a particular database but
> on the common aspects. . . . Then there are other classes, the
> analysis of algorithms, just sitting down and doing, writing out
> algorithms and figuring out problem solving. I hated those three
> classes. They were too theoretical and impractical for what I would
> be doing, what I envisioned myself doing. The problems we were
> studying weren't the kind of problems you would ever face in a real-
> world environment. I was more interested in solving a database
> query, or writing an operating system that handled high disk I/O or
> what were the best methods to handle process queueing, something
> that you could program in and see if you . . . say I changed the
> algorithm on this, then what happens, spit it out. You had to create
> the situation, try your algorithm out in several different situations,
> and see how it compared to other algorithms in every situation. I
> found doing things like that interesting.

    The most engaging aspect of computers for many programmers, whether
student or professional, is programming *languages*, the symbol systems used to
communicate instructions to the machine. One way or another, anyone
programming a computer must learn one or more of these languages. At some
schools many courses are devoted to programming languages, while at others
(typically more prestigious technical universities or universities with doctoral
programs in computer science) languages are merely an expected part of one's
background, rather like the ability to read and write English. At Cornell, for
example, Ed said, "They really don't [teach languages]. They expect you to
learn it yourself. They teach problem solving." Stuart, an MIT graduate and
employee, said that in order to learn languages, he "primarily sat down with the
manuals, read them through, and played with [the computer]." The aim of the

computer-science program was quite unrelated to this, as Stuart found in his first computer-science course:

> The introductory course . . . was one of the best courses in computer science. It's not programming computers: The approach that MIT takes is that programming is something you pick up on the side. [The] focus [is] on computer science, and programming is simply a way of expressing that. So in that course, usually the first day . . . they have people come in and they ask what sort of background people have, what do they know, how many know this, how many know that, and then they make a point of saying, "Well, first thing we want you to do is forget everything that you've ever learned, we're going to start from scratch." And they did.

At MIT computer science emphasizes method and principle over concrete application. Typically, as one progresses from vocational programs, community colleges, and state schools into more academically prestigious institutions, the aims and course offerings become more abstract. Kraft (1977) linked the academic stratification to the economic class of students and to their eventual careers. He was right, but only to a limited extent, about both of these links. For example, though Joyce took eight years to complete a bachelor's degree and went to two state colleges, complaining that Worcester (Massachusetts) State College did not teach computer methodology and that she couldn't afford a better school, both Ed, the son of a medical-school professor, and Stuart, the son of a policeman, attended computer-science programs at highly regarded universities, and all three are successful in their careers, Ed and Joyce at Cellsoft and Stuart in an academic computing environment.

On the other hand, there are people who enjoy the more intellectual aspects of computing. Dave is a thirty-five-year-old programmer at a company specializing in research for the Department of Defense and for the military. Like Stuart, Dave attended MIT, but he studied linguistics rather than computer science. His first exposure to computer languages was LISP, a language often used in artificial intelligence and considered by serious "hackers" to be the "purest" language (Turkle, 1983). Unlike COBOL, the language most commonly used by business programmers, which is written in a verbose, "English-like" syntax, or FORTRAN or BASIC, scientific languages written to resemble mathematical formulae, LISP is a language conceived in terms of functions rather than of computations. Its style, consisting mostly of terse variable names grouped by large numbers of parentheses, is quite daunting to the uninitiated. Dave said of being introduced to programming through LISP, "That's got to warp one's personality, but it was quite common around MIT, that's what people programmed in."

Stuart also began with a somewhat obscure scientific language, APL (which stands for A Programming Language). For him,

The systems that we had were very small, in many ways were somewhat limiting. The first one was an IBM 5100, which was actually the first desktop computer manufactured by a major company. [It] ran the APL programming language. So that in itself was part of the challenge because it was something absolutely new, not only was it just learning the idea of expressing thoughts in a methodical way, but it was also a completely new language because it uses Greek symbols instead of English text. And so it was a game, it was a challenge.

For Dave, beginning with LISP was not a deliberate decision, but a function of the way the computer-science department at MIT was organized. When Dave was a student, a decade before Stuart,

the intro [language] course then at MIT was a subset of PL/1, which I took, and I found the course abominable. It was punch cards, it was all the wrong things at the wrong time, so you could literally walk down the hall and hack with LISP in a very interactive, fast environment or you could take a course and wait for your runs on punch cards, so I quickly got out of paying much attention to computer science at MIT, with the exception of some of the artificial intelligence courses. I sort of got it out of my system my freshman and sophomore year and went back to things like what I was originally interested in, mathematics and stuff.

Unlike most professional programmers, who just want to get out into the world and start working, and who therefore find much of the course work simply something to get through, Dave was actually drawn to the more academic side of programming because of his interest in linguistics. "Within linguistics I did a lot of . . . the foundations of computers, I mean formal grammars, automata theory, very useful stuff if you're gonna do computer science academically, but for totally different reasons other than what people normally did. Aside from that, I did not do a whole lot with computer science, let alone software engineering, at MIT."

Different people learn languages in different ways, just as people learn anything. But for almost everyone, learning to program means a lot of practice and experimentation. "Playing with the machine," "trying things out," and "tweaking" are important components of learning to program, probably more important than anything taught in a classroom. However, the "code" (the instructions that compose the computer program) is ultimately a small part of what constitutes a software system. One program may be enough for a game or a class project, but typical computer systems comprise hundreds or thousands of separate programs, or modules, linked together to form a composite. In industry it takes a great deal of coordination among several individuals to build a complete system; in large military projects coordination among teams totaling hundreds of people may be required. Perhaps the most important part of building a system of this magnitude is the overall system design, or architecture; and academic computer-science courses seldom, if ever, address this topic. In general, school programming projects are for one person or a small team of students. The emphasis in courses is on practicing discrete skills (such as mastering the programming language) or on demonstrating understanding of the principles taught in the course (whether abstract, such as using mathematical algorithms to solve a problem, or more practical, such as writing a small database-management system), rather than on writing code that another person can pick up and modify, or on creating the initial specifications from which other people can write a program. Conversely, there is little if any training in the important practical skill of understanding programs and systems that others have written; and since all programmers begin their careers by maintaining other people's code, this is a serious lack in those academic programs that view preparing students for jobs as one of their goals.

For students, then, programming is an individual endeavor, while in corporations it is a collective one. The programs an organization already has form a library, to be drawn on as a standard and as a template for new work. A great deal of learning in the workplace comes from copying and modifying preexisting programs, but there is little preparation for this in courses. There is also little attempt to teach students how to work in groups. Group projects in classes tend to be somewhat superficial. Judith, a twenty-seven-year-old programmer/analyst at Cellsoft, did a class project with her boyfriend (whom she later married). The two of them programmed a line printer to produce a graphical display, something she would never do in the real world. "It sounded good, and we figured it'd be easy, and it was. There were different types of calls to the plotter, and you'd plot and you'd draw pictures and that's what we did. We did banners and we did pictures. Why would I draw a stupid thing like that?" Judith and her boyfriend worked together but not in a formal collaboration or division of labor on an industrial model.

In general, Judith found little of interest in her courses. "The stuff I had in school, at least the programming, I guess it was supposed to exercise your mind, but I mean, I think the class after me wrote a calendar program. Where are you gonna go write a calendar program, if you're gonna do applications programming?" On the other hand, her introduction to computers in high school was much more stimulating.

> We had this teacher, she was Chinese, her name was Mrs. Lee and she was really funny. That was a really fun course, I took it my senior year, it was a good teacher, there were good people in the course, that was my first introduction to the class. Although I remember, it was on a PDP [computer made by Digital Equipment] . . . , it was an 11/70 and we had line printers, you didn't have VT

[Digital's video] terminals. We did some programs, I don't remember what we did, I just remember that she was always giving out fortune cookies and stuff, and she was very hyperactive, hopping around.

In this case it was a teacher who made programming come alive for Judith and eventually led her into a career in computers in spite of dull university courses. For some women in this study, the role of the teacher has been very important. Leslie, who installs programs at customer sites for Cellsoft, started college as a music major, then switched into business and hated it. She later worked for an accounting firm that paid for her to get a master's degree in accounting, but she "despised the whole experience." Like Judith, Leslie's first experience with computers was in high school, but it was a very unpleasant one: "I remember in high school, a few times sitting at the terminals to do a few things—I was completely, I was just perplexed, somebody explained it to me, I just didn't understand what on earth it was." Her first experience in college was no better, and Leslie attributed this at least in part to a poor teacher, but later a more empathic one enabled her to learn at last.

And then, . . . I guess it was my freshman year of college, I signed up for a Pascal class, I remember I dropped out of that class in a couple of weeks. I just had no concept of, you know, I'd sit in the class, and then we had our first assignment and I had no idea how to approach it because I graduated from a high school where we were spoon-fed our whole entire life. So, I mean I couldn't understand [how after] hearing one thing in the lecture class, . . . you're supposed to go and write this program. There was no method, there was [sic] no examples to follow, there was no nothing. Yeah, this was a teacher, more high-leveled, professor, also, than you might get for that type of a class. . . . Anyhow, finally, I got the nerve up to try it again, one or two years later, and this time it was a very, very successful experience and that's because I had a professor who was much more, more toward the example side of life, and towards nurturing, and holding your hand as much as he possibly could. But yet still leaving, you know, some kind of a challenge for you, so that you felt good about it and felt like you learned something. And then after that I felt more comfortable.

To many programmers, such as Dave, it is the extracurricular aspect of programming that is most important to learning and to developing interest. Course work provides theoretical background, which may or may not matter to the student, but the fascination with the act of programming and with interaction with the computer plays a much larger role in the making of programmers. Barbara's comment that "I would start writing a program and I would look at my watch and as if by magic it was five hours later" is typical. The work is absorbing. One is driven to succeed at it. Small problems in making a program work will not let the programmer rest (Turkle, 1983; Weinberg, 1971; Weizenbaum, 1976). There is an intensity to programmers' focus that does not fit the standards of a classroom. Steven, a recent graduate, recalled a class in which people spent up to seventy hours a week getting programs finished, in spite of having other courses or jobs. Another programmer, Henry, remembered spending an entire weekend in his college computing center finishing a class project. Often, what matters is not simply completing the required work for the course, but the excitement of getting something to work exactly right, or of adding ever more technically interesting features to a program.

The methodology of "structured programming" or modularity taught in computer-science courses is often used as a standard in industry. It is also a technique that many programmers and engineers adopt instinctively. Stuart, the MIT graduate and employee, describes the process as follows:

> There are several classical forms of attack. Typically what teaches is showing you how to break things into pieces, typically called divide and conquer, in terms of mathematical algorithms or [the] computer-science part, but it's more, when you go to solve a problem, first think about the requirement, what are you trying to solve, think of how to describe it sort of in larger areas, and keep bringing it in smaller and smaller, so that you can think of, you can think of describing things at a variety of levels, and each time you can peel off a layer and go deeper and deeper into the details, but the goal is always to try not to get mired in details when you don't have to. One of the buzzwords for that is abstraction, or building black boxes, or modularity.

Adult programmers who learn this style as part of their formal training, either in school or at work, often find it congenial to their way of working. I asked Stuart, "If somebody were to have asked you, before you went to college, how you solved those, would you have described it in similar terms?" He answered,

> [You] figure out what you're trying to do, build a model of it in your head so that you understand what you're doing, and then just start off taking little pieces at a time. One of the things that people who don't do this sort of work, or who try and get frustrated, typically have problems with, what I've seen is that they get in and they start worrying about lots of little things and don't really get the big picture, and a lot of it in computer science is geared towards getting the big picture and breaking things down so that you can easily do things in little pieces.

SCHOOL VERSUS THE WORLD

School and the world have different demands, and people adapt from one to the other in different ways. For Jack, one of the important differences is a change in standards. In business, it is not sufficient that something works well enough to run once to satisfy a professor; it has to run repeatedly under a wide variety of conditions, and it has to be readable and maintainable by other programmers. Also, a job lasts (one hopes) much longer than a course, so time invested in meeting standards can have value to a programmer later on.

> Usually when you go to school, it's a perfect world. And you do things the way it should happen. When you get onto the job market—supposedly in a scientific lab in school, you shouldn't fudge your results. You should be, you should go all the way through. I just felt that we . . . followed the standards better in a classroom or on campus than we would ever outside. And I felt that was true in computers as well. And in my experience [in contrast to expectations] that hasn't been true. Since I hit the job market, I will follow standards much more now than I ever did in class. And I think that's because in class, you have thirteen weeks. And it doesn't matter what you do now. Whatever you do, in thirteen weeks it'll be over. On the job market, if you spend more time to do something today you're going to get a return on that investment in time.

For Jack, the difference between school and world was a shock. Other people just accept the difference. Bill, the former co-op student, said, "School is where you learn theory, and you learn the tools. Now how you use the tools, you learn that at work. You learn that by asking your questions, as far as, you learn how to theorize about how to take a problem but, as far as practically doing it coming into it . . . they don't tell you, you have to learn someone's business before you try to help it."

Jack also noted that school does not teach programmers how to modify other people's programs, or how to work on large systems. He said, "I don't think you'd ever see [a full-scale business problem], because you're not gonna have someone learn how to modify, enhance, or maintain a system. The best you're gonna get is write one from scratch, which is much easier." The systems students are assigned may be quite large. For example, Ed had a semester-long project of writing a database-management system, and Henry had to "basically write MacPaint [a popular drawing program for the Apple Macintosh computer] from scratch." But there were no assignments simulating a business condition involving enhancing or fixing errors in a preexisting system.

Stuart said that his course work at MIT was valuable "primarily in setting a foundation. Not a lot of it is directly applicable." For Colleen, a forty-five-year-old systems programmer who studied mathematics and philosophy in college, this is actually one of the pleasures of the business:

I think most of my formal education had nothing to do with any of this. Probably the mathematics would have the most to do with it, but it's actually surprising how little mathematics you really need to do this. Maybe a course in logic, the one I took as part of the philosophy training, would have been the most useful, formal logic and syllogisms and all that, and just thinking in those precise terms.

I think another thing that appeals to me about [working in computers] is that training seems to have very little to do with it. When I look at these people who are computer-science graduates today, they know certain bits and pieces and they have a thorough grounding in, you know, what are databases about, and various ways of organizing things, what kinds of sorts can you do and so on: things that are helpful, I'm sure, but I think you can get by remarkably well without them. I may be totally wrong, but I've seen people with excellent academic backgrounds who've been grounded in all this stuff, who aren't particularly good programmers.

Robert is a manager of a group of programmers at a large computer-manufacturing company. Members of Robert's staff work on computer-aided design (CAD) programs to aid electrical engineers. He himself holds a degree in electrical engineering, as do many programmers, and he actually draws on his academic background as part of his work.

I do have to use it to listen to our end users, who are all electrical engineers and are saying to me, "well, we need to look at the electromigration problems here in this chip." I need to know what they mean by electromigration, and the volts and watts and amps and currents and resistances that cause it to happen. But that pretty rapidly gets translated into the computer-science domain of what do we have to process and how do we process it, and how do I program it? It's a necessary but minor part of the job.

Some programmers, like Jack, found that methodologies learned in school were more useful later than at the time. Judith

used methodology since I've gotten out of school. We tried to use [structured programming] at [my last job], maybe not the exact, use this form maybe, we tried to use things like that. . . . Yeah, we learned stuff like this in college but it's hard to apply it when you're doing stuff that you know is useless, like a car-inventory system. I learned it in school but I really applied it at work. It's almost like if you can read the instructions you should know how to do it.

Of course, one never knows what part of one's training is going to prove useful at work. Dave was able to take advantage of his linguistics background to write a grammar for a system to process messages. But perhaps the most unlikely application came from Alyssa, a technical writer. Before entering the computer field, Alyssa had spent several years teaching severely handicapped children. In working with these children, she said, "you had to examine every step of the learning process in order to make the steps small enough and repeat them and repeat them and repeat them so that they after a while learned it and assimilated it." Recall that computer programming involves breaking down operations into many tiny steps:

> I did great as a potty trainer. We started the child, gave him a lot of water, we spent the whole day, one whole day in the bathroom, and we put him on a little chair, we had toys and stuff right in the bathroom, try to put him on the potty every couple of minutes, and if we succeeded, if he actually eliminated on the potty we made a big deal of it, you know, a lot of clapping and hugging, and during the day as he had a successful elimination on the potty we moved him a little farther away, so hopefully by the end of the day or the end of the week we'd be walking from outside the bathroom and, I mean with a normal kid you don't have to go through all those steps but I was dealing with six- and seven-year-old children who their parents had given up on, did not think they could be trained, and it was an intensive experience. That's what we did for many of the kids, but it was a very important step, obviously, the parents had been diapering the children for six or seven years [and] were delighted when their children learned the skill. But it was progressive, little steps little steps little steps, repetition repetition repetition, and it took a lot of reinforcement.

"Little steps little steps little steps, repetition repetition repetition": in some ways the essence of programming, but here referring to a totally different setting. Alyssa's account captures the kind of skill and the kind of understanding that make for a successful computer professional.

SUMMARY

A predominant theme sounded by this group of programmers, especially those at Cellsoft, is that their formal education, even in subjects used in their careers, was largely irrelevant to their professional lives. Formal course work provided at best a grounding in method but did not give them the hands-on experience and room to play and to experiment that draw many people to computers in the first place. Lectures were boring, and the pleasure and true education in programming lay in what people did in their off hours, not in what they did to satisfy course requirements. The exception to this occurred when, for some of the women in this study, a particularly inspiring teacher brought the subject matter to life.

Training also did not prepare these students for life in a real-world programming environment. There was no emphasis in anyone's course work on learning systems as opposed to programs; there was no training in how to draw on a library of resources; and no one described any academic training that provided an understanding of real-world programming as a corporate, collective activity.

It was mainly the graduates of elite universities among my respondents (but not all of them) who recognized a value to formal study in computer science; and they saw the value precisely in the methodology and approach to problem solving they had been taught, not in any skill directly applicable on the job. What Stuart called the "divide-and-conquer," top-down method, the structured programming Kraft condemned as a management tool to stifle software workers, is a valuable technique to these programmers. Interestingly enough, those programmers with no formal academic training in the field learned this methodology on the job, and most took to it quite competently, leading me to wonder what the point of learning it at an expensive technical university may be, at least if one is going to work at a place like Cellsoft. However, one noticeable contrast between the Cellsoft employees and the system programmers and other elite-trained people I interviewed is that several of the latter expressed a fondness for relatively esoteric and intellectual aspects of computer science (LISP programming, formal languages, artificial intelligence), while no Cellsoft employees mentioned anything of the sort except as part of the boring background material they wished they could skip while getting on to the practical business of playing with machines or working on something with some practical application.

4

Learning the Environment

Whatever their education and work experience, all new employees of any company face a particular set of challenges. They must come to know not only the specific tasks that make up their jobs, but the other elements of "the system" as well: their company's business, their co-workers, their clients (at least, on the technical level, the end users), and the overall culture in which they will work. In this chapter I discuss how software workers find their way around the work environment: their orientation and formal training within the new company, their formal and informal introductions to the culture of their organizations, and their first activities in "learning the ropes."

LEARNING THE BUSINESS

One would expect that learning the actual business of a company is an important matter. For the computer workers at Cellsoft, much of this learning is incidental rather than formal and is not of primary importance. Programmers often use the phrase "Garbage in, garbage out." This has at least two meanings in the industry. One, the more commonly heard, is that the best program is no better than the data that it processes. No matter how well designed a program may be, if the data are invalid, the results are useless. The other meaning is more like "I don't care what the inputs to the program look like. Just tell me what you want done to them, and I'll do it." A related sentiment appears in an office cartoon: "Job control never makes mistakes. We just process them and see they get out on time." For applications programmers, the "garbage" is the raw material of their programs. Whether the subject matter is shop-floor control in manufacturing, an accounts-payable system in an engineering firm, or a billing program for a cellular telephone company, the important matter is the manipulation of the material, not the material itself. Therefore, while it certainly helps to know the company's business, it is not absolutely necessary.

In some cases learning the business is a matter of inference. The programmer begins with a problem. Presumably the program he or she is working on would not exist if there were not a business need for it. Therefore, the programmer can infer the need from the function of the program. A program is basically an implementation of a set of rules. Sometimes the rules are internally imposed: A program can work in one of several ways, and the developer (or management or sometimes the client) has chosen a particular one of these. Sometimes the rules are external: What and how much to tax on a phone bill, for example, is a matter of the laws of various jurisdictions, not of programmers' tastes.

There are many components to a cellular telephone bill. Some of these—monthly charges, taxes, service fees—are similar to the charges that appear on a regular telephone bill. The charge for a call to or from a cellular telephone has two components. One, the *land charge*, is the charge the local or long-distance carrier would impose for the call. This charge is the same as it would be on a regular phone bill and is based on a set of tables standard throughout the industry. Cellsoft, like any other company in the business of making phone bills, buys these tables from a standard vendor for the industry. The other component of the call is the *airtime charge*. This is the charge the cellular carrier levies for the cellular phone service. Almost all calls, whether they originate from the cellular phone or come into it, are assessed the airtime charge; the exceptions are the *special numbers*, such as the emergency number 911 or calls to customer service, which are always free. Airtime charges, like land charges, are assessed on a per-minute (or fraction of a minute) basis and may vary depending on the time of day or the day of the week. A cellular company has various *rate plans* that subscribers may select. The rate plan determines the airtime charge per minute in every time period and may also allow a certain number of free minutes. The airtime charge for any given call is determined by a process called *rating*.

A subscriber is assessed airtime charges regardless of whether he or she calls another phone or someone calls him or her. In fact, the airtime charge may begin when the called phone begins to ring rather than when someone picks up the call at the other end (so-called *ring time*), or even when the subscriber picks up the phone to start making the call (this is called *seize time*). Though these charges are not always made, the switch keeps track of them. Programmers working on rating consider this a rather sleazy practice; as one programmer, Guy, put it, the charge "shouldn't include dialing time. What the hell, it shouldn't include ring time, either. I'll tell you why. What the hell good is a phone you can't dial and it won't ring?"

Programmers at Cellsoft have learned these facts about cellular rating and billing in a number of ways. There have been formal training programs that include an introduction to the cellular industry (jokingly called "Cellular 101"). More often, however, people have picked up the information simply from working on the programs. Because the cellular industry is still very young (see chapter 1), most programmers come to Cellsoft with no experience with cellular phones. None of them have telephones in their cars. What they do possess, as we have seen, is an understanding of computers, programming, and business systems in general, and it is largely up to each programmer to apply that knowledge and figure out the cellular business in his or her own way. The learning may not even occur.

Barbara said that "unfortunately the programmers that have a clearer understanding of the business needs are more valuable than those that just know programming. Unfortunately, because that learning is incidental." She tried to learn as much about the business as she could when she started at Cellsoft: "I just sort of jotted down lots of questions. Not only did I know nothing about the cellular phone industry, I didn't even know anyone who had a cellular phone. So I wasn't even aware of the fact that when you're in your car and you have a cellular phone and someone calls you you pay for it. So I didn't have any prior knowledge. I knew billing from [my last job]."

Barbara believes that it is important to know not just the company's business but the industry as a whole: "If you know something about the industry, you will also need to know how your company fits into it, because that gives you rationale for doing what you have to do here. You need to know your company's position in this industry, so that if something happens, if you need something really quickly, that gives you more motivation, because you've got a competitor over there."

Also, even though one can program without knowing the business in detail, Barbara, as a senior programmer/analyst, is also interested in understanding the business issues and in writing the specifications from which the coding is done, and "if you don't know what the business requirements are, you can't do the analysis. I think you can code it, if the analyst knows what they're doing."

Before coming to Cellsoft, Jack had worked for a large software vendor doing government contracts. His company "had to report, on a monthly basis, moneys spent versus moneys allocated and projections, and it's got to be really tight. And my function was to come in, and in addition to looking at the money issue, also start looking at the staffing issues, so that we could better hire or not hire people." Jack learned about the business needs

> very quickly, because no one else knew about this, and of course being it was concerned with money and eventually staffing, a lot of people were asking questions, so I was the one answering questions. And it was good 'cause people [in management and government] didn't care that it was gonna take me an extra month to get out their monthly reports. They were going to give me that leeway initially,

but then they expected that I was going to be able to answer their questions. So because of that, I had to know what was going on.

In Jack's case, understanding the business needs made him more valuable to his employer.

For Bill, the system became clear through the process of watching a program run. Bill's first task at Cellsoft was a batch edit program—that is, a program that reads a large file of data (in this case, records of *roamer* calls, cellular calls made by a subscriber outside his home area) and decides which of them to process and which to reject, based on a number of conditions. Bill would go through the program with a *debugger*, a programming tool that allows one to run another program in such a way that one can stop after every line of code, or as often as one likes, inspecting data along the way. Bill is very enthusiastic about the debugger as a tool (see "Using the On-Line Debugger" in chapter 8). What is interesting here is his use of the debugger and the edit program to learn aspects of the business:

> See how the program runs, and see what gets kept and what gets tossed. And also, once you've gone through a few of the programs with the debugger you see where it gets tossed and then you know exactly, and you go in, and because you've seen certain values, you can go in and check it. Or you can go to the CTIA CIBER manual [an industry standard manual detailing data conditions], and say, Ah, you had these five conditions, you go in, oh let's pick that record out. Why did this record get rejected? You can have, bang, right away. And that's when you have a feeling, you know, I'm starting to understand this system.

Another way to learn the business is from records, or file layouts. A *file*, in computer parlance, is an organized set of data. Files are built from *records* containing information of a standard kind. For example, one file consists of *call-detail* records, information about each call that cellular subscribers make. The *record layout* describes the contents of the records in the file, broken up into *fields*. A field is a fixed number of characters, or *bytes*. Call-detail fields contain information such as the cellular telephone number of the subscriber, the number called from that telephone, the duration of the call, the land (or toll) charge, the airtime charge, and many other attributes of the call. Cellsoft follows an internal standard that says that all fields in a record description are to be *commented*; that is, preceding each field is text describing the field's purpose, possible values it can contain, and the meaning of those values. Therefore, it is possible to learn a great deal about Cellsoft's business simply from reading the comments in the file descriptions. Judith, who had to write report programs based on the call-detail file, used it as a learning device in this manner: "I learned about the call-detail record and the reports and the fact that there were interlata calls [long-distance calls between area codes] and intralata calls [long-distance calls within an area code] and local calls, and you know there's RBOC [Regional Bell Operating Company—the local telephone company, or 'Baby Bell'], and . . . I think I learned more about the applications side than our systems side. [I learned a lot about] the cellular industry."

GETTING STARTED IN A NEW JOB

People become oriented to new jobs and companies in a variety of ways. At Cellsoft there was no formal orientation to the company until mid-1989, so many employees were left on their own to figure out who was who and what was going on. People may have gotten an introduction to the industry through the training overview ("Cellular 101"), which was just starting at that time, through conversations with their managers, through reading programs or documentation, through reading a book (Bernard, 1990) used informally as a textbook about the industry, or simply by being given a task that introduced them to many features of the system.

In most cases a new hire would be given at least a chance to find his or her way around, rather than being started cold on a task. Barbara, for example, was hired to work on billing programs. Her manager "sat down with me, I think on my second day and gave me a twenty-page document on how billing and rating work. And he also gave me a three-or four-page schematic on what files are input to billing and what files come out of billing and sort of a general picture of how billing worked." Barbara's manager wanted her to read and learn all this, "and he made it very clear that he would be available for questions. So I just jotted down lots of questions . . . and then he gave me a task and he said, 'what I want you to do is, there's a biller program that has lots of calls in it and that generates the data for our bills, and we have two different versions, we have Boston 1.4 [that is, version 1, revision 4 of the software running for the Boston client], and he said we have other versions of 1.4, and what I want you to do is take those two programs and compare them for functionality.'"

The project that Barbara's manager assigned her was a *conversion*, a translation of a program from one version of a system to another, in this case for two different clients: a program working for a client in Boston had been modified to meet the requirements of another client in Washington, and in studying the differences, Barbara could indirectly learn how the biller itself worked and what functions it performed. A task of this nature, designed as much to teach the system to a novice as actually to perform some useful work for the company, can be thought of as a *forcing function*. Robert, the electrical engineer who manages the CAD group at another company, explained how he orients employees, using terms that describe Barbara's experience at Cellsoft to some degree, though he added another element:

Typically we try to use a mentoring approach where we find a senior person who's worked in the area and pair that person on a buddy-system mentoring approach. Typically [we] start the person off for the first quarter at least doing maintenance tasks on similar coding so they can become familiar with the system. First of all, it gives them a task which they have to achieve, and so, there's a forcing function which says, "Ah, I'm new to this group, I want to prove that I'm a good person, and my manager has told me I must repair the bug in the XYZ module." OK, so that's the forcing function. We have the mentor to offer guidance and suggestions, and in performing the task, which means, "Oh, I have to learn how to log into VMS [the operating system, or controlling program, of the Digital VAX computer], I have to learn how to use the Language-Sensitive Editor." They encounter a set of skills that they need to be successful in the environment, and they keep bumping into these barriers, and hopefully we provide, through documentation, through formal classroom training, and mostly through the mentor and other colleagues who are willing to lend a hand and help out, provide them access to the information or pointers to it so that they can . . . get over those hurdles. The assumption is they come in being basically good programmers and they have to learn the local applications.

Cellsoft does not use the "buddy system" as Robert described it, though at least one programmer wishes it did. Jack, when speaking of the limitations of the four-week training program he experienced, said, "I think if I was able to work with someone, if [in] that last week of training [they would] allocate you to a peer, who could answer all your questions, I'd be all set."

While Jack feels that his manager gave him little help during his first few weeks at Cellsoft and expected the classroom training to provide a thorough orientation, Barbara's manager served as a mentor for her. He provided her with conversation (actually formal presentations) about the system, tasks to teach her aspects of billing, and time for questions. "So I thought about that, and ten minutes later I'm back and I said, OK, if you were me how would you approach this task? And he said, OK, this is what I'd like you to do."

Barbara's style incorporates an iterative process of taking in information, absorbing it, coming back and asking questions, going off by herself, writing down notes, and asking more questions until she feels she understands everything. Stuart, at MIT, used a similar process in learning the X Windows system, a set of programs that allow a number of *windows*, or small screens, each with its own work, to appear on one workstation, giving a user the ability to work on multiple projects concurrently from the same terminal. Although he worked on his own rather than with a manager or colleague, his internal process of building the system for himself was much like Barbara's, though he described it in terms consistent with the formal training that he had, and Barbara did not, in computer science:

At the time [the system] was very small and so it was still the same
method of sit down, read what documentation there is, understand
how the pieces fit together. The key thing is building a model in my
head. I liken it to a chandelier: What I do is I keep reading, looking,
trying to build a lattice or something, again putting the pieces of the
chandelier together, until I understand how all the different pieces fit
together, and then at that point, once that happens, then suddenly it
all works that you can then take it apart, you can understand what
you can do, what you can't do, and then, when you start breaking
problems down, you then can figure out how to keep breaking them
down to the smallest little pieces.

Formal training has its virtues and its limits in orienting people to new
jobs. Cellsoft programmers who did not go through the introductory training
program, whether because their managers didn't allow them the time or
because they started with the company before the training existed, regretted not
having had the formal introduction. Arthur, who was hired at Cellsoft to
speak with customers about problems they were having with the system, and
who had little programming experience when he started, said of the training, "I
think everybody could use that. I certainly could. When customers call, a lot
of times they say, 'Wow, our system can do that?' or 'What key are you
hitting?' Just working with one little aspect of it, I never have time to go play
around with it and see what you can do and how the whole thing works. I don't
know how you make time for that, I think it has to be structured."

Jack started at Cellsoft a year after Arthur. By that time "Cellular 101" had
expanded into a four-week course, not just describing the industry and
presenting an overview of the company's software, but going into considerable
detail from both a customer's and a programmer's point of view. The first
four-week class began on Jack's first day, so, unlike Barbara, he was immersed
in training before acquiring any direct experience of the product. While he
appreciated the value of training, he found himself wishing for a chance to get
to know his co-workers and the culture of the company:

This is my fifth week here. I might know three people, because I got
to see some of the people going through training, but they would be
in the class with me for three or four days, then I'd have a new group,
because a lot of people who've been here for a while, who need this
training here, are going through the classes now. So I've met the
people in my department, and that's it. Somewhere along the way
someone needs to say, "If you're going to get a new employee, then
you need to give them an organizational chart so they know who's
who." So there needs to be in some ways a little bit more—maybe
at this point it needs to be management training. They need to go to

the managers and say, when you hire someone, take him out for lunch that second or third day, and tell them what your department is doing, how it relates to other departments, etc., etc. Yesterday I was [looking] for the accounting department. Didn't know if there was one. Had to find that.

So even with the training, Jack found himself on his own and isolated to some extent, and he added, "I'm not sure that's really efficient for the company. Today I just realized there are distribution lists out there. So that's why I wasn't getting any of your mail. Oh. So that's where I think we need to be more formal." What was missing for him was an introduction not to the cellular industry or to the software, but to the company.

The extent of this training, concentrated as it is, can be a drawback. Joyce, who left college because she wanted to get direct experience on the job, had similar feelings about attending classes at Cellsoft for several weeks.

If you learn all the concepts first, in classes, you wonder how is this really used, and how would this actually fit into some problem that you have, so the application isn't there as much, the real-time application. You know, a lot of times they'll simulate things, but it's not the same as when you're given a problem and you need to solve that problem. So I'm not saying that you need to take all the training before you do anything. Because I think that has some negative aspects too. So probably if you found the right mix, that would probably be a good way of learning.

Horace, a professional instructor at another software company, echoed this view:

I would say the thing that mitigates against the effectiveness of five-day training is, first of all, the fact that it's five days. If it were every other day, its effectiveness would increase by at least 30 percent. We used to have [a] two-week course, and the effectiveness of the second week was almost nil, because they just had no chance to absorb all the [material]. [But] when we split the two-week course into two one-week courses with the idea, perhaps they return to their work site, . . . it worked better, because there was some real world in between. Of course for those who weren't using it on the job, it worked worse.

On the other hand, some things can be learned only from experience. Leslie's job is not to create or change programs, but to customize and to install the system for new clients. There is no direct training for this kind of work, only immersion in the problem: "Getting in there, getting incredibly frustrated, and figuring it all out. And you know, it's like going into the war, it's the best kind of training there is. But, you know, up front thinking about having to go through that is not always the most appealing thing."

To a more experienced programmer, formal orientation and training may be unnecessary. Guy is a senior programmer/analyst with twenty-eight years' experience. The only programmer in this study without a bachelor's degree, Guy learned his craft through some formal training but largely by experimentation. Guy has a unique, linguistically based approach to learning that will be discussed at length later in this chapter. He came to Cellsoft at the beginning of 1989, before the company had instituted any formal training programs. His manager, Clark, is also Barbara's. Guy was also working on the billing system. He sees learning as a matter of finding out the meaning of words he doesn't know. Here is how he described starting out at Cellsoft:

> Well, I started by goin' over to the guy that hired me, and, what is it he told me to do, he told me to read, there was a manual. No there wasn't a manual, he told me to read the code. OK, so I started out getting a listing of BILLER, reading the code, and lo and behold, didn't I run into a lot of words I didn't understand, OK? When I found out what those words were, I went off and I figured out what it did. I went to Clark and said, "Hey Clark, you got the original specification on this program?" He happened to have not the original specification but an overall functional spec that he loaned me, so I sat down and I understood conceptually what it is we were trying to accomplish, and then from reading the code, you know, and things that got me where, techniques in COBOL that I never used before and some of the Rdb [relational database product manufactured by Digital Equipment] stuff. So I just sat down and read the code and tried to figure out what the heck was goin' on. And once I figured that out the rest became history.

Guy first received formal training on computers in 1962. He had been employed as a technician. He was given classroom instruction, first in the hardware, then in assembly language, then in FORTRAN. He found his early training immensely helpful, recalling the instructor's approach as particularly straightforward:

> So a guy says, "Look, a computer can only do one thing, it can add, that's all it can do. There are people'll tell you computers can subtract, forget it. They don't know how, they just add. Very fast, though." OK, and they said, "All right, there's instruction registers, there's memory registers, there's program buffers," actually they called them program registers at that time, "there are some counters involved," and some other bull, OK? So they sat down, they drew a

hierarchy and they said, you wanna do this, let's say I wanted to do an LIA, Load Into A, from a teletype for instance, OK? I gotta turn this bit, this bit, and this bit on, because that's the instruction that says LIA, OK? So, that's what happened, they taught us those things.

By the way, the way they taught was very interesting. . . . It was interesting the way they taught, because what they did, I think I probably oughta thank 'em for this, because they taught me something, more than they think they did. But the very first thing they did when they started to tell us, started to teach us, was tell us what they were gonna teach us. Then they taught us, then they told us what they taught us. That's education 101, right?

The very first thing this guy did was sit up on the board and said, "Here's the problem. And I'm gonna teach you how to solve it." So . . . there was something, a task that had to be performed, and this guy was gonna give us the knowledge.

Guy, then, wasn't just getting theory; he had something to tie it to from the beginning. Like Ed, Joyce, and many other programmers, Guy could benefit from classroom learning only because it was tied to practical problems. Also, at each step Guy was able to build on what he already knew, based on the sequential nature of the training, which paralleled the logical, sequential nature of programming itself.

One of the things that happened was, I began to recognize that, as the guy set the task up on the blackboard, . . .   that before he started to teach me something, I knew about 60 percent of what had to happen anyway. I wasn't gonna pay particular attention to that 60 percent, but I sure was gonna listen to the other 40, if I didn't know that. And that's what taught me how to get the way I am now, and that's how I do.

What triggers the learning, what enables Guy to flag something as unknown, is unfamiliar terminology. In this particular problem, Guy already knew

the instructions. For instance, when somebody described to me Load Into A, I want to take a character from the teletype and stick it in this register 'cause I wanna do something with it. So I know that if I'm gonna take a character from the teletype and the task is to generate an interrupt routine that says when the character's done . . . putting it out to the teletype, cause an *interrupt*. A who? A what? An interrupt, so now we go into finding out what an interrupt is. But I knew one thing, I knew that I had to do a Put A or a Load Into A first to get the character into the teletype, then I had to put it out to the teletype to get it out there. I already knew that because I knew, . . . three instruction sets, what the hell's an LIA, it's Load Into A, OK, load into accumulator A, actually. But, you know, next thing that, I don't know if it's osmosis or what the hell happened, but I always look for words that I don't understand, OK?, because that's the stuff I don't know. The other stuff I understand, well, OK, that's no problem.

Bill also started off by reading, but in contrast to Guy, "I read through everything because it's a new job, and I didn't know what I was gonna be doing, exactly." Whether by training, mentoring, questioning, having a particular job to do, or simply immersing themselves in whatever they can find, programmers get started and find their way around. Which of these things they do, and which they choose to do, help to define them as individuals and as learners; and the relationship between their styles of learning and the jobs they are set, or their managers' approaches to training and orienting them, helps or hinders their achievements and their feelings of satisfaction on the job.

LEARNING THE CULTURE

In addition to learning the specific tasks they need to do, new employees need to grasp the culture of their organization. Most people do not think about this dimension of their work. Those who do may see it as a contrast with other companies for which they worked in the past, or they may see learning a culture as consistent throughout their careers.

Stuart, who is especially interested in organizational behavior, has worked at two companies. The first, now defunct, was a small firm that made graphical software for mechanical engineers. Stuart was brought into the company soon after it was formed; his job was to write graphics programs. Here is how he described the atmosphere at that company:

One of the things that was very special about [that company], that most of the people that I knew there all agreed, was that there really was a sense of striving to get something done, and that everyone was pulling together and was part of a team. That manifested itself by having everyone from the president of the company on down working together if there were problems. I always liked to quip that if the floor was dirty and the president was standing next to the broom, he got to sweep. That's mostly geared towards being a startup. But I think there are a lot of lessons there that any organization that really is striving to meet a goal should have.

Stuart favorably contrasted the teamwork at his first job with the more individualistic, academic atmosphere at his current one: "The goals of the lab are different. This is a research laboratory, it's very academic, and in some ways people here don't value working together, they don't actively try to work together and they honestly don't care what other people are doing. They're really focused on their own particular interests. And I think some of that is counterproductive." What the two organizations have in common that does please Stuart, regardless of the differences in cultures, is that each is "an organization that wants to succeed": "Part of our goal is to spread X [the windowing system] as far and wide as we can, and so we do that in certain particular ways some people agree with, some people disagree with, but in general it works. I tend to look upon it as part of being an organization that wants to succeed, and you do that by really making people want to use what you're doing, and if people don't want to use it, then you're not gonna succeed."

Barbara saw the contrasts between Cellsoft and the other company she worked for less in terms of people's interactions and more in terms of the differences between a small, fast-moving organization and a large, bureaucratic one:

> I think it takes a very special kind of person to work in this environment. Things are very volatile—[the last place I worked] was always very much into process. You'd analyze something to death, you'd sit around and meet for three weeks and you'd have flowcharts and you'd have pretty eyewash, and then maybe a month after you started your analysis, maybe you'd get around to doing it if you got cleared for it, but your boss would have to check with three other people to see if it was clear.

Barbara liked the fact that Cellsoft is much smaller than her previous company: "It gives you a chance to have an impact." Jack noted the individualistic nature of Cellsoft and of his former employer, like Barbara's a large computer manufacturer, but one with a different sense to it. Jack's last company expected individuals to fend for themselves and to build their own networks of people for support. It was a culture built on individual initiative, where "there's a very high value placed on you knowing as much as you can so you could be as productive as you *could* be. That meant you've gotta get your own network, because your manager's not gonna get it for you. That meant you were gonna get yourself into any classes you need to because, especially like in my department where I was bouncing around a lot, I could easily be setting myself up, and three years from now be ignorant of any changes because I was so busy going from one to the other." Unlike Cellsoft, however, Jack's last company was sufficiently large to offer its employees the structure needed to enable them to succeed as individuals:

You know, it was such a large company there was a formal process where people would actually indoctrinate you, if you will. I even went into a corporate culture training class. . . . I do remember they had said, "You can do nothing for five years and no one will ever notice. But five years from now you'll still be what you are today. Or you could go out there, and raise the flag and just do it all, and you'll move accordingly." Which was interesting to me because I had expected that but I hadn't expected that if you do nothing nothing happens. No one was responsible for you other than yourself. That was a very, very strong part of the mentality. And if for one reason or another you need any type of assistance, there is support out there for you.

At Cellsoft, on the other hand, since it was much smaller, "the support is not there. And I don't think you should expect it to be there. That's part of the overhead that a large company has." So Jack continued on his own the practice of building up networks. "I'm finding that I do because of the fact that, being that there is not that formal support, if I have a question, and my manager's not here, I gotta give it to someone. So that's why a network is being built up."

It is interesting to contrast Jack's jobs with the picture presented by Kraft (1977). Although Jack noted the contrast in working environments, he described neither his first company nor Cellsoft as the impersonal, regimented bureaucracy Kraft described. While there was an indoctrination, as Jack puts it, into the culture, it was not a culture where employees were told to follow orders; rather, they were explicitly encouraged to display initiative and to learn on their own. Though there are no doubt constraints on this in practice, even the espoused values differ from those of Kraft's world.

For Guy, who also worked for a much larger company, but who has many more years in the industry, the similarities between Cellsoft and his previous jobs outweigh the differences. He sees cultures, as he sees other aspects of his work, as a matter of learning the language. For example, Guy, like most programmers at Cellsoft, had never heard of cellular phones before working there. The word "cellular," in the industry, is often used interchangeably with "telephone," as in "Suppose a customer has five cellulars" or "What's his cellular number [meaning telephone number]?" When Guy first heard the word, he figured out from the context what it means and how it is used, and then

what happens is, the very next chance I get a chance to use the word cellular, I use it. 'Cause I want to be a part of the in-crowd too, I don't want people to know I don't know that a cellular's a phone, I don't want to say phone, I say cellular. [Then] I sound like I belong. It may or may not be true at that particular juncture, but at least that's what you do. 'Cause the sooner you assimilate into the group, the more you can learn. So, in order to do that you gotta talk the same language. . . . [It isn't that] necessarily you think you know what you're talking about, but at least you have a common ground to discuss things. If a guy's given you a detailed description of what he wants you to do, OK, and he says I want you to go, and I want you to take the cellulars out of accounts and take those in with the transactions, and whip them in using this thing to do that thing, and there are fifteen words you don't understand that he just got through talking about, guess what? You don't understand anything! So what you have to do is, you have to back the guy up and say "Hey, OK, what is a cellular? What is a transaction?" or "What is a woo-hoo?" or whatever. So, in order to move more quickly, be able to understand what's going on or what's developing, you have to learn the vocabulary, and once you learn that, then you got it made. It becomes a lot easier.

Culture as a network of support, culture as new terminology, culture as the rate of change and the degree of impact a person can have on his or her work: one way or another, new employees must grasp all this as part of learning their jobs and as part of learning "the system." "The system," again, is not just a set of programs: it comprises the hardware, the software, the organization, and the needs of customers.

SUMMARY

For the participants in this study, learning the business of one's company is an interesting, to some people an important, aspect of learning one's job, but it may not be as critical as one would expect. The programmers who consider it important are most often those with greater experience and certainly those with greater desire to perform more analytically oriented tasks, that is, to move beyond being what Kraft calls "mere coders." Those who are interested in the business elements of their work can acquire them deductively through formal training, attending business meetings, and reading company documents, but more often they learn them inductively through careful attention to what the programs they work on are doing. For programmers who learn in this way, the code, rather than just being what turns the "garbage in" into the "garbage out" (or, in Guy's words, what turns "gazintas" into "gazoutas"), becomes the key to what the business itself is all about. For most of these programmers, however, business learning is incidental learning, not a formal requirement of their jobs, and management is at least officially indifferent to how, or even if, such learning takes place.

When these employees started their jobs, they were generally given a chance to find their way around. They would typically be assigned a first task that would provide the "forcing function" to make them learn a large part of the system. This is congruent with the programmers' own emphasis on practical experience over abstract learning and represents one distinct consistency (though probably an accidental one) between management's need for practically trained workers and programmers' need for specific tasks from which to learn.

The role of supervisors is inconsistent and ambiguous. Some bosses, especially those with technical training and orientation, serve as teachers and mentors, while others let their subordinates drift and learn in any way they can. In view of the strong emphasis management literature places on the role of the supervisor (see, for example, Schein, 1985), one would expect this to have a strong impact on the amount and success of employees' learning, but at Cellsoft, at least, this does not seem to be true: Although the *pace* of learning may be affected by the amount of attention the supervisor places on it, the overall *extent* and *quality* of learning appear more directly tied to each worker's individual motivation. They will use whatever styles and inclinations they possess to learn their jobs exactly to the degree they wish, which is generally at least as much as is needed for them to do their day-to-day tasks.

The importance of formal training (that is, in courses within the organization) and its balance with practical work also vary with individuals. Although some programmers at Cellsoft considered their formal training valuable in laying a foundation for their work, nearly all felt that the practical work experience was more important in teaching them the company and the system. Even the one professional trainer interviewed felt that extensive training not broken up by bouts of practical experience is a waste of time for programmers.

Learning the culture is generally an informal task, typically not articulated by the programmers. Where cultural values are formally inculcated, as in Jack's previous company, ultimately each employee must still ferret out the "theories-in-use," to use management theorist Chris Argyris's term, as opposed to the formally "espoused theories" (Argyris and Schon, 1980, pp. 6-19). With a few exceptions, such as Jack and Stuart, the programmers and others in this study absorb organizational culture passively and do not think of it while doing their jobs. In part this may be due to the technical emphasis of programming (long considered a "machine-oriented" kind of work), but it may also be due to the fact that at most companies, including Cellsoft, no one brings such matters to the employees' attention; and just as most people are not aware of the sociology they practice in everyday life (as adumbrated by such theorists as Harold Garfinkel [1967] or Erving Goffman [1959, 1967, 1969, 1974]), so do the employees interviewed here seldom pay attention to the social backdrop of their work. This is not meant to downplay the importance of organizational culture to the employees' lives, but at least for these particular workers, as they define their own world, the culture of the organization is not a significant part of their awareness.

5

Repertoires of Thinking

In learning the systems they work on, the programmers and other computer professionals I interviewed draw on a range of mental activities. These activities may be grouped into informal and formal thinking modes. *Informal* modes of thinking are those of which the thinkers are generally unaware, those that arise semiconsciously from past experiences and that draw on analogies between the current activity, system, or problem and some other event or association in people's lives. *Formal* methods, by contrast, draw on training in techniques of problem solving or of thinking about computers and programming. These may be grouped into *analytic* (top-down) and *synthetic* (bottom-up) modes. It is also worthwhile to examine the notion of *design* in these programmers' thinking: that is, whether they believe there to be, and if so, whether they look for, any overarching set of principles in the system as a whole. This chapter discusses both formal and informal methods, as well as the problems that arise when a programmer cannot identify design problems and cannot make sense of the system as a coherent, unified entity.

INFORMAL THINKING: EXPERIENCE AND ANALOGY

"Experience" is a highly valued commodity in the world of work. Programmers' salaries, like many professionals', are tied to the number of years of experience they have. Salaries and employment opportunities are also linked to experience in particular areas: specific applications (payroll), industries (insurance), manufacturers or machines (IBM, Digital VAX), or languages (COBOL, C). People are supposed to learn from experience, and what employees learn is expected to contribute to their productivity and usefulness to their employers, though sometimes experience can actually get in the way of adapting to new situations (Weinberg, 1971). Experience, then, is widely agreed to be a good thing. But what is it? How and what do people learn from experience?

One of the simpler, though less obvious, skills gained through experience is the ability to work in a group setting. As stated earlier, students program in isolation on small programs or systems, but programming in industry is a group activity, and "the lack of experience in programming becomes more evident as the size of the system to be produced increases" (Weinberg, 1971, p. 67). Stuart, the systems programmer at MIT, saw experience as the result of personal and professional growth, rather than as an accumulation of technique or knowledge:

> Like most young hotshots I came out of school figuring I knew everything and boy, get out of my way, I know what I'm doing. And I look back now and I shake my head because I didn't realize really that what it means isn't just learning any techniques or learning additional theory or other things like that or learning how to program because yeah, most people when they come out, especially somewhere like this, they already know that. But that's not the issue, the issue is more learning how to work with people, learning how to design things that other people can pick up and use and dive into, and the real mark of a software engineer is that he can do something that is easy to come back to later or for someone else to walk up to, get into it and figure it out easily without having to really muck around. [That's] the classical distinction between [a software engineer] and a hacker, which is just throw it together and make it work, and God help anyone who wants to try to touch anything in it.

When Stuart and others speak of software engineering, they are referring roughly to a concept matching David Parnas's description:

> Software engineering requires the ability to program well, but it requires more. In software engineering it is usually true that (a) more than one person is involved in the construction and/or use of the product and, (b) more than one version of the program will be produced. It is as a consequence of these facts that the software engineer should possess abilities that are not required of one who produces a program for his own personal use (the solo-programmer). (Parnas, 1984, p. 303)

This distinction between software engineering and programming is similar to Weinberg's differentiation between amateur and professional programmers:

> Perhaps the deepest differences emanate from differences in the ultimate user of the program. Almost invariably, the sole intended

user of an amateur's program is the amateur himself, whereas the professional is writing programs which other people will use. To be sure, the professional oftentimes finds himself writing a program for his own use—to generate test data or to evaluate the performance of an untried algorithm, to name but two instances. And, indeed, when doing this kind of work, the professional commonly slips into amateurish practices. But the main thrust of his work is directed toward use of the program by other people, and this simple fact conditions his work in a number of ways. (Weinberg, 1971, p. 122)

To a large extent, the difference between the two styles is much of what experience accounts for. As an illustration of inexperience, Gary, an MIT-trained systems programmer in his mid-thirties, described a bright, relatively new person in his office who worked hard and could learn very quickly: "We . . . got this young guy right out of master's, and he has a master's degree and he just reads the stuff, he'd go home with manuals and come back the next [day], so he can read them over the weekend but he's young and unattached, and has nothing else to do. The young guy is brilliant, must be brilliant, given his background, [but] the point is that he doesn't have the judgment to know how to write maintainable code, easy-to-understand code." A company needs a balance between brilliant people and those with the greater judgment and perspective that experience brings. There is no way of conveying that perspective to the newer people; "They have no reason to believe [that more experienced people know better], because you have to live through it, you have to live through unmaintainable code."

As a part of this perspective from experience, Gary has found that as he has grown older and has been in the business longer, technical issues seem less important, and he has been focusing on issues of management and on the development of an organization rather than on individual skills. Contrasting himself with his younger colleague, he said:

You've gotta have some firsthand experience. . . . I think part of it is that . . . [at] a certain point in adulthood you recognize limits, and you recognize, either limits or just lack of interest or something that you say, "Yeah, I could learn this. Let's say that binder there was five thousand pages of code for some program. I could learn all that code, and I don't care how complicated the code is, I'd learn it." Or you could say, "I don't want to spend my time learning a program. It's a waste of time, it's mostly trivia. If it were well written, I wouldn't need to have this amazing set of knowledge."

More generally, experience gives one a backlog of past transactions of all sorts. It is useless without the ability to draw analogies from the past transactions to present situations. Previous encounters with computers become *standards*, or *templates*, on which to base later work. Gary put it this way:

> Well, a lot of it is, at least for me, that I take what I already know and I expect things to work that way, and then I figure out how it isn't like that. So, for example, getting back to the beginning of my career, the first system I learned was Unix when I was in a professional setting, so I learned how to understand the system as a set of function calls with manual page. And also the user programs, you expect a certain form of manual page where each function gets described.

The Unix operating system (Kernighan and Pike, 1984), as originated at Bell Laboratories in the 1970s and enhanced at the University of California at Berkeley and many other places, maintains its identity largely through a standard way all features are documented (an on-line manual, called **man**) and a standard format by which new features are added. Unix programmers have become accustomed to seeing things presented in this way and expect to see this style when they encounter either Unix itself or other programs built on it. For example, the X Windows system was built under the Unix operating system, and X documentation follows **man** format. Microsoft Windows, a windowing system similar to X that Microsoft developed for the IBM PC, follows the same format. Gary continued, "And then Windows pretty much copies, is a minor change over that kind of thing. [For] Microsoft Windows, the manuals are pretty much like the Unix manuals, for each function they have a description that's fairly . . . similar to it."

Sometimes the concern is not going from one program to another in the same system (in this example, the Unix operating system) but moving between systems of similar type. "Systems" here is used to mean common types of programs (operating systems, programming languages) or common applications (for example, learning two different companies' payroll software). This discussion focuses on operating systems and languages.

Joyce, the quality-assurance analyst, came to Cellsoft from a company using Data General (DG) computers. Data General began as a spinoff from the Digital Equipment Corporation (DEC) when Edson DeCastro, a Digital engineer, started his own company to develop a machine whose design Digital had rejected. As a result, DG operating systems have commands that are somewhat similar to DEC's. This made it easy for Joyce to apply her twelve years' experience with DG machines to the VMS operating system that runs on the Digital VAX computers that Cellsoft uses. For example, both companies' operating systems have an on-line help feature. If someone doesn't know how a particular command works, he or she can type "HELP" followed by the name of the command and see an explanation.

An important difference between operating systems, from a user's point of view, is that any given function may have different names on different systems.

There will always be some way, for example, to display text on a terminal; to copy, rename, and delete files; to send a copy of a text file to a line printer; and so on. For commands of this type, a programmer simply has to learn synonyms, but they are not always easy to find, and on-line help (called simply HELP in the Digital and DG operating systems, more cryptically **man**, short for "manual," in Unix) provides one common way of getting to them. Joyce continued, "What I normally would do is use the on-line help. Because I've already had that background at DG, I come here and I need to learn the VAX stuff, I need to learn a particular command, I know it's gonna be something like PRINT, and then I find it. And sometimes it's very easy, a lot of times it is, and other times it . . . does not resemble what I had used previously at all, and that's more difficult to find."

Guy described learning a new name for the command to display a list of files, the DIR or DIRECTORY command in VMS. Perhaps the most obvious method of learning new things, or new ways to do old things, is to look them up in manuals (see "Books, Manuals, and Other Documentation" in chapter 6). However, programmers seldom use manuals at Cellsoft, because, as Guy said,

> usually the accessibility of those kinds of materials is not what you'd call readily available, they're just not. I mean, that's a big expense, to look at all the manuals that a company has to buy for every particular kind of equipment that it has and multiple copies that are required because some guy pilfers one and takes it home with him or whatever, so short of buying every employee involved in th[e] . . . project . . . a manual for everything that he will ever conceivably need, there needs to be an alternative way. So the alternative way is to call on the experiences that you already have, or try similar things like you know, DIR is a nice word for directory but the very first one [I learned] was not DIR, it was CAT. For Catalogue.

> OK, but, so now what happens is you get into a foreign BASIC, OK? So you get into some guy's BASIC and you say, OK, I want to look and see what I got for files so you do CAT 'cause that's the first one I learned, CAT. Catalogue. It says, syntax error. So you try DIR. That don't work. So you say, OK, what is it that I'm trying to get this thing to do for me? I'm trying to get it to show me what files. Oh, let's try FILES. OK, here comes the stuff. So now I know that there's another one, there's another word in back that'll get me a listing on the screen. There's DIR, CAT, and FILES. OK? So next time I run into that problem I'll try those three. And if that don't work I'll look for another word. Keywords, all the time, that's why they call 'em keywords.

When Guy mentioned "a foreign BASIC," he was referring to the fact that not only are operating systems different from one another, and not only is one programming language different from another, but the same language is different on different operating systems, and in moving between machines a programmer has to relearn the idiosyncrasies of each language. Here again, experience becomes a matter of drawing on the right level of generality. It is as if the programmer is saying, "I know what I need to do because I've done it before, but I need to know the new way to do it."

For Guy, this is far more than a programming issue. We have already seen the importance of words and language in Guy's approach to learning. In his case this actually goes back to his childhood. Guy came from a fairly poor family and was partly raised by his Italian grandmother. He learned Italian because

> well, it was a necessity, I had to talk to her. She didn't know any English and I didn't know any Italian and the likelihood of her learning English was remote so I figured I better learn a little Italian, right? So I learned it. Same way as anybody else. I didn't know there were things called Italian-to-English dictionaries and backwards, [so my grandmother] says to go ask my mother, Ma, what's a gavon [an Italian obscenity], you know, and my mother tells me, so next time my grandmother says that I knew she was swearing at me.

Guy drew on this experience to continue learning languages: French and Spanish in high school, and later Korean when he was in the army. This was not difficult for him because of his background in Italian. "French was a high-school subject, I picked French because all the words in French are very similar to the words in Italian, so I only had to learn 45, 50 percent of the stuff. Same thing with Spanish. Once you know French and Italian, Spanish becomes, you know the only problem you have is the same problem you have learning programming languages. [Sometimes there is a] problem with syntax, and sometimes transposing the wrong keyword."

As with spoken languages, programming languages are generalizable, within limits. Guy was hired at Cellsoft to program in COBOL, a language he did not know, but he had no trouble learning it. The major difference between BASIC and COBOL to Guy is that the latter is "more verbose. From a programming perspective, it's not what language you use, it's all technique. The syntax changes but the technique doesn't. BASIC does FORs and WHILEs, and COBOL does PERFORMs. Whoopee-doo. Same thing. So syntactically something has to change."

Guy also draws on experience in a more general way. From his background as an electronics technician he learned a basic approach he calls half-splitting, identical to what computer scientists call a binary decision tree:

You plug your TV set in the wall and you turn the knob on, OK? And it doesn't work, [so] what do you do? The very first thing that I do, is, I go, take the back of the set off, . . . right? [Check for] DC power and see if I got any. If I don't have any, I know where the problem is, it's from there back. Go halfway again. How 'bout if I do have some? Then I go the other way.

If I'm trying to evaluate something, I half-split it. What happens here, where does it go? It diverges, or it converges. It diverges, it goes on these two tracks, so I develop the paths that it goes to, then I watch it . . . all back together again, then I handle one path . . . .. If I got a problem, that's the way I work on it, I work at it at the juncture of the divergent paths. I look there and see what the data looks like. Does it look like this is what these guys want to see? Yeah. Oh, OK, then I'm cool there.

Drawing on experience farther removed from computing, Leslie, a trained pianist, related learning software to analyzing music. Music theorists Heinrich Schenker and Felix Salzer, for example, have developed approaches to music that parallel the hierarchical structure of systems analysis. Leslie does not like to study music, or computer software, so systematically. Her style is more holistic: She is inclined to play a whole piece of music over and over rather than to break it down. Similarly, her introduction to Cellsoft's products was total and unsystematic:

I was taught also how to break things down into chord structure. . . . That would aid in memorizing things if you looked at each measure for its chord structure. And if I was forced to do [that] then I would do that. But I never liked doing that. I didn't want to systematize; you had to think about that. I'd like to do things, sometimes without thinking, and then ultimately the thinking might catch up with me. But I like to do things, I guess blindly at first, just sit there playing the same thing over and over again and finally, after I finally know it, and it's part of me, then I'll go back and I'll analyze and say, "Oh yeah; that's the progression there and now I see it."

That describes pretty much how I went through that whole [cellular management] system. . . . I'm just finally getting the concepts, you know, like I was asking Harriet [the training manager, who teaches the "Cellular 101" course] about them the other day. It's like I've seen everything, I know where everything is, but I have no idea really, where would you go first, what interconnects with what, when would you look at what, I wasn't thinking about that at first when I

was going through it. I was just going through everything blindly.
I just wanted to see everything. I didn't want to think about it. . . .
You know, either flip myself out or overwhelm myself or
something, and then [laugh] start to think about it.

It's like a magazine. I won't read a magazine, I won't go right in and
read a magazine first, first I have to flip through, and see what's in
there. Look at all the pictures first, look at all the different articles
first, know what's there and then finally I'll start reading.

Sometimes specific experience interferes with learning new software
because principles learned in the past may be inapplicable, or even
contradictory, to the new situation. Horace discussed a problem that arose as he
was learning PostScript, a formatting language used in printing text in different
fonts, as contrasted with other systems:

I have examples here somewhere of one of my early exercises, in
which . . . the text as I typed it goes *up* the page, the first line is at
the bottom [points on a piece of paper to illustrate], . . . actually
that's not true, the first line is near the top, [the] second line is above
it, the third line is above that, and the fourth line ran off the top of
the page, because I was incrementing Y instead of decrementing,
because I forgot that PostScript does the rational thing of putting the
origin at the lower left corner of the paper, which is what math does.
Well the thing is, on a Symbolics system and on many systems that
I've dealt with, (0,0)'s up here [in the top left corner]. And the
reason is, that when you're doing text output, it's more natural to
increment . . . the Y position than it is to decrement. Well, that
makes sense on a Symbolics machine, because [on] the Symbolics
machine, screens have the form of [an] infinite strip of paper with a
top but no bottom. And you could go arbitrarily far down, adding
text to the bottom of the screen. . . . Take a look at this [points to
the right side of the screen]. You see, that's a bar, and that bar
shows, on our system anyway, the system maintains a complete
transcript, everything that happens, I'm scrolling backwards now,
[types] through the, I could show you I mean, way up here, we'll
find, not where I logged in but where I cleared the output history, and
it goes on forever. Anyway, in PostScript, since it's a page-
description language and a page is not taller than eleven inches, we
don't have to worry about that. The coordinates are not going to go
negative, because paper stops here. And, and so they, not having this
problem of the infinite sheet that we did, they dropped back to the, I
believe, correct thing to do, that's to agree with mathematics and put
the origin [at the bottom of the page]. I forgot this. I'm so used to
going the other way.

So experience, which did give Horace a guideline of how the line count should work, steered him precisely wrong. Curiously enough, contrary to what one is never supposed to do, he did make the same mistake twice, but the value of experience in this case was that he caught it much sooner the second time.

What's funny is, that I've learned PostScript in spurts. And I had this [same] bug . . . once, I had to stare at it for about ten minutes before I realized what was causing it. I had to stare at it for about forty seconds before I could even figure out what had gone wrong. The text looked so strange. And then it took me five or ten minutes to figure out what had gone wrong, what had caused it. And then, very recently, I sort of picked up PostScript again, 'cause I had some other case that I needed to print out. And I found that I made the same mistake, but this time, as soon as I saw it, I knew what it was, it didn't take me any time at all.

However, some errors recur regardless of knowledge that would presumably avert them, and here too the virtue of experience is in improved speed of recognition and correction:

There are programming mistakes that I make in LISP, that I have made from day one, I've never stopped making these programming mistakes. And I have gotten so used to the symptoms, that as soon as I see [them] I can almost without thinking charge in and fix the typo; it's just something that I do. This involves setting up a loop. You initialize the loop, and then you have some expression that you use to initialize a variable, and some other expression that you use to step the variable. And usually the stepping expression is something like $I + 1$, where I is the variable. Well, so you say, "let I = start," and then . . . now there you go and you say well $I = I + 1$. But I continue [instead] and I say "let I = start + 1." So the loop . . . consists of 0, 1, 1, 1, 1, 1, and it does that forever. And I've learned that, it's not just adding one, it happens in all kinds of domains, it's sort of like, you know, for each line of text in a file, I find myself adding [the initial] variable . . . [instead of] the looping variable, and I do this constantly. But I've learned to recognize this sort of 1-2-2-2-2-2-2 pattern.

There is a theory in education that "bugs" in learning are the result of incorrect mental models, and that "debugging" a pattern of thinking involves getting at the erroneous thinking at the base of the problem, not simply correcting a mistake (Schoenfeld, 1983, 1987; Senge, 1990). However, when this idea was suggested to him, in an attempt to elucidate the model underlying this particular error, Horace said, "I think I've never paused to analyze it because the obvious explanation that it's just stupidity is so convincing to me."

FORMAL THINKING: ANALYSIS, SYNTHESIS, AND DESIGN

Programmers try to understand both the overall structure of the systems on which they work and the details they need in order to work on particular problems within those systems. For each programmer, the balance between overview and detail is different, as is the balance between analytic (top-down) and synthetic (bottom-up) approaches. For many, system knowledge (like God) is in the details, and in some cases all knowledge is derived from inferring the relationships between small pieces of the overall system. Other people find it more important to grasp the whole picture before going into details.

Also, some but not all programmers think in terms of *design*, the idea that there is or should be a controlling form, idea, or style underlying an entire system, and that grasping the underlying design is important in understanding the system. This way of thinking is clearly tied to programming methodology. It is not automatic, however, that programmers will apply this approach to preexisting systems, and in fact some do not. Whether and how well one can apply the notion of design to a system, moreover, is a function of the system itself, not just of the programmer's learning style. One can only grasp the internal organization of a system that its creators have constructed in a "systematic" way. Many software products were haphazardly constructed, and one must impose a design on them retrospectively. While doing so may in fact be an excellent idea when one is constructing or understanding a finished product (Parnas and Clements, 1985), many programmers do not make the effort when they are simply trying to solve particular problems. As a result, they may not see what consistency exists within a set of programs, or they may not realize how much the lack of clear design is hampering their ability to solve problems without creating others and without assuring that the problem will remain solved despite changes elsewhere in the system.

Analysis: Top-down Thinking

Before Bill was allowed to change any code in his first task at Cellsoft, his manager had him analyze and describe what the system did. His manager gave him "the heart, the program which really is the heart of the financial settlement system, although I didn't know that at the time." Bill figured this program out, and his manager "reviewed it with me, and he said I analyzed it very well. Which made me feel good because I still didn't feel quite on the level of confidence that I really was that sure of myself. . . . I didn't feel that comfortable with BASIC yet, and I was still unsure of myself with it." Once Bill had the overview, he could proceed to the details:

> And from that you could explode the system into subsystems, and do the same thing again for each subsystem . . . until you get to a program-by-program level, where, as far as documentation all you really need is a paragraph if that, probably two, three sentences for most programs, and if you need more detail than that go look in the program because you really, it seems like you're gonna be either looking for something or making the change in that program and you need the detail of the code.

Bill described the same process when he had to add a new routine to an existing program within this particular system:

> I also had to include right after I accepted the input a validation routine, to validate what had been entered by [the operator], and if it was incorrect to return and prompt her again and not to go on. Or in this case actually it would return with an error and it wouldn't perform, since this was done in batch later on. . . . What I did was I dissected it into functions, where things were performed, I analyzed them to see, well, can I fit this in or will it have to be restructured? It was a fairly good program to make a modification to because I didn't have to do any restructuring to the existing code, very little, but there was no way around that, it was more or less structure of how the control was now going to work. It was not ripping apart [the] code's function . . . , it was mostly just adding and replacing code.

Henry acquired his top-down understanding of his system neither through training nor through coding, but rather as a system manager. He saw how the system functioned because he had the job of setting up the hardware and dealing with operational problems. "Just from my system administrative duties I've known how the whole project works together, expert system, the talkers, and all the other things, and how the talkers function."

A *talker* is a program that passes data from one machine to another. At least one of the machines is a computer; the other one may be some other type of computer-driven hardware. Henry's company makes credit-decision software that allows a client (such as a cellular phone company; this company was started by the founder of Cellsoft) to enter identifying data on an applicant, such as his or her name and social security number, call various credit bureaus to get credit information, and then, based on that information and on a *policy*, a set of decision rules provided by the client, either grant the applicant credit, deny credit, or suspend a decision until a manager can review the application directly. The credit-decision program feeds the applicant's data to talkers that call the credit bureaus. The credit bureau returns the information to another program, called a *listener*, which passes the data to the decision-making part of the system, called the *doctor*. Sometimes the credit bureau reports come in through a fax machine rather than directly through a computer; Henry had to write a talker for the fax.

Before he started on this particular talker, Henry had to learn how the other talkers worked. Henry started his current job as a system manager and then moved into programming. From system management, "I got an overview of how the whole system should work, and then how the talker should work. And then, analyzing the lower levels, and then, that fax project I told you, was a form of talker. Started with a bare-bones talker, and I built up all the pieces around it, specific to a fax, instead of calling a credit bureau."

Stuart uses an iterative process, alternating between studying a system and playing with it: "Read, figure out the areas in which you need to play, and then go and play. Some people do it by effectively walking into a dark room and then stumbling around. I like to at least get some notion of topology, some notion of the layout of things."

Dave described his analytic process as follows:

> The way I tend to break down systems these days is into sort óf a bunch of cooperating, active processes. I design it that way even if for the sake of performance it ends up being inefficient. I design it that way and then I . . . sort of take the tasking or the processes out and build a standard kind of cyclical system after having designed it as autonomous processes . . . and each one sorta does one thing, like one guy [program] listens at the command line, one guy listens at the port where the messages were coming in, and everybody had one job to do.

> Each guy was an active thread of control. And I ended up having to mesh three of 'em into one task: the command-language interpreter, the error-correction guy, and something else all ended up being one, I think I called it the interpreter task. Just for efficiency reasons. But . . . that was almost a straightforward code transformation, once I designed them as autonomous things.

> I guess my conception of a design was organized around [the idea that] . . . all things are concurrent until proven sequential. I was saying earlier how I operate around basic principles? That's one of my basic programming principles. All things are autonomous unless proven dependent, or something, is one.

Dave here was referring to analyzing a complete new system that he was asked to develop from government specifications; we shall look at this system in more detail later. When the problem concerns fixing a system rather than creating or enhancing it, the analytic process is different. Guy saw that sort of analysis in terms of discrepancy:

> What I do, when I look at a program, I've got to get in and modify [a program called] BILL_MONTHLY_CHARGE, I'll look and say OK, what is this turkey doin' now? What do we want it to do? And is there anything structurally different? And if there is, can I set up a qualifier to go to a different part of this thing and rewrite that part only? And if the answer is yeah, that's what I do. So that you'll find a new procedure somewhere that does something based on this condition. So they'll leave all the other conditions alone, right? Sometimes that's not possible. You have to rewrite the whole thing. . . . You know what the gazintas are, you know what the gazoutas are . . . [so you try to isolate the problem.]

("Gazintas" and "gazoutas" are programming slang for inputs and outputs, as in "what gazinta the program and what gazouta the program.")

Because of the sequential nature of programming, no task is too daunting. Analysis is what saves programmers from being overwhelmed. As Guy said, "I can't . . . remember, . . . seeing things that were difficult to do . . . that I couldn't reduce to a series of simple tasks. If you try to look at them as the overall thing, I think it [would] probably overwhelm you, but you know, what's the first thing you need to do? What's the second?"

Synthesis: Bottom-up Thinking

In contrast to the approach of starting with the problem or the system and breaking it down into details, the synthetic method amasses the whole from the parts. This is often a result of a programmer's work assignments rather than of his or her style. That is, there are few people who would deliberately choose a random, pointillistic way of learning a system, developing their understanding from a collection of discrete pieces and problems scattered across many modules of a complex product, but this is what maintenance programmers often have to do. People whose work mostly entails finding and correcting problems ("bugs") in software may never have a chance to see the system as a whole and may have to build their knowledge from the many separate parts on which they work. In some cases they never develop a sense of the whole system at all, and this failing can at times have serious consequences when corrections to one part of a system cause another part to break down. In other cases no problems result. This is sometimes because the system is sufficiently modular, or the particular problem is so isolated, that there is no global impact. On the other hand, it is just as likely to be due to pure luck.

Like the assignments themselves, the programmers' learning may be randomly scattered throughout the system. Arthur was hired as a customer-service representative. His job at that time was to handle customer complaints and to deal with problems as they arose. Later he became manager of a maintenance-programming group. Arthur said, "I think this is what works for me: I think you start with little pieces and if that works put another piece on and another piece and another piece. Just makes sense logically." He did have some overview of the whole process, but it was vague: "I think, yeah, I have a general idea . . . how things are gonna go together, unless it's something obviously huge and then you can't, you just want to deal with one little piece at a time."

Arthur recalled his first task at Cellsoft as very detail oriented:

Find out why programs didn't run for our [service bureau] customers, and debug them, or find out what had to be done to restart jobs, and how do you submit a job interactively to a batch queue rather than using ACMS [the software used to run programs interactively], and what logicals have to be assigned, and so forth, what directories have to exist. More of like a production, firefighting, learning experience than being able to sit down and go through it and talk with somebody who knew anything about it.

Arthur did feel he understood, after about a year at Cellsoft, how the parts of the system are connected. His understanding came from "just working at all the bugs that our customers report and tracing it back to, you know, where did it originate, what caused it?" He learned by "running DEBUG, and inevitably you find out that we allow things on the ACMS side that we never thought of, whoever designed billing."

By the time of the interview, Arthur had worked mainly on the interactive aspects of the system: primarily the Customer Information System (CIS) and the Equipment Inventory System (EIS). In dealing with CIS and EIS problems, Arthur learned "what other part of the system might be affected. Whereas I don't feel that kind of competence with the rating and billing system. And I . . . try to avoid ever touching it, other than just helping to, you know, fight a problem, but I just don't know enough about the interaction between CIS and billing." This is in contrast with Guy, who focused on billing programs but claimed to understand the connections with the rest of the system, the "gazintas" and the "gazoutas." As a manager, Arthur felt that the people who worked for him often lacked that knowledge as well: "I don't think the developers understand the interaction right now between rating, billing, and CIS, and how you can affect something." Thus he focused on the limitation of the bottom-up approach, though it has worked for him to some degree.

Henry, like Arthur, focused on one piece at a time, but unlike Arthur considered it a matter of style. When he was working on the fax talker, Henry "built up all the subpieces knowing how the flow should work." However, he did another project from more of a bottom-up perspective:

Another project I did, which is now being incorporated [into the product], was some probability matching routines, where you're given a group of fields, like name, address, state-city-zip, and you use a fuzzy matching technique to compare them and determine, well, are these two people really the same people, if their addresses are the same and their social security number is two digits off and their last name isn't quite spelled right?

Henry began by programming a limited, specific case before he made the program more general: "The approach I took to that was, initially it wasn't required to be record-independent. We were only comparing these two, this one type of record with the same type, but I designed it so that you could pass it any type of record, with any different named fields and anything and it would compare the fields you'd want." Henry wanted to make it more general, "but I knew that, well initially . . . I just wrote it to work, but then, as I had more time I started changing the program, to do it that way, 'cause I knew, someday, we may want to use it for other types of purposes. And we are."

Henry had to set up the conditions for determining what constituted a match. "There was a very crude [algorithm], and I looked at that and started, used that as my base for determining [a] matching technique. Mostly [it] compares strings of characters and determines if they're rotated, or shifted or transposed or simply the digits don't match up. And so I applied, and uh, I kept using that same function, but applying it to different types of fields." He continued:

The way it works is, [my boss] developed this Bayes' theorem algorithm, which is . . . you match two fields, say, or two records together, or one field at a time, and you have a probability for each field, based on how well they matched, and then using Bayes' theorems you multiply all these probabilities together to get a final result. So if a lot of them don't match but one of them matches exactly, [that] alters the probability. . . . I had taken a statistics course but I really didn't grasp the concepts too well, but now I have a better understanding of it. It really helps for the matching routines.

So Henry then had a table of conditions, with each condition assigned a probability.

The way it works is, it returns an error code, either one digit was wrong or digits were transposed or whatever, and based on that you have a set of probabilities associated with that, those types of errors and how they affect an exact match. An exact match has a probability, and then, if you allow more errors, then the probability becomes greater that the two records will match, 'cause you're allowing more fuzz, but also the probability that you'll screw up and say they're the same when they're not also goes up. So what you want to try and do is have the probabilities that the records will match increase, without increasing the incorrect match. . . . And then that's different for every type of field, for example, social security number, it's often screwed up by two or three digits, yet a human looking at it would say, Oh, these are the same. But a computer has a harder time. And even if everything else is wrong, but the social security matches exactly, you're pretty much guaranteed that that's the same person.

The reason this program is necessary is that credit bureaus are not very systematic in how they gather or store information on people:

When [the "doctor" program] gets back information from the credit bureaus, it gets a list of possible responses, or possible variants, of the person you inquired on, but sometimes they return the wrong information. If they return three specific records on a person, each record may contain, or two records may contain, duplicate information, so you have to determine if the information in each record is the same, and if so you throw out one of them. I think they base a lot on the last name and the social security number. So that's why we need all of our matching and stuff, to handle all of the credit bureaus' errors.

Henry's technique for building the program is a synthetic one known as *prototyping*. A prototype is a small, working piece of a system. Rather than design a whole system before programming any of it, in a prototyping strategy the developer designs and codes a small piece, and when that piece is functioning, he or she builds upon it. Henry described his use of prototyping in the probability routines in the following way:

I think I focus on one piece, which may or may not be good, instead of focusing on the whole problem. But in the probability routines I started with the simple procedure that just compared two strings. And then from that I extrapolated out to the larger view: well, I have these two fields which may contain anything, and they'll call this generic string-matching routine. And so I'll expand that further: well, I'll need something that'll have a whole list of fields I need to compare, that will call the string-matching routine. So I build outwards from that small detail.

Henry acknowledged that even in this prototyping approach it is necessary to keep a larger picture in mind, even though he may not lay it out formally: "Yeah, you have to do both, you have to build the macro structure, how things will be laid out, and then I can build from the individual pieces outward, and meet in the middle."

Design

Underlying synthesis and analysis is the idea of *design*, the notion that there is a basic structure to a program. This is not self-evident; it is also not always true. Especially if a program is built up from small sections, like Henry's prototype, there may not be an overall design by the time it has grown into a full system. In that case code may branch to many points indeterminately, making it hard to follow and to debug (so-called spaghetti code). If there is an overall design, it will not necessarily be clear to anyone other than the original developer, or to someone joining a programming project after it has been going on for some time.

Whether it is possible to find or to infer the design of the system depends on a number of factors. One possibility is that the original developers have provided documentation on the structure of the system or are available to explain the design to new people. Ideally, a system can be documented in the form of functional and technical specifications before any coding has taken place. If this has not happened, one can retroactively create documentation implying that the design that ultimately developed was actually conceived in advance, even though it may not have been (Parnas and Clements, 1985). Specifications described as written "for historical purposes" fall into this category. There may also be documents that provide an overview, though not a formal description, of the system design. Most commonly, however, none of this is present, and programmers must infer the design from the code itself and from how the system works (the "black box" approach).

Dave bases all his work on what he calls "principles." He said that this is what drew him to studying mathematics:

Well, I think I like the orderliness of it. . . . I have a terrible memory, so I always liked the idea that, unlike going to a biology class, if I was in a math exam I could derive most of what I needed from axioms, from first principles, whereas if I'd ever had to take a serious course in biology or something, I would've been adrift, because I just couldn't remember, I don't have a way to organize facts

that way. I can organize simple principles and then derive
consequences, you know, so, and I would go in, and if I had a
calculus exam, I couldn't remember fifteen to twenty different rules
for how you integrate different things, I'd have to figure it out in real
time.

Dave said that he programs from basic principles as well. He admitted that
having to go back to basic principles slows him down, but

> I think . . . I still program that way. I program very much by
> principle. . . . I probably program very much by sort of combining
> simple principles rather than idiomatically. Or, this is how I did one
> of these before and now I'm gonna perturb it a little bit. I mean, you
> end up perturbing things 'cause you don't want to write tremendous
> amounts of code from scratch, but hopefully the way you do it is by
> having left yourself enough parameters in the time you wrote it last
> time that it's easy to plug in new ones.

Sometimes a programmer really cannot learn "the system," cannot find a
design. Newton is a programmer in his mid-twenties from Hong Kong. He
has been with Cellsoft for two years. He has fixed problems and maintained
programs for Cellsoft in both the billing and the customer-information
systems, but he does not have a sense of the system as a whole. Changes he
makes to code in one part of the system often lead to problems in other parts.
When he was asked if he saw any kind of unity in the system, he said that it
"depends on which function you're talking about. For some small function,
OK, say cellular number change, . . . even though you don't have the proper
design it won't be too far from what it's supposed to do, right? But say for
customer inquiry, it's a big function, and it ends up [with] a lot of bugs . . .
due to the design problems." However, when he was asked to identify a design
problem, he came up with a trivial example: "You cannot get rid of
equipment. Because, I'm not sure, OK, what I said may be, may not be 100
percent accurate, but is something like this, OK? Because in the past they
think every cellular only get one equipment record. It turns out that's not the
case. So now, if you access equipment for a particular cellular, it only find the
first one. But in fact a cellular could have several different ones. So you
cannot see the others."
What Newton was describing here is a minor feature of the customer-
information system. When a subscriber begins cellular phone service, he or
she may either own the phone or lease it from the carrier. This is the
"equipment" Newton was referring to. This piece of the order-entry subsystem
was designed with the assumption that a subscriber would only be renting one
piece of equipment. However, someone could also rent the antenna attached to
the telephone, and the system made no provision for that. There is no way to
enter that second piece of equipment, and even if there were, there is also no

way to refer to it from the terminal or to delete it. As design problems go, this one is not significant, and Newton was able to program a way around it soon after this interview.

A more significant problem emerges with a feature of the system called BILL_WHAT_IF. BILL_WHAT_IF allows a user to tell subscribers what their bills would cost under alternative rate plans. For example, a customer on rate plan A, with no free calls, a monthly charge of $10.00, and twenty minutes of airtime at a peak rate of $.50, would have a charge for the month of $20.00. He or she might find it advantageous to switch to rate plan B, with a monthly charge of $15.00 and fifty free minutes. The customer-service representative could bring up a copy of the subscriber's bill on the terminal and then go into BILL_WHAT_IF, enter the alternative rate plan, and see whether the subscriber would benefit by changing rate plans.

Logically, the BILL_WHAT_IF function duplicates the work of the billing software, merely substituting one rate plan for another. However, the programs for it were written as part of customer inquiry, which was conceived as a separate system from billing and did not use the same code. As a result, every change in billing logic—and there are a great many of these, because cellular phone billing is highly volatile in response to client demand— necessitates a change to BILL_WHAT_IF. Often, however, the billing programmers and the customer inquiry programmers are not the same, and the latter would not know that the former had made a change that required modification to BILL_WHAT_IF.

Thus there are design problems at several levels here. At the first design level, the programs should have been written in tandem and should have called the same subroutine. If this was not the case, at an organizational level the same person should be responsible for billing and for BILL_WHAT_IF. Finally, even if this failed, there should be communication between the programmers so that the BILL_WHAT_IF programmer would know that a billing change must be acted on in order to make BILL_WHAT_IF remain consistent with the biller. Because no one ever analyzed the problem, and because BILL_WHAT_IF was not considered an important part of the system until one customer began to use it extensively, the difficulty persisted for more than two years, until Newton, a relatively inexperienced programmer responsible for other customer inquiry functions, was assigned to fix BILL_WHAT_IF. He succeeded in fixing it a number of times, but each time the biller was changed, BILL_WHAT_IF stopped working correctly.

Although he studied computer science in college, Newton does not recognize BILL_WHAT_IF as a design problem in the sense just described. He is well aware of the connection between BILL_WHAT_IF and the biller, but just said, "If [the] biller is [frozen—that is, has no further changes], certainly, then once I get it to work, then BILL_WHAT_IF is all set. . . . I don't think it's hard to fix WHAT_IF, OK? Spending two weeks or four or five days is not a big deal to make the function work. But the problem is the biller is changing all the time." The idea that BILL_WHAT_IF should change automatically if the biller changes has never occurred to him. Because he is aware of the connection between the two programs, however, he has begun reading the biller program:

> Because, if you just look at the BILL_WHAT_IF, it won't help you, because it displays new data on the screen you don't know whether it's right or wrong, so the only place is you look at [the] biller, and try to find out the difference between the programs. Of course, first of all I would check the comments in [the] biller [at the beginning of the program, indicating what has been changed and when], . . . [but] they don't usually put it there, in the past at least. . . . And you don't know whether it's in [the] biller or its submodules. Or they add several lines to it, like the GET_SYS_ID, remember?

GET_SYS_ID is a subroutine that had recently been changed. Called by both the biller and BILL_WHAT_IF, this subroutine requires a number of inputs, or parameters, to be passed to it. The recent change to the program had increased the number of input parameters, but the programmer who changed this was unaware of all the programs that used this subroutine and had neglected to inform anyone of the modification. This is another common problem in systems with more than one programmer. Again, Newton is not aware that this lack of communication is a problem to be dealt with; rather, he simply said,

> I can't find [the] changes in the comment section of the program. If they put it there, OK, it will be very very easy for me to find out. [Or] if they let the one who change [the] biller to fix BILL_WHAT_IF, they will do it in a minute. Do you agree? It's much easier. See, if whoever puts the GET_SYS_ID in the biller, then they will know they will have to put the same thing in BILL_WHAT_IF. But I don't know, I don't know there's a program called GET_SYS_ID in the first place, and I didn't know someone put this into the biller because they didn't say it in the comments section. Even one line will make it very hard for me.

There is a utility in the VMS operating system called DIFFERENCES (DIF for short) that compares two files and prints a list of the differences between them. This utility, however, cannot show the changes to the biller and to BILL_WHAT_IF because, as Newton pointed out, "the two programs are totally different." It is difficult even to compare two versions of the biller because sometimes the older version has been deleted. Newton, then, has to look through perhaps several modules of billing code every few weeks to make BILL_WHAT_IF consistent again; but he could never see the problem at the most basic level, as a flaw indicating a poor conception of BILL_WHAT_IF from the start.

SUMMARY

The thinking that these programmers bring to their work combines formal and informal modes of understanding and inquiry. It is from a broad, usually uncategorized repertoire of past experiences that they identify individual problems as members of *classes* or *types*. Following Schutz (1962, pp. 59ff.), who applied the notion of typification more broadly to all sorts of experience, one can see programmers freely associating their current work either to clearly similar work in the past ("this is another billing program like the one I worked on yesterday") or more distantly to other aspects of their world (learning a system as one learns a piece of music, programming a computer as one toilet-trains a retarded child). This informal, metaphorical typifying of experience is necessary before one can proceed to a more formal mode of inquiry because it is impossible to identify the appropriate mode until one has categorized the experience. The programmer must invoke the most suitable technique by typifying accurately at the most appropriate level of analogy, or the application will not be useful. When we consider that these programmers are masters of the practical and do not pay close attention, as a rule, to their methods for typifying reality, their consistently accurate choice of analogies must be appreciated as a practical accomplishment.

Proceeding to more formal modes (analytic and synthetic), these programmers employ one or another mode partly as a matter of personal style, as when Henry opts to build prototypes and move from small systems to larger ones, and partly from the exigencies of work, as when Newton or Arthur must construct a system by relating small, discrete assignments to one another. The programmers accomplish analysis through reading, careful thought, and sometimes (following Parnas) constructing a system whether it exists or not; they accomplish synthesis through experimentation, prototyping, play, and a somewhat osmotic, less-than-conscious merging of pieces into one another to form a mental model of a whole. The danger in the synthetic approach, as we have seen with Newton, is that sometimes the system is apprehended at an inappropriate level of generality, or perhaps it is not grasped at all. If a programmer cannot find (or invent) the design in the system, this greatly increases the potential for breakdown in some area of which he or she is unaware.

6

Written Materials

In chapter 5 we examined the repertoires of experience and methods that computer professionals use in identifying and analyzing problems. Next we shall look at written sources of information. Beginning with the specifications that often serve as blueprints or instructions for programmers, in this chapter I discuss references written by others to aid in the work—that is, textbooks, reference manuals, and tutorials—and the occasions for reading them; and I also describe programmers' use of their own notes. Another form of documentation, namely, the on-line help provided by the computer itself, will be described in chapter 8 along with other uses of the computer as an aid to learning.

PICKING UP THE DETAILS: WORKING FROM SPECIFICATIONS

Typically, a programmer starts to work from a written *specification* (or *spec*, as it is commonly known). A specification is a document describing the function the program is to perform and may also include technical details about the program. A programmer's job is to translate the specification into a working program. There are different types of specifications: A *functional specification* is simply a description of what the program is to do, while a *technical specification* outlines how it is to work. These may be combined into one document. Reading and understanding specifications are important parts of programming; writing them is part of the analysis function. Someone with the common title of *programmer/analyst* may be expected both to read and to write specifications.

Like other resources, specifications have their virtues and their drawbacks. Ideally, a specification provides enough guidance so that a programmer is clear about what is expected, but it should still leave the details of implementation to the programmer. For Emily, a programmer/analyst three years out of a computer-science program in a state college, Cellsoft was the first company where she had to work from specs, and she appreciated it. "It cuts down on . . . doing something wrong the first time"; that is, it makes it clearer whether something is right or not. It also serves as a check on the sometimes fickle demands of clients. Clients often change their minds about what they want once a program has started. A great deal of time and money is wasted in rewriting programs if they have been improperly specified. However, the programmer cannot be faulted if what he or she did matched the written specification. As Emily put it, "If you have a spec and you program something that way and if someone comes back and says 'no, that's not what we wanted,' you can go back to the spec and say 'that *is* what you wanted.'"

As stated in chapter 2, the client is really part of the system, in many ways its most unpredictable element. To programmer/analysts, who often have little direct contact with clients, they appear capricious and often frustrating, and specifications serve to provide programmer/analysts with some control over this volatility. Bill also appreciates this aspect of a specification. Two specs from which he was working "sorta got modified though halfway through, not due to the people who wrote the specs or anything, just due to changing the business idea," but at least his manager did not hold him responsible for the original deadlines, whereas at his previous job, "you still get it done on time."

Wayne is a computer-science graduate from Taiwan. After three years of programming in the United States, including nine months at Cellsoft, he decided to return to his own country, giving up the programming field to work in his father's business. At Cellsoft Wayne worked on the promotions subsystem of billing. *Promotions* refers to a special feature of billing in which cellular subscribers receive discounts if they use the system a certain amount (for example, 10 percent off the total bill if the subscriber uses one hundred minutes of airtime). This feature was developed for a specific client. The specification, written by an analyst working for Cellsoft at the client site, was hard to understand and constantly changing. Also, to an inexperienced programmer with limited fluency in English, the specification was incomprehensible, and there was no one to explain it. Originally it was only three pages long. The spec, Wayne said, "tells me nothing. I cannot start it, you know. Because I think the point is, I don't understand . . .the spec, for the promotion. For the spec, I don't understand it, so I have to ask people, ask Clark, and Trevor [another programmer from Taiwan], sometimes they can give me the answer but lots of times they cannot, they don't know what the customer wants because they are not [on site], so I have to talk to Greg [the analyst at the customer site], but sometimes Greg [does] not understand very well." Even the analyst working with the client did not understand the problem well enough to write a decent specification for Wayne. Some of the difficulty could be the volatility of the client environment, but in Wayne's case the language barrier also played a role. In any case Wayne eventually left the company, the industry, and the country out of a combination of frustration and homesickness.

Specifications are written for a number of reasons. One programmer reported that at a previous job he had written them "primarily for historical purposes, so someone else who came into the group would have something to refer to and say 'Why were these changes made?' and they would be able to refer to the spec." More commonly, however, specifications serve as blueprints for programmers to work from. They may also be written as the basis for competitive bidding on contracts. Dave described a specification for a government contract. Though quite detailed, it missed what was for him the essence of the problem it described:

> The specification that the government had in place was your typical sort of functional breakdown. And I didn't really build it that way 'cause of the implicit need for the concurrency. . . . The spec . . . described, at a systemic level, what this thing, what the government at that point in time imagined they would do. You know, so the typical thing [is that] it talked a lot about the fact that it had to do error correction. It gave a character- or a byte-level, if you will, characterization of what a message was, but it didn't give you any of the grammatical aspects of a message. And it at best implied the requisite behavior of the system, the notion that, you know, if I'm correcting a message, while I'm doing error correction on this message that I've got in my hand, obviously the rest of the world can't come to a halt waiting for me. That kind of stuff's never in the spec, at least in government specs, you know. So that was the value added, or whatever, from my architecture was the fact that well, obviously they can't mean everything else comes to a stop, so we've got to keep going, especially if this performance requirement here is to be taken seriously.

The spec Dave described, though detailed, contained the wrong kind of information. Specifications can also be ambiguous. Guy uses specifications to understand "what the business wants to accomplish." As long as the specifications are clear and well written, there is no problem. "Now, if there are some things in that that you don't understand, then you go understand what they are. And if there are some things that you do understand then you got it made. The problem comes into being when people try to be very clever and they write things with a great deal of ambiguity, and then, you can get caught up. And a lot of times people write 'em that way to cover their yoyos, you know?"

The following example shows how three programmers, Barbara, Perla, and Judith, collaborate on specifications. They used an initial functional specification from a client as a basis for more detailed programming specifications, which later became the basis for actual programs. The client requested a report showing different types of calls accumulated from rated call-detail files over a period of time. "So [the client] wrote up a whole functional spec as to what they wanted in these reports, and then my job," said Barbara, "was to try to figure some kind of high-level feasibility study or high-level technical spec. And they really take their information out of rating, and so I had to learn about rating and I had to learn a little bit more about the usefulness of the reports from [the] customer's standpoint."

Barbara's approach to this specification from the client illustrates her learning style, as did her initial orientation from her manager:

> OK, the first thing I did was read over [the] functional spec and try to make some sense out of that. [This client] has a habit of singularly saying "this report" when actually they mean eight reports within that report. So I tried to understand on my own what the spec said, what their functional spec was, and [that] was just a matter of poring over the detail, and that I didn't need anyone for, but it took me a good day and a half to understand what they were saying. I mean, even at that level, just understand what they wanted, and then maybe try to figure out why they wanted that, but the first thing was to understand what they wanted. . . . So then, after that, that took about a day and a half, I sat down and tried to figure out from the spec what they meant by these fields, you know, what do they mean by billed minutes, what do they mean by toll charges, how do we calculate toll charges, how do we calculate billed minutes?

First, then, Barbara worked at the top level: What did the client want to know? Only after spending a day and a half on that did she go into the technical details that would relate the client's business needs to the files, records, and data of Cellsoft's billing and rating system. To do so, she looked both at the specification, as written by the client, and at the record descriptions of the files containing the data the reports would use: "I was looking at, also a record, the call-detail record, to see if some of those fields matched. But it was only after, let's say, two or three days of looking at that spec did I have questions about what they wanted." This is consistent with the other example we have seen of Barbara's style: She would study something as long as necessary in order to furnish herself with a set of detailed questions. She could not formulate the questions until she thought she understood the specification. She was able to derive a summary of what she gleaned from the specification:

> [The] functional spec said, well, this report should be divided into four sections, and each section should have this, this, and this data, but this section should have that, that, and that data, and this section should have this, this, and that data, and that type of thing. So, what

I did was, I just had a piece of paper and I just sort of took it down and wanted to just define all the subsections and the major sections and started matching it with their spec to make sure I was getting all the sections and all the pieces in the right places . . . and trying to define . . . some sections should be summarized, some should not be, and I was trying to clearly define in my head what the summary section should contain. That was all totally on my own, but then, after I got through with the general structure down, of what they wanted, then I could look at it in more detail and figure out, OK, well in this one piece of this structure they want something known as billed minutes, what does that mean? How do I get it?

I sort of had to look at it at two levels. One was the general structure of the report, OK, and what they wanted not only included these four sections and these subsections within the sections, it also included, we want to run this monthly, and we want it to include this, this, and this data, and we want it to tie to our billing cycle. . . . OK, so that's sort of a general, sort of system flow. And then I had to kind of look at it specifically as to what data they wanted.

But it turned out that the desired data were not merely billing data, with which Barbara was already familiar from other work she has done over the past year, but rating output as well; and Barbara had never worked with the programs that rate (that is, compute the airtime cost of) calls. Cellular subscribers are billed on a monthly basis, while calls are run through the rater once a day.

When a cellular subscriber makes a call from a car phone or a portable phone, he or she does not call the actual number. Rather, the subscriber's phone is connected to a computer called a *switch*. The switch validates the calling phone's *electronic serial number* (or ESN), which is a number wired into the telephone by the manufacturer. The validation process ensures that the caller is not a fraud, or someone using a stolen telephone, or a subscriber whose service has been cancelled for nonpayment. The switch records the date, time, and duration of the call. Once a day a tape of all the calls tracked by the switch is made and processed by the cellular telephone company (Cellsoft's customer), or by Cellsoft directly, acting as a service bureau for the cellular carrier. Then the customer or Cellsoft runs the *rater*, the program that computes the charge for each cellular telephone call. The switch also contains data from two other types of calls: *reseller* calls, those from numbers that the client has sold for use by another cellular company, and *roamer* calls, those from cellular users who live in another cellular area but are visiting the client's area, such as a customer of Cellular One in Boston who is authorized to make cellular calls in Minneapolis. (Incidentally, the commonly used name Cellular

One is not copyrighted. There are many Cellular Ones across the country, not necessarily owned by the same company.)

Once a month the rated calls are aggregated and run through the billing software, where the rated call details are but one of the numerous inputs used in calculating a subscriber's cellular telephone bill. The reports that this client wanted required both rating and billing data. Barbara continued:

> These reports would take the output from rating, and rating doesn't know anything about the billing cycle. I mean, rating runs daily or sometimes twice a day, [and] has nothing to do with a specific customer's billing cycle. These reports were really switch reports. They were reports that took the output not directly from the switch, but took the output from rating, which took the output directly from the switch. It had to be translated into a meaningful format for [the client], that somehow could be run coincident with their billing cycle, even though a lot of the data didn't have anything to do with the billing cycle.

The reason for this was a matter of timing. Recall that there are two components to the cost of a cellular call: the airtime charge, calculated by the rater and due to the cellular carrier, and the land charge, which is really the toll charge levied by the local "Baby Bell," the Regional Bell Operating Company (RBOC). In this case the client had to pay the RBOC at the end of the month for all toll charges accumulated on the switch, while the billing cycle ended on a different date. Therefore, the report needed to cover all rating data for a given month, which would not be directly related to the results of a billing cycle. This created the need for the report Barbara was working on, and she only came to understand this by reading the specification and by discussing the format with the client and with other programmers.

At this point Barbara had tried to figure out the client's general requirements and what the fields meant, had outlined what the reports would look like, and now could put together a list of questions. "And some of them were very general questions, like 'How do we tie this information that's output from rating to their billing cycle when rating doesn't know anything about billing cycles?' If they want to tie it to a market code in the future, we have a problem because the switch data can contain data from many market codes, and rating doesn't know different market codes," making it necessary to separate markets if a carrier served more than one. "So, do they want to do that? So, I had lots of questions, some general design issues and some more specific questions. Because the spec, although somewhat detailed, was not super-detailed. And Greg [Cellsoft's representative at the client site] either answered them on his own or found people to answer them."

Barbara divided her questions between Greg at the client site and Trevor, the company's expert in rating programs, back at the home office. From Greg "I got as much as I needed in terms of the functional requirements. I got help from Trevor or I elicited help from Trevor in terms of the technical design, the more practical matter of, well, let's say this customer runs rating every day, and the output from rating is three files, home, reseller, and roamer, and I need those three files every day. How long are those [switch] tapes held? How long are the roamer tapes held? Can I run this once a month, or should I run it every day? Well, it turns out I should run it every day." These were the practical details that Trevor would know.

When Barbara felt that she had a sufficient grasp of the material, she wrote a high-level functional specification of her own, which she kept refining until she had "maybe fifteen iterations of the spec." Finally, "I guess at one point I just knew that I was satisfied with the level of detail and sort of like the grand plan for these. And I don't know how I knew that except I guess I sensed that all my pieces were sort of fairly answered, for that level. I still had many other questions as to how, technically, we were going to do it." This was still only the functional phase, however; the technical details would come later. "The functional spec did include file formats that need maybe a little bit more work, but I was satisfied that my questions had been answered at that level of detail and Greg looked at it and the user signed off on it, Trevor has read it, so there's many other people involved, too."

Another programmer, Perla, became involved in the process as well. Perla had spent some time analyzing this problem at the client site and now helped Barbara with the specification. She was part of the iterative process of generating questions: "Initially she would read, actually she read the specs, the iterations, and commented on them. That generated more questions, so she was sort of a helper in that. She [also] sat in with meetings with Greg, because I needed another mind on this" for the technical details:

> I felt unclear, and I felt that I didn't really know anything about rating, and also from a technical, even though it's a high-level sort of design, it does mention the fact that we're gonna be writing to RMS files [a type of file structure used on Digital Equipment computers], and reading RMS files, and my background is not RMS files. So, I didn't even [know] how RMS files are physically stored, and how you access them, and how you set up your keys [fields for sorting and accessing records in files]. That was not in my background at all.

After this the work was divided into pieces, with Barbara, Perla, and Judith taking different aspects of writing more detailed technical specifications. Judith described her introduction to the project:

> I was shown the spec for [the client] that would need to produce these reports, the intralata usage reports, and they were basically usage termination reports, depending on how calls were terminated, where

they started from, where they ended up, and how much they were
billed, and the primary reason for these reports was so they could
settle with AT&T their long-distance charges. And in doing that . . .
it was decided prior to me becoming involved that we need history
files, to store, to track the information so that then these reports
which are summary reports for the billing period could be produced.
And so I was given the original request from the client to read and
specs that Perla and Barbara had drawn up. And then from there, [I]
continued working.

Judith's task, then, was to write a specification for the history files and
subsequently to write a program to create and populate them. Judith pulled the
following information from studying the client's request and from reading the
record layouts of files that already existed:

Well, the call details pulled information, such as call origination, the
calling phone number, the called phone number—you know, who
you're calling—the duration of the call, and the billed duration of the
call. And then since these are cellular phone calls, it broke it up, it
also specified the airtime amount because the cellular companies bill
you for airtime, and then it had the amount that was billed for that,
and then the total toll charge. And what we had to do was track the
information depending on the report and history file, if we wanted it
summarized by NPA-NXX [area code and exchange], or by calling
destination or if it was a land-terminated call or a mobile-terminated
call, or a directory-assistance call. We just basically had to track the
information in this history file and then write reports from this
history file.

Most of that information was from the call-detail file, taking a
specific field and . . . routines would determine what that field meant,
but everything was based on the call-detail record. So [the client's
request] didn't have a file layout, but it addressed the call-detail fields
that were needed.

When Judith got the assignment to write this specification, she read the
client's request several times, without taking notes or outlining it. Judith said
of rereading that "probably each time you read, you know, maybe another
paragraph worth of knowledge gets absorbed into your brain. It depends on the
complexity of what you're reading or how much you need to know, or what
you were told already prior to reading this, or . . . what you're coming into
this situation with a background knowledge of."

This was only Judith's second project at Cellsoft. In the first she worked
on a set of programs that keep track of a cellular carrier's supply of phone
numbers that have not yet been assigned to subscribers. The project was not

closely tied in with other major subsystems of Cellsoft's, so Judith had not been exposed to billing or rating information before. Therefore, she brought very little directly applicable background to this project.

Once she had read over the request several times,

> I think at that point then Perla, Barbara, and I got together and we talked about . . . where we had to go from there, and I was given the task of writing the detailed spéc for one of the history files while Barbara took care of the other ones. And basically Barbara and Perla decided on what the layout should be so I had to work from that, and it was basically writing up a specification of how you accumulate that information when you're reading the history file—when you're reading the call- detail files to create the history record.

> I don't remember having specific questions, they explained what we needed to do. I remember that they said this is what [the client] wants and we had layouts of the reports and we basically knew what type of information we had to track, we knew where we were coming from, that we had point A, that we had these call-detail records that we had summarized, and it was basically just figuring how we could accumulate them. . . . I had to determine the layout of the history file that I was working on, so I wrote up, I guess you could call a mini-spec of that, describing what the fields would be in the history layout, and then from there, I wrote the spec of how we would get the information into that history file. . . . And then from the layout, I just wrote the spec of how we would get it. I mean, basically determining the layout was more difficult than the spec because you had to think through about how you would do the spec in order to do the layout. . . . I mean, if you said you wanted to accumulate billed minutes . . .based on NPA-NXX, you had to make sure that information was available.

At this point Judith had the end result—the contents of the report—and had to reconstruct the data that would be necessary to produce it. "We worked backwards to a point and we had to work forward to a point to come to the middle where you got the specs." So it was at that point that she actually got into the layout of the call-detail file and figured out what was in it. "And based from testing, after we did the coding and then doing the testing and then utilizing all those fields in the call detail you become pretty familiar with it, when you work with it on a daily basis."

Compared with Barbara's approach, Judith's is slightly less iterative and more straightforward. She spends as much time reading the requirements as Barbara, but asks fewer questions. Of course, the fact that she had a smaller part of the overall problem to work with may have made her work appear simpler. Because this was her first exposure to cellular billing, she had to acquire as much knowledge of the system as she could from her work on this problem. She had not been to classes on the system, and she felt angry about this:

> I guess a month or so ago Barbara got to go, this is when I still worked for Perla, and no one else was allowed to go, and I forgot the reasons why. But then yesterday we were told that, I guess [a contractor who was working for Cellsoft temporarily] wanted to go to the next set of classes, but [my boss] told us that, you know we're under such a tight schedule we really shouldn't go, you know it's not good. And I just said that's a good attitude [laughs]. I really wonder why. I mean I can understand [his] saying that about [the temporary employee], if she's a contractor let her do her work, but they really should encourage employees to go.

Judith had been assembling her knowledge, then, from the record layouts and from both reading and writing specifications, but she diid not feel she understood most of the system. Also, she likes to work on a project from beginning to end and therefore found it frustrating that after she wrote the specification for one of the reports, another programmer, Jennifer, was assigned to write the actual code: "Well, I think if, for that . . . report if they had had Jennifer, I mean I don't know what her level is, but I thought it was pretty ridiculous they needed three of us to write a spec that someone else was gonna program. They could've had one person write the spec and that same person could've done the programming . . . [but] I don't design the hierarchy here and I don't care to."

In this example, Barbara and Judith wrote the specifications before they, or someone else, wrote the program. For Henry, on the other hand, program and specification combine in an iterative loop as thinking and questioning do for Barbara. Programming is part of his thinking process. Henry has a bachelor's degree in computer science from Princeton and a master's degree from Harvard, but little actual work experience. Like Ed, he had only recently become acquainted with the need for serious specification writing. His style is, in Kolb's terms, highly convergent rather than assimilative. He has to log in and play before beginning to theorize about a problem.

> I've always heard the best way to do something is to write a nice, complete spec that has everything you're going to do, and all that, and I've never had to do that. But I know I will be . . . doing that in the future, writing a specification, a complete one about projects I'll do. But [in] a lot of the [projects] that I've been apt to do now, mostly the specifications are written by other people. And so I know what I'm supposed to do, . . . and so I start prototyping immediately.

In this conversation Henry was talking about his first project at his new job as an analyst for a small company, at one time part of Cellsoft, that makes credit-decision software for cellular carriers. This particular project involved establishing communication between the main computer and a fax machine. To find more to say on specifications, he thought about

> some projects I did in college. I would kind of outline the whole problem in pseudo-C-code, . . . and I'd also have a specification in my head that I would have mostly worked out but not completely, and the more I wrote pieces of it the more I would complete this specification. . . . I know I should write the specification down on paper but I always keep it in my head, keep changing it. . . . [But in a] lot of the experience I've had so far I haven't needed to do a lot of paperwork, and I never liked to. But now that I'll be getting into bigger projects of the system, I will be doing that. So that'll be a new learning experience for me, how to write specifications.

Henry always referred to the connection between actually writing and trying out the programs and keeping a written model. "I write down sentences about what are the major pieces of the system, and how will they communicate, and write down some of the details I know that I will need, but not all of them, and then I'll build those pieces and develop more understanding of, more of the details I need."

BOOKS, MANUALS, AND OTHER DOCUMENTATION

Documentation provides another important source of information for programmers. Whether it is in the form of textbooks, reference manuals, tutorials, comments in programs, or on-line help (see chapter 8), documentation is meant to serve as an essential tool in programmers' mastery of their work. In fact, programmers do draw on written texts in a number of ways, not necessarily those imagined by technical writers.

Though programmers certainly use written materials, at least at Cellsoft reference manuals provide less utility than the great effort and expense that writers and vendors put into producing them would warrant. At Cellsoft any programmer wishing to use manuals for learning or for reference would encounter two problems from the start. At the time of this study, the company owned very few copies of the software manuals provided by the manufacturer, and those copies were not centrally located. People would take manuals from the shelves and not return them, and there would be no easy way to locate these manuals. Electronic mail messages requesting the return of the manuals would often go unanswered, so someone would have to walk through the rows of cubicles hoping to find a particular manual on someone else's desk. Eventually most people just gave up and found some other way to learn what they needed to know.

The second problem is that Cellsoft's own manuals, those written within the company to document its software, were often inaccurate. The writers may have lacked the technical knowledge to document the programs properly, and in any case the product changed more quickly than the writers could update the reference materials. Here again, documentation was less useful to programmers within the company than it should have been. Also, the manuals were oriented to users and operators of the system and so did not contain the technical detail that programmers would find useful in their jobs.

Even with these limitations, however, programmers did use documentation for a variety of reasons. A distinguishing aspect of computer documentation is that it is practically useless without the thing it describes. That is, no one reads a reference manual to a product without having the product available to work with. What is important is not the documentation itself, but the relationship between the reference material and its referent, that is, the computer software that it documents.

Why Programmers Use Documentation

Documentation can be useful in learning a system or a program by providing an overview as well as by showing people how to use individual commands or features. Several programmers and other computer workers at Cellsoft use documentation as a way of teaching themselves the purpose and general functions of software. Jack, for example, described this use of reference materials. Here he was talking about learning to use a Digital utility called Datatrieve: "You can walk over to your bookcase and pull out the manual. And in there they usually will have . . . your very technical reference manuals, and your general user manual, and . . . usually the first section is like fifty pages of very top-level documentation as to what Datatrieve is all about. I usually try to get through that. And then, sorta like quickly go through their sample, and see what they're trying to do."

Similarly, Perla, when she started to learn the VMS operating system, relied on manuals extensively:

> My learning came by picking up the system stuff because I really had nobody to talk to about that. The system manager that I initially was working with would show me how to use the add-user utility in a very basic way. . . . The earlier versions of VMS manuals were much more technically oriented. By reading manuals you could find out a lot about how the system was working, so I would read the manuals and look at the code on line, to see the procedures they had set up.

Note that in both these examples the programmer did not work with documentation purely as an intellectual reference. Jack followed examples, while Perla used the manual in conjunction with reading the programs that embody the information it describes. This interrelationship is a distinguishing feature of nearly all uses of computer reference materials.

Of course, if one can use a manual to get the big picture, one can also use it for learning details. Most reference manuals are in large measure dictionaries for looking up specific commands or functions, and it comes as no surprise that people use them in this way. For Emily, reading is almost always oriented to a specific task and is not very useful otherwise. "For me, sometimes I read, it goes in and it goes out, but if I have a task and I need to go to a book for a specific reference and say, what does this command do, . . . I'll go through the book and that's very helpful. But to sit there and read it from cover to cover, I don't find that very [helpful]." This does not mean, though, that she only reads for very limited commands; rather, she will read larger sections of the book in order to learn more fully. However, for her the important thing is that the reading must be tied to specific work. Guy expressed this similarly if more colorfully, reflecting the pragmatic approach to learning so common among people in business computing: "You don't need to know anything more than you need to do your job, and you know, you don't need to know a hell of a lot about the manufacture of gyros to fly a plane, although it certainly would be interesting to know about gyros."

Programmers use reference materials to verify and to reinforce what they know, and also to refresh their memories when they need to recall something they haven't used in a while. Thus Leslie, in speaking of classroom learning, referred to the interaction between hearing a lecture and reading textbooks: "I like to reinforce what I've read. I'm not the kind of person who would go in to a training class without having read every manual there was before it. So, reinforcement is very important for me. I need to hear something—read it, and hear it. I need reinforcement constantly."

Joyce provided an example that illustrates the use of a reference, here a math textbook, as a memory refresher. She could not casually recall information from her college calculus course,

> but, when I go to refresh my memory, when I go back to look at the subject matter again, I pick it up very quickly. . . . If I go back, and just look for a few minutes in a book, I'll remember it. I can recall it all back. Someone that I worked with had some requirement, math courses. She started asking me some questions, and . . . I can't remember these polynomials, and I can't remember how this works, and, and she's saying "Gee, you know you're a math major, can't you help me out?" Let me see the book, let me take a look at this.

Well, it ended up, I'd look at the book, and within five minutes I could get through all her problems.

Manuals can also function as resources for incidental learning. Just as one can learn words by browsing through a dictionary or find an interesting book in a library by skimming the card catalogue (a process made more difficult by automated cataloguing systems), programmers looking up something in a manual may be diverted by other material. Ed described his process of using manuals this way:

Usually I'm going for something specific in a manual, something that I've scanned the index [for] and I'll find a section on it, and if I find a whole section on it I'll try to find the subsection on what I'm looking for and try to get more specific. . . . [But I also find myself] picking up things along the way that I didn't expect. If I'm scanning a section and [it] refers to, like, See this command or See this section, then I'll go back to that section even if it doesn't relate to that problem.

Although these purposes and methods of using manuals and other references are significant to programmers, by far the most important function of written documentation is as a source of examples and templates. People learn more and do more work by copying and following examples and by working their way through exercises than by any other single activity. For example, when Bill started at Cellsoft, he had to learn the BASIC programming language. Starting with a textbook in VAX BASIC, he would "go home, read the book, read it at work, go over the exercises in it, and basically become more familiar with the BASIC commands." Jack did the exercises in the book at work, typed in programs from the book, watched them run, and then modified them to do his work and to learn different functions of the program.

Some manuals contain tutorials as well as examples, so people can learn by following every step in the manual and then take the example as a guide to their own practice. This is how Judith learned Datatrieve. The Digital Equipment Corporation's documentation set for Datatrieve contains a series of examples carried through a number of reference manuals, so that as someone learns different aspects of the program he or she can continue with the same reference database. In addition, the Datatrieve software comes with the examples in the documentation actually included, so one can use the practice data as soon as the software is installed. Judith used the manual as a workbook and picked up enough knowledge of Datatrieve from using the sample personnel system provided with the software to be able to use Datatrieve on the job competently. Perla and Emily learned the Digital ACMS utility by using a similar workbook and following examples in the book while trying them out on the computer.

Examples are also useful as a way of clarifying command syntax. One of the most difficult things to remember in programming is statement syntax. Sometimes programs fail because the programmer forgets a comma or a semicolon, and examples, when they are followed carefully enough, can show exactly how commands are supposed to look. Emily grappled with this sort of problem and went to examples in a manual to try to find the solution. The problem facing her involved selecting a number of records with a set of attributes, and she was having trouble remembering how to group the attributes in order to select them properly:

> I was looking at it and I said gee, I don't have anything wrong here, because you can do several ANDs and ORs and parentheses in a record selection and I had all my parentheses in in the right way and I was thinking about it and I . . . tried to translate it into an IF statement and write it how I would write it in normal COBOL, which helped to clarify where I put my ANDs and where I needed my ORs and where I needed my parentheses, but it still didn't work. So it was at this point, actually, I had looked in the book and I had looked at example programs and I tried every possible combination that I could think of.

In this case even the examples were not sufficiently clarifying, so Emily eventually asked Perla for help. This case shows Emily's typical use of documentation in learning and problem solving: She reads for specific facts and examples and always in conjunction with specific tasks or problems.

Programmers use examples not simply as tools for learning, but as templates for copying. What would qualify as plagiarism in scholarly writing is common and accepted practice in the computer industry, at least when carried out on a small scale, using documented samples designed for the purpose. (Of course, one must be extremely careful when copying, or even conceptually borrowing from, copyrighted material. For a thorough discussion of software copyright battles, see Clapes, 1993.)

Horace described one of the two manuals he uses for the PostScript language:

> One of them is called *Tutorial and Cookbook*. And the last half of the book is just a gigantic collection of example programs, and because PostScript is a page- description language, they show the output of the example program. So what you do is you want to figure out how to do something, you just leaf through that section till you see something that looks vaguely like what you want to do, then you look at the program. I've found that to be wonderful.

Horace simply copies what looks useful and modifies it to suit his needs, though, as a software instructor, he doesn't feel that this limits his learning: "Especially since I'm not so lazy, I will go back and learn the principles." Just as Beethoven learned counterpoint by copying Bach's fugues, programmers can often learn their craft by copying and modifying examples, and this is a critical use of programming documentation.

Occasions for Reading

People read manuals and textbooks in class, sometimes in conjunction with listening to lectures, sometimes to get ahead of them. Leslie prefers classroom learning to what she calls the "self-study" (that is, largely unsupervised and unfocused) way she has to learn at Cellsoft: "I like the interactive classroom style: having people around me, talking about things, reading on your own, having someone push you further, take you the next step. The book takes you quite a ways, somebody else takes you further along. You feel like you're moving along, while [with] self-study, you have no idea how far you've gotten." By contrast, she finds the approach she took in her first few weeks at Cellsoft, "reading manuals, looking at the system, reading the manuals again, looking at the system again," much less productive, as one could tell from the bored, slightly whining tone in her voice as she spoke of it.

On the other hand, this is a person who loves to read on her own, one whose boyfriend gave her a book on the impact of computers on the workplace as a birthday present. More typically, she reads books completely, rather than skimming for specific information, even in a textbook: "I'm the kind of a person, when I do something I hate if I can't do it from scratch, like if the answer's [on] the last page of the chapter, I really feel funny just going to that last page, I feel like I really want to read everything before this, 'cause I'm probably gonna miss something that was said at the beginning of the chapter that would make what's said on this last page even more meaningful."

Emily, by contrast, only makes sense of what she reads if she can tie it to a particular task, as we have seen. "If I sit down with a book, that's not the way that I learn. I need to have a task in front of me even if it's overwhelming because by the time I get through it, I've learned so much that [it] isn't that bad, and if I can do that then I can do something else." Joyce uses manuals and texts as memory refreshers. Guy, on the other hand, was the only person in this study who reads technical documentation as a leisure activity, because he works with computers and electronics as a hobby as well as a job. Many years ago he took an Evelyn Wood reading course, which has been useful in teaching him how to skim a page for important words, but he has no use for speed reading. He reads faster than he did before taking the course,

> but I don't read two thousand words a minute. But the stuff I read
> you can't read two thousand words a minute anyway. I don't read,

Tom goes out with Jane, grabs her by the hand and passionately kisses her on the right earlobe, I don't read that kind of junk. I read how to set up a Novell network, Dbase 3+ reference manual, BASIC. . . . I read things that challenge me. I don't find reading particularly entertaining but I find it tremendously informing. . . . I don't have time to read for fun, my eyes hurt when I get done doing what I have to do just to stay on top of things, looking for new words, man.

For Guy, as we have seen earlier, actually reading in order to learn things at work was "probably the last resort" because reference materials were so scarce at Cellsoft:

If you need to do something, the utopian way . . . is to sit there with all the possible information you could ever need at one little beck and call. Obviously, with computers it's getting closer every day, you press a button and it tells you everything you ever wanted to know about everything, you sit back there and absorb it. Next best thing is to have a library [so] that you can read it all. But those are utopian worlds. We don't live in those, as you can probably tell from around here, we don't have enough manuals to go around.

NOTES AND VISUAL AIDS

One would think that note taking is an obvious part of learning, but in fact only eight of the programmers interviewed referred to the practice. Notes are used in a variety of ways: simply as an aid to clarifying thought, as material for reference and review, as a retrospective test of understanding, or as quasi-specifications to show to others for confirmation that one grasps the material or the problem correctly. Visual aids include diagrams, flowcharts, and any sort of pictures used to improve learning. Programmers use visual aids supplied by others to help them see the relationships between parts of a system, and they also on occasion draw their own pictures either to enhance or to confirm their understanding. No one in this study, however, uses flowcharting or any other formal graphical technique.

Weinberg (1971, p. 194) recognized note-taking differences among programmers as a component of their individual styles. Though he was describing note taking that people do while sitting in lecture courses, his observations are also applicable to self-paced, individualized learning:

The individuality of the learner is not only reflected in his passive acceptance of information from a book or lecture, but also in the activity he performs while using these media. For instance, some people cannot learn effectively from a lecture unless they take notes, even if they never refer to the notes again. The very act of writing while listening enhances retention for some. For others, however, taking notes during a lecture is merely a distraction, and they retain best by concentrating on the lecture as it is given. Such learners are handicapped by being forced to take notes in a course, as when the instructor requires that each student turn in his notebook at the end of the term. When learning individually, however, no such outside pressure is present, yet many people continue to take notes because they were forced to, or taught to, when they were in a formal school situation.

Writing down material helps to clarify difficulties and to alleviate confusion. Emily used her notes in this way when she was starting at Cellsoft, because she had to contend with a plethora of utilities and programs that were new to her. "At the beginning [I] had all those RDUs and ADUs and FDUs and all that [was so] confusing, I wrote all that stuff down. So I do have notes, I have a folder of just miscellaneous notes, and if something trips me up once, I write it down. I may not go back to it, but I know it's there. Sometimes writing things down, too, reinforces it; even if you don't go back and reference it, just the act of writing it down helps." Emily referred to her notes frequently at the beginning, but then decreasingly, and after a short time stopped looking at them. "I'd have to say I've gone back, maybe in a week, three or four times, you know, the first week I went back a lot, the second week I went back a little less, [the] third week even less. I haven't gone to them at all this week." Perla's use of notes is similar to Emily's. "I don't make a great attempt to memorize everything. I write, I take notes, and I refer to notes. . . . So, I take notes, refer to my notes until I've gotten it just through rote, [until they] become . . . familiar."

While Emily uses notes for initial learning and for brief reinforcement, Arthur can be described as almost a compulsive note taker, at least when he started at Cellsoft.

I kept every note I ever took, you know. As people . . . gave me something to do, modify a report . . . I just asked questions. I tried to do things on my own, and if I didn't understand something, I'd ask a question. Every time I would ask somebody something I wrote it down, and that was the system basically, writing notes and back then they didn't all make sense but now if I go back and look at them I realize that I didn't write down the whole explanation or I wrote down . . . the procedure but not the explanation of what it was doing, but now 99 percent of them all make sense.

Note taking was a study skill that Arthur had acquired in school.

> [My] standard procedure, I guess, [was,] I would just always read, read
> the text or read the chapter or read notes, then I'd condense, write
> notes. If I was reading a text [I'd] write notes from the text, and if I
> was reading notes I'd condense those notes down into the real, what I
> thought was important stuff, then I'd condense those into even more
> important stuff until I only had a little bit of things written down,
> but they all related to bigger pieces, and that's like—as far back as I
> can remember that's the way I always read and then write.

However, Arthur's notes remain in an unprocessed state; that is, he did not
attempt to outline them, rewrite them, or reduce them to summary form, even
though, he said, "I guess that would've been beneficial."

Another Cellsoft programmer, Doug, who has worked as a consultant at
several companies over ten years, takes a more systematic approach to writing
notes. Doug learns through a combination of reading code and working at a
computer terminal.

> As far as notes that I would make to myself, . . . as I'm going
> through it I would typically be doing something on line, if possible.
> Searching through modules, or with an editor or with a search feature
> if it's there, and I would probably just take little notes with a module
> name, and sort of a brief description of what it does. I have on
> occasion made tree structures that sort of indicate a flow. But not so
> formal as flowcharting, which is just a personal quirk for me, I don't
> really like flowcharting.

Doug refers back to notes after writing them, though the discipline of writing
them fixes things in his mind as well.

When Colleen encounters a software system that is new to her, and she
needs to develop a new piece or fix problems in an older part of the program,
she uses notes as a way of identifying and clarifying knowledge.

> How I usually approach it, is first try to specify what my
> understanding is of this piece that I'm trying to add onto, because
> usually I'm not the one who's defined what that piece is but someone
> else has this need, and often not very well specified, so a lot of time
> and effort goes into getting as much information as I can about that.
> And I've learned the hard way to spend a lot of time on that and to
> write that up, and to pass it by the people who are gonna be using it,
> so that they can sign off on it. Because, as you well know, very
> often people hear what they want to hear, and even if you put it in
> black and white and get them to sign on the dotted line, they don't
> always admit that that is what they meant all along after all. Then, I

look at what information there is about the preexisting stuff. Often, that's very sketchy, people have left [the company], and the only information you have is the code itself, sad to say. And often that code, if it's [the] MUMPS [medical programming language], is pretty opaque.

Barbara's use of notes is the most comprehensive. She uses notes iteratively, as Arthur and Emily do, gradually lessening her dependence on them as she internalizes her new knowledge. Like Colleen, she also uses them to clarify and confirm knowledge as well as to acquire it, and like Doug, she builds specifications from her notes. She described her first job at Cellsoft, moving a client from an older to a newer version of the billing software:

> Part of what I'm working on now is upgrading Boston to [the] 1.5 version of billing, and part of that task involves changing how Boston in 1.4 currently processes their taxes. So the first thing I did was look at the program in the current version of 1.5 that processes the taxes. And I looked at that program and wrote down all the steps it took, the different files it looked at, the different files it found based on the information it found in the prior file, and I wrote it down. And I sort of looked at it, and I thought I knew it, and then later on in the day I was trying to abstract that and I was sort of, OK, well don't look at your piece of paper and see if you really know how that processing occurred, and I didn't so I looked at it again.

In effect, Barbara was giving herself a test on what she had learned. "So I read it again, and the next day, I thought about it that night. I read my notes. I read my sort of watered-down version of the program . . . and the next day I looked at it again and I sort of owned it a little more but not totally. And then the weekend came, and Monday morning I felt like I was back at Thursday morning. My notes were Greek. So I went back and looked at it again." So she needed to review the information she had written down, which even over the course of a weekend had become obscure to her.

However, by reviewing her notes she was able to relearn the material more quickly than she had originally acquired it, and within a day she was acquitting herself well at work. "We had a meeting on Tuesday about the whole Boston conversion and we were talking about the tax processing, and at that point I could talk about it in a way that indicated that I understood it. But it was sort of like a curve like that, because at one point I really thought I owned it on Friday too." As the knowledge became more secure, Barbara could reduce both how often she referred to her notes and the amount of detail she needed: "So I'm sure I will not look at it for two more days, and I'll have to redo it again but maybe not quite in this detailed a way." When she was asked for clarification, she rephrased, emphasizing the iterative nature of learning the material:

When I was rereading my notes on Friday, at one point it really clicked and I understood why it was happening and what was happening. And then by Monday I had lost it. So I redid it in my head and tried to figure it out and Tuesday I did the same thing again. By Tuesday afternoon I was able to explain it but if I sort of leave it for a couple of days I will have to rethink it in my head, maybe not from square one, . . . but maybe from halfway through and [in] shorter and shorter time.

When Barbara was learning material from scratch, as in the specification she later developed for the Minneapolis client, she again used systematic note-taking to organize her work. We have already seen how she derived the structure of a specification (see page 94). Her notes became the basis of the specification. Visual aids served more as an organizer. For some people, like Barbara, they can be useful when others present them and also as a summary of one's own knowledge. We have already seen that Barbara's manager gave her a diagram of the billing system. When she began to analyze the two versions of billing for the conversion project, "I did a DIF on them and I got a wealth of information, printed out the two programs, and a week later presented Clark with a chart of the functional differences, a rough draft of a chart. He said he was impressed, and I was real pleased [because he's] hard to impress . . . [even though] I don't think those charts told him anything he didn't already know." The point, however, was not to impress her boss, but rather to schematize the knowledge she gained from printing out the differences between the two versions.

A number of programmers claim to make little drawings for themselves. Judith is a case in point. She described her use of time lines to figure out the sequence of financial programs: "That's one of the ways I sometimes do designing, at least at [my last job] it was easy to figure out, if you say, OK, here's a time line, here's January, here's March, you've got February, . . . this should happen in this period, and they made their loan payment here, and they couldn't pay ahead we could . . . interest . . . here, how would you calculate . . . interest, you know, . . . pictures like that." She has used diagramming at Cellsoft as well. After describing (and drawing on a whiteboard) an overview of the first system she worked on at Cellsoft, she said, "There. See, I got this from a picture. Pictures help me. [The people who worked on the system before her] drew me this picture, and I remembered it because I had a picture."

At times, however, the use of drawings can go to extremes. Although books on programming and introductions to the field describe and advocate flowcharting programs, in practice no one does it unless it is required by management. Bill described the situation at one job that overdid both documentation and flowcharting:

You did a system, you did the whole system, you made a change, you documented your change. You wrote a new system, you wrote a new program, you documented that. One place I worked was a bank and they I think went overboard on documentation. They wanted each and every program flowcharted. I don't think it's necessary. I think once you want to look at that you should be a good-enough programmer to go in and understand it by looking at the code. And if the program's so large that it can't be, then it shouldn't be one program any more.

I thought it was utterly ridiculous. One of the other guys [said], "You like doin' that?" I say I don't care what I do, as long as I'm getting paid. I said, it's a waste of time though, I mean, I don't mind it. Most people despise that. I didn't mind it, but I knew while I was doing it, it was a waste of time. Yeah, that's one more way to reinforce that system, but again, as I said before, you're gonna walk out and within three days you're not gonna remember it. It's great to go look at ... but   ... I don't think you get anything out of it, I think you read the code. . . . I don't trust flowcharts 'cause I think they're dated.

SUMMARY

The programmers in this study use documentation for a variety of reasons: as a memory refresher, for functional overviews, as a glossary, and primarily as a source of examples. The importance of examples in programmers' work styles cannot be overemphasized; it appears, along with reading programs and testing functions on the computer, to be their primary learning mode.

In an environment like that of Cellsoft, where reference manuals are scarce and hard to find, programmers look for other methods of obtaining information--primarily asking one another (see chapter 7) and experimenting on the computer (see chapter 8). Specifications are in a sense the most important form of documentation these programmers use; they serve as organizers for their work and provide a library of system functions.

As we have seen elsewhere, these programmers are eminently practical people, drawing on whatever resources are available to the extent necessary to get their jobs done. If a book can be found, they will use it; if not, they will ask someone for help or try the machine. Many keep libraries of notes to serve as references as well as organizers. Although the manner and extent of note taking is a matter of personal style, it is also a way of maintaining a private reference library not likely to be borrowed or stolen by others.

For all the emphasis in courses on formal visual representations such as flowcharts or system-flow diagrams, the computer workers in this study seldom use them and tend to dislike them. Perhaps this confirms a model of programmers as conceptual thinkers who do not often express themselves or think visually, a model distinguished, say, from that of mechanical engineers, who, according to a colleague who teaches them, can seldom hear a concept described without drawing a picture of it. Although programmers' notes may include simple diagrams (usually hierarchical drawings of functions, with boxes linked by lines or arrows), visual representation is not a primary learning or thinking mode for them.

7

People as Resources

In this chapter I examine programmers' and other computer professionals' use of people as resources for learning. Weinberg (1971) devoted a chapter to analyzing "programming as a social activity," but that is not the focus here. Without asserting that programming is primarily social or individual in nature, and without analyzing the intersubjective experience of working in a programming environment, this chapter treats each programmer as an isolated individual. It artificially views other people as resources in the environment, and skills for dealing with people as tools in the programmers' repertoire. Of course, this follows the model used in the vocabulary of business, in which personnel departments are called "Human Resources" and managers can be heard to say, "We need to add two more resources to this project," by which they do not mean a computer and a new tape drive. If the unfortunate result is to treat human beings as objects, this does not mean that that is all they are, but that is the artifice to which the project of seeing the world from the perspective of individual learners confines this discussion.

From this limited point of view, programmers use other people in one of three main capacities: model, source, and foil. A *model* is someone who serves as explainer or exemplar, a source for notes or someone to copy. A *source* is a referral: someone who answers questions, can find the right place in the right manual, or knows someone else with the answer. A *foil* is someone in whom one can see one's own knowledge confirmed or refuted: a person whose knowledge is perhaps less than one's own (the *fool*) or greater (the *sage*), someone who confirms one's own knowledge by seeking it out (the *student*), or someone who serves as audience while one thinks, works, or explains (the *dog*). In this chapter I discuss each of these three roles—model, source, and foil—in turn. Also, I describe how programmers use questions—what sorts of things they ask one another, when, why, and whom they ask—and provide an example of how one person integrates another's questions and concerns (in this case, mine) into her own learning framework.

THE USES OF OTHERS

People as Models

Models and examples play a large and complex role in learning. Much of programmers' informal training consists in copying, modifying, and following examples. In chapter 8, we shall look at programming models; here we are concerned with human ones.

A person serves as a model for another by doing a task the latter will subsequently perform, by embodying experience the latter will eventually possess, or by defining and describing the activities that compose the latter's task set. Robert, the manager of the CAD group described in chapter 4, uses a "buddy system" for orienting new employees; senior people serve as mentors to junior ones. Robert "typically start[s] the person off for the first quarter at least doing maintenance tasks on similar coding so they can become familiar with the system." Robert envisions the mentor, however, more as a source for questions than as a model for the role.

Here is an illustration of how Jack used his boss as a model:

I was in the business office and they needed to get some things out very quickly. The person I had replaced . . . had left about a month or so before. So all the work that he should be doing my manager was forced to do. We were learning . . ., sitting next to my manager watching him do what he has to do. And take notes real quick. . . . It was fairly easy to mirror what was going on [by copying the commands my manager typed in, because] I could relate the commands he was using to commands I had previously seen.

Jack used his office mates the same way as he used his boss: "We all had offices as opposed to cubes. The two other people in my office were junior people as I was then, too. And very quickly they were very helpful so that, this was like, 'all right, I'm just gonna sit here and watch you go at it for an hour, OK? And I'll ask you questions.' So that was very useful."

Another type of model is the *role model*, as that term is commonly used to describe a person of one's own background in a similar situation. Although the role of women and minorities at Cellsoft (the latter almost entirely Asian—the company employed one black woman and two Hispanics at the time of my research) was not generally germane to this study, one important exception involved the language barrier faced by the three programmers who were native Chinese speakers. Newton, from Hong Kong, was the only Cantonese speaker in the group and spoke only English at Cellsoft, but Wayne, from Taiwan, was able to learn a great deal from Trevor, who also speaks Mandarin. This helped to acculturate Wayne into the company, because Trevor is both a highly respected programmer at Cellsoft and a role model as a Mandarin-speaking Chinese who had been in the American business world for several years.

The role of explainer is far more common that that of exemplar. People learn a great deal from formal and informal explanations, and much orientation occurs in this way. Perla described how her manager, Clarissa, introduced her to the ACMS application-management program:

> She had given me . . . an ACMS how-to intro manual. Clarissa had given me the task and marked the areas. I think another thing that was really helpful is that Clarissa had pointed out the main steps that I had to go through, and she gave me samples, I mean I didn't initially have to go out and find my own code, and she gave me the code to modify, and set up my test environment for me, and, during the first task, stepped me through some of the procedures that I had to modify. I think that's a big help. She definitely was holding my hand for the first two tasks.

Gary described another kind of model, someone who represented for him a way of acting and learning on the job rather than a direct teacher:

> I was working with this woman Donna, and she didn't have a computer background. But she had an enormous amount of energy and she was very bright, and she was into it, and she was learning stuff. And basically, she had a six-month head start on me or whatever it was, she had a lead on me, and she was always ahead of me, and she was always jumping into stuff. . . . She was the kind of person that she would read through the manuals, [and say], "Oh yeah, this awk [Unix utility], boy, this is really weird. Well, let's figure out how to use it."

While Donna's style was to get as far into a problem or a text as it went, Gary sees himself as merely learning as much as necessary to solve the question at hand. When Donna would encounter an obstacle, she would do everything in her ability to track it down and overcome it:

> But wait a second, that won't work because of this, and then you have to go, and solve another problem and then sort of nest down . . . to another problem, another problem, another problem. And pretty soon there's a certain point where I say, this is getting much too complicated to just get this thing done by computer. . . . At a certain point you say, forget it, I'll do it by hand, this is too much

trouble. Where Donna didn't care, I mean she just kept on going deeper and deeper and deeper and deeper and she'd hit bottom, and then she'd work her way back, and she'd get the thing going. I usually am not that motivated. It's like enough of this already.... And part of it is just memorizing, learning all this trivia, how this particular program works, how *this* particular program works, if you're only gonna use it once. So, I have limited tolerance for that. But just being around her was helpful because she was always digging into stuff.

Donna served as a role model for Gary because of the intensity of her learning and of her involvement in the work, and although "she wasn't a teaching sort of person, you could look at what she had done, you can follow her examples and ... talk about stuff and figure things out."

People as Sources

The most common use people have for one another in programming settings is as sources. Whether as references to oral tradition, as referrals to other knowledgeable people, or as answerers of direct questions, people constantly serve as sources for one another, both inside and outside the organization. A few examples will suffice.

We have already discussed the occasional difficulties programmers experience when they are learning a new operating system and are unable to figure out the right command to perform a familiar operation. Robert described one such snag and how he overcame it:

I'm starting to learn Unix. And in fact, just thirty minutes before you came in, I was talking to a colleague, I wanted to know how to set process priority in Unix. In VMS I call the SET PRIORITY system service. So I pulled out my Unix manual and said "Priority? No. Set? No." OK, you know I'm in trouble here, I can't think of anything else to say. Looked up process, no, that didn't help. So, you know, Unix in its typical cryptic way said, Oh, you use the nice function. You know, so now I had a keyword I could go and look it up, and sure enough, nice is what sets process priority. [I learned this] from my colleague.... I ask somebody.

Robert used other people to find out information that would be inaccessible given his still-limited grasp of Unix's vocabulary. But in other settings oral tradition is even more important. Colleen described her experiences in an organization in which very little is ever written down, and in which programmers pride themselves on their knowledge of arcana, specifically of the medical programming language MUMPS:

> [There was] one particular application I've worked on, began using this thing called go-strings, [where] . . . if you're gonna call a module off here you'd never name it and go to it. You would put the name of that module and other places you were going in a variable, and you would execute that variable to go to that place. All very clever, I'm sure, but awful to maintain. I'm not sure of the motivation of doing it that way. Job security for the people who wrote it, perhaps. [The code was] sometimes [commented], but often not. Often not, and in the early days of MUMPS, the comments were not stripped by the interpreter [that is, by the program that translated MUMPS into machine-readable form], so they took up space in the partition, and . . . the symbol table was built up from the bottom of the partition and the routine down from the top, and when they met, that was it.

How, then, would Colleen or anyone else learn this? "If you're lucky, there's some word of mouth around, and if you're very lucky there's somebody still working in the group, not maybe your group, but the laboratory that you have access to, who can dredge up ancient memories."

Colleen worked similarly on a more recent project when she had to convert her MUMPS system from an IBM computer to a Digital VAX:

> In doing this VAX conversion the first thing we wanted to do was find out what tools were available on the system, and . . . in many cases we were pleasantly surprised by things that we discovered, that we'd wished we had, and hadn't had before. [We found] some of them by looking at the manuals, some [by] word of mouth, and that's I think my preferred method, but that only works if you've got people around you who know.

Colleen drew on people outside of her organization as well as within it:

> There are a number of alums from my laboratory who now work at Digital on DSM [Digital Standard MUMPS] products. And I resorted--when I was really stuck and I felt that there should be some way to do something, that I didn't have, I called them up. And . . . there were undocumented features that they could tell me about. And they did, and it was terrific.

For Colleen, using people in this way is a hallmark of effective programming technique. "I think, often, what distinguishes a good and effective programmer from one who's just sort of average is the ability to ferret out and to talk. I think the schmoozer does better than the person who lives in a corner of his office and doesn't find out from others what's going on."

Jack also made use of contacts with people in his previous job. We have seen in chapter 4 how he built up a network of people. He was able to do this not just through direct personal contact but through electronic mail as well.

> You'd be surprised how you can learn a lot in three months. 'Cause when you're working on that first project, say, you can—especially at DEC you just VAXMail to three or four people who have said, yes, I really know Datatrieve real well, and sure I'll get time and I'll help you out, no problem. So you just start mailing your programs and then saying look at this, these are my record definitions, this is what I'm trying to do; any suggestions? Usually that'll cost me a couple of lunches.

Jack built this network not just through formal requests for help but through other uses of electronic mail and used it not just to answer his own questions but to become another type of resource himself: a referral to others. He described this process and its value to him:

> I used to . . . every day get seven or eight different jokes from different people around the country, around the world. And every day I would send those jokes to ten other people. So you start building up rapports with different people based on different things. For a while I was commuting with a commuter van for about a month, so you met like twenty people there, and it was very important to me that I always keep in touch with as many people as I could, and that helped me—because of the Datatrieve aspect, but also, there are times when, my group needs—my group needs to be hooked up to the New York Stock Exchange. They don't know how to do it, and it certainly is not my function to know how to do it. But if I can get them in contact with someone who can, my worth to them has just increased. And I realized that my worth to the company was a lot, based on who I knew. That's why I kept my contacts as heavy as I could. And whenever anyone would ask me for help, then, if I could help them I would try, if I can't I would try to point them to someone who could. Networking, even informally, is very important. That network of course has fallen apart now, but I still use some of the people in there. I can call someone there, and get things much faster than I can from anyone else in this company here.

People as Foils

In speaking of people as foils for one another, I use the word in its literary sense. The *American Heritage Dictionary* defines a foil as "any person or thing that, by strong contrast, underscores or enhances the distinctive characteristics of another." People at work use others as foils in a number of ways. First, the foil may himself seek the information one has; thus the subject confirms his own understanding by conferring it upon another. Second, the foil may highlight the subject's knowledge by contrast with his own ignorance. Third, the foil may be a more experienced or more knowledgeable person who blesses the subject's understanding by confirming it. Finally, the foil may be a mere sounding board in whose presence the subject develops, demonstrates, confirms, or recognizes his own ability or confirms an error but who contributes little or nothing of his own to the conversation. I call these four types of foil respectively the *student*, the *fool*, the *sage*, and the *dog*.

It marks a gratifying stage in the recognition of one's own growing expertise that one can answer other people's questions. Sometimes this is a way not merely of demonstrating the extent of one's knowledge but of becoming aware of it. Bill described his experience of becoming an answerer rather than merely an asker in this way: "[A new person in his group] starting a month, a month and a half ago, hounds me with questions all the time. I get a little scared because I start realizing how much I know. Wow, I can't believe I picked all this up." Thus the new person served as a student for whom Bill could be the teacher or expert.

Bill's manager, Barry, serves this role for Bill in a related way. Barry has come to rely on Bill for finding and solving problems with the system, and in his ability to locate problems and to resolve them quickly Bill verifies his expertise and his system knowledge for himself as well as for his boss. For Bill, this is closely tied to the gratification and insight he experiences from being able to answer less knowledgeable people's questions, though his manager has been a source of knowledge as well.

> I feel I know [the system] pretty well. [When] we run into problems I research them, I know what's goin' on between Barry and myself, and he [laughs] this is scary from Barry's standpoint 'cause he relies heavily on me to go research bugs, but we're getting them out. We usually address an issue within a day. I can't remember the last time something took us longer than a day to address. When they have bugs I get them and I can figure out where to go now. Before it was like, you're out in the middle of the ocean, someone threw you a life preserver. Now it's like, which way do I swim? There's nothing in sight, you don't know where to look. Not only you don't know where to go, you don't know where to look how to get there

eventually. Now I'm at the point where, OK, let's take a look at this, let's rerun it, you know what steps to take to get to it, and I feel comfortable with it now. Not enough where I'm not a little apprehensive sometimes but I feel much more comfortable than I did three or four months ago. And it's funny some days, it happened when [one of the users] asked to explain a problem to me. And it was that day when I said, oh, I know where to go look for this, and I went and looked for it. And that's when I said I really am starting to understand this system.

If one way of identifying one's own ability is in answering other people's questions, another is in recognizing that someone else knows less than oneself. This is the *fool* role. It does not mean that another is necessarily foolish, merely that he or she is clearly less knowledgeable than the subject. Jack illustrated the value of information gleaned from the training classes he sat through during his first several weeks at Cellsoft, and he contrasted his own knowledge with the relative lack shown by another programmer, Tom:

I had a really good example of that yesterday, because [Guy and another experienced billing programmer] were talking about a problem in the source. They then took [Tom] and myself and they said, "Why don't you guys come in and listen to us, and get some idea of what's going on?" And going in, I could see the questions that Tom was asking, as opposed to the questions I was asking. The little piece of code way down there that they were trying to look at, I had already understood a lot of the assumptions that were being made. Tom didn't know those. So I could see that I was much more productive in that meeting than he was.

More common than using someone's ignorance is using his or her knowledge as confirmation of one's own. While most people practice this to some degree, for Barbara it is a deliberate technique. "I do that with Trevor a lot, to run things by him. This is how I think it works, correct me if I'm wrong." She also uses this method as part of her iterative process of thinking, asking, and thinking some more: "My style is that I tend to confirm what I hear, and sometimes I heard wrong, but I will try to do that. . . . The only loop involved is that sometimes after I confirm what I've heard, it generates another question." Similarly, she tries to get a number of readers for her specification, both for confirmation and for correction.

Greg looked at it and the user signed off on it, Trevor has read it, so there's many other people involved too. Perla has also, Perla and I sort of [did it] together . . . because I needed help on it. Initially she would read, actually she read the specs, the iterations, and commented on them. That generated more questions, so she was sort of a helper in that. She [also] sat in [on] meetings with Greg, because I needed another mind on this.

In this example Trevor, Greg, and Perla served as *sages*, possibly providing correction or feedback but just as likely saying nothing and by their silence indicating that Barbara in fact did understand the problem or task correctly. For the last type of foil even this much is unnecessary. A software instructor explained the *dog* in this way:

> Sometimes in a lab a student will have a question. Maybe his program has a bug, or he doesn't understand something. While you stand there he explains the problem to you. While he explains it he looks over his code again, something doesn't quite look right, and oh yes, there's the problem, now I've got it, thanks very much for your help. And I didn't say anything to him at all. You might just as well tell your problem to your dog.

This method of using another person simply as observer of one's thought process (for which I have coined the term *dog-checking*), is really an informal variation of the *walkthrough* practiced in many programming organizations, where the act of describing one's logic to a group can help spot problems before the coding is done (Weinberg, 1971).

THE USES OF QUESTIONS

Questions form an important part of programmers' interactions with one another and of their learning. Programmers and other on-the-job learners use questions in a variety of ways: to save time, to fill in gaps in their learning, for overviews, and for confirmation of what they already know. We shall look at the uses of questions by answering basic questions about their use: how much people use questioning as a learning technique, when they ask questions, and why, whom, and what sorts of questions they ask.

How Much to Ask

In a way, to work in a programming environment like Cellsoft is to be a ceaseless asker and answerer. People constantly approach one another with questions of all sorts: technical ("How does the COBOL compiler handle string delimiters?"), administrative ("I've finished coding and testing this program, now how do I check it back into the system?"), experiential ("Take a look at this bug; have you ever seen anything like it before?"), and many others.

However, people differ quite a bit in how often they will consciously question others.

For example, if Bill is to be believed, he never stops asking. He said that part of learning how the system works is that "you just pound people with questions," or

> I will ask a question at the drop of a hat. [If] I don't understand something, I'm gonna ask it. Because I'm a firm believer [that] the most stupid question was the one you didn't ask. No matter how ridiculous it is, some things can be hitting you right in the face, and you can't pick 'em up. But that's somebody else's viewpoint, they're hitting *them* right in the face. Obviously they're not hitting me right in the face, otherwise I wouldn't have asked the question! Yet there are other things I pick up so easy but somebody else has so much trouble with, and it's not that they're less intelligent than me, it's just—I happen to pick something up faster. I have always asked questions though and I always will, and when I don't understand something I will, and [if] it's important to me I'm gonna find out.

Curiously enough, Bill also espouses another view, apparently in contradiction to this, that it is important to find out as much as possible on one's own, "because once you learn it yourself, if you have trouble you won't forget it. If you try an easy way of [asking] 'Hey, what does this mean?' you will rely on that crutch." The two approaches are really complementary, however, in that Bill relies on a combination of questions and experience, as all programmers do to some degree, to put his picture together.

Other programmers are similar to Bill in asking a lot of questions. Barbara, for example, when she was first learning the billing system at Cellsoft, "jotted down lots of questions." Arthur said, "I probably ask more questions than anybody." On the other hand, Guy said that when he learned the biller, "I didn't have to ask that many questions." However, Guy also felt that very few people around Cellsoft had many answers for him; this is understandable given Guy's much longer experience in the industry than that of any of his colleagues.

When to Ask

What determines the occasion for asking questions? Again, this varies with individuals and with the types of questions. For example, Bill would begin learning a new project by thinking through his own ideas and then asking his manager, Barry, as much as he could, in almost a stream-of-consciousness process:

Actually the first thing I do is I sits [sic] down and start running my
head. What about this, what about this? I start running through my
head about different instances, different types of viewpoints, well, are
we looking at this if the sending carrier? Or if the receiving carrier?
A better way to phrase that is, the home carrier or the serving carrier?
Whose viewpoint is it? How do we look at this in a different light?
I want to take a view from both sides of the business, the serving
SID [System ID—an industry-standard number uniquely identifying
each cellular carrier] and the home SID. I want to look at it from
both viewpoints. . . . For all the tapes we get, you're gonna have
two different companies, for each SID that we get. . . . If they were
inter-SID, we don't get them. So we're gonna have different SIDs
each time we get a call. And what if one SID belongs to company 1,
and the other SID belongs to company 2? And the serving SID,
who's the one whose tapes we're gonna get, he's not enabled for
duplicate call checking. So my question was, What if the home SID,
company 2, what if they are [enabled for duplicate call checking]?
The answer was, we do it. So if all but one company has duplicate
call checking, that one company basically will still get it for free.
But do you want to gamble that?

The way I go through it, I bounce all these different ideas and
questions through my head. After that, I bounce 'em against Barry.
What do you think, how should we handle this? My idea is, let's do
it this way. Most of the time, . . . if he says I can't think of any
other thing, he lets me do it the way that I want to. If he has a
different idea, or a different method he'd like to use but he can't shoot
a hole through mine, he lets me do it my way. If he's got a damn
good reason though, I get shot down. Which I don't mind, [because],
even though we've covered all the bases, he will come up with a
better method of doing something and I just sort of, OK, I didn't
think of that, you know? Or jeez, that's something I've never seen
before, and that's how you pick up a lot of things too. That's why I
bounce a lot of questions off somebody else.

While Bill begins a task by asking as many questions as he can, others
only ask when they have exhausted what they can do on their own or when they
already have a general idea of what they are doing and need to fill in details.
Joyce described her approach:

I usually . . . try to figure out as much as I can of a problem till I get
to a point where I just don't know . . . where something's coming
from or what, and then [I] ask. . . . Sometimes, if I've been working

by myself and I come across a problem, I would go through and try to resolve it as much as possible and then go back and ask a specific question like "I don't understand what this file is," or whatever. Oftentimes when I was working right beside someone, and they're gonna do the next step and the next step is something I had not seen and had never used before, I would just ask and then get a general explanation of it.

The most common time to ask questions is when one's own resources are exhausted or when there is not enough time to pursue the subject. Often the pace of work at Cellsoft makes it imperative to cut one's own learning time by asking someone else for help. However, programmers often consider this a poor substitute for doing the work themselves. As Barbara put it, "Sometimes if I'm in a crunch I'll ask Trevor. If I know that this thing is due and it's gonna take me at least two hours to figure out on my own, I'll ask Trevor if he's available prior to spending the two hours. It's not quite as good because I don't think you learn it as well if you haven't figured it out by yourself, but if something is due by 5:00 I'll do it that way." Similarly, Judith said, "I've learned that you can try figuring out answers for yourself just so long, and there comes a point that it's more of a waste of time for you to sit here, it's better to ask someone a question and use two minutes of their time getting an answer than for you to spend an hour trying to read this document."

Leslie described the process of grappling with a problem and of asking and processing questions this way:

Well, first, . . . I try to go to the manual and make sure I entered the right piece of information. If there's an error section I'd look there. And then ultimately I—well, I tend to ask questions quicker at this point in my life; I'll ask people instead of spending too much time spinning my wheels. . . . [Then] I'll take the information somebody tells me, and then what I will typically do, unless I just don't really give a damn, or I just don't have the time, I . . . try to think it through and make sure I completely can understand why and to the point where . . . I can figure out a way to backtrack and realize that I could have found that answer . . . on my own. . . . So I will try to give myself the knowledge that I might have been able to get before.

For Barbara, also, questioning, like other aspects of learning, is iterative. She will take time to digest answers and then come back with more questions. When one programmer explained something to her, "I made sure I understood it, or I thought I did, and then he went away and I went back [to him] and I said, 'Wait a minute, I don't understand this,' and he explained it in more detail and then I did it."

Why Ask Questions?

Probably the most important reason programmers ask questions (other than "to find out the answers," but this has a why-did-the-chicken-cross-the-road quality not intended here) is to save time. We have already seen this response. Work has a certain pressure that militates against the systematic search for knowledge, and while this is frustrating to people of an assimilative bent, who want to understand things in great detail and to explore their work fully, most programmers, at least in business settings, are more interested in solving immediate problems than in delving into their subject matter, and even though they value the process of finding out for themselves, they would sooner ask others and get on with their work than waste a lot of time.

Another important reason for asking questions is to fill in gaps in a programmer's schema of knowledge. Questions come out of a framework. Barbara studies specifications, develops a partial understanding, and then uses questions both to confirm (or disconfirm) and to complete that understanding. On the other hand, some programmers, such as Bill, ask as much to gain an overview as to fill in details.

Whom to Ask

Another important aspect of asking is knowing and deciding whom to ask. Sometimes this is a matter of chance, or simply of proximity to people with the answers. Thus Arthur said of his first days at Cellsoft, "I was lucky that I was in an office [with] programmers that you could turn around and ask a question, but everybody has a specialty I guess, and eventually you learn that. . . . Ahmed would know Datatrieve questions and Phil RDO, or whatever."

Ahmed, a Tunisian programmer in his mid-twenties, specialized in switch-interface software. Soon after this study began, he became a manager supervising Doug and Ed. Arthur often turned to Ahmed with questions because he shared a small office with him, an example of work space influencing learning strategy. Doug turned to him as an employee would naturally turn to his boss, as well as because of Ahmed's expertise with switch software. From talking to Ahmed, Doug found other people by the fact of their talking with Ahmed as well, and by some coincidence they were Ahmed's office mates, Arthur and Phil.

> Well, primarily, I've been turning to Ahmed, because I know he knows the switch software and he's my supervisor. There have been occasions where he hasn't been around, and I've looked to other people for information that wasn't directly switch related. There was one point where I had a problem with one of the CDD [Common

Data Dictionary] utilities, and I turned to people that I guess I thought would have some knowledge or expertise in those areas. I'm not sure how I identified those people. . . . I guess I went to people that I'd seen talking with Ahmed on various issues, and sort of had a feel for what sorts of knowledge they had.

As we have already seen, Guy, being more experienced than any of the other programmers, asks very few questions, but when he is stumped he finds the people with the greatest knowledge. "I guess maybe the key is knowing who knows, huh? I mean, it's not something that happens, I don't think you'll find anybody to tell you, you know, as a conscious effort what they do. It just happens. I mean, I don't say 'I need to learn this,' I just say to myself, automatically, 'Who knows this stuff?' or 'Who should know this stuff?'"

As important as knowing whom to ask is knowing whom not to. There are people who are virtually useless as resources. Sometimes they simply don't know enough to be worth asking. Then there are people who simply don't want to be bothered. This was how Bill felt about Jason, his first manager at Cellsoft. Jason, Bill said, "is unapproachable quite often. His style is to be busy. He . . . wasn't around a lot either, and he is someone who blows you off quite easily, and I've been burned by him . . . which is nice to know. I wish I learned it earlier."

In another incident, people wouldn't answer Dave's questions because they disapproved of his project or saw it as an encroachment on their professional area. Dave was working on a program that could translate code from one programming language to another. Dave was to modify this program, which had originally been designed to translate from the LISP language, so that it could also translate from another language, called Ada:

The core team who had done the LISP implementation . . . would answer questions, but they hated to be[cause]—there was sort of a psychodynamic there that was interesting—they absolutely hated Ada. And management had suggested, somebody other than they themselves had suggested that there be an Ada code generator to this. So they hated when I came into the room to ask a question, they hated being reminded that Ada was part of this system. There's a lot of strong feelings about Ada in the community. A lot of the questions that I had, sort of, "How would you do this?" or "How would you do that?" was often regarded as thinly veiled—"Adaspeak," was the phrase one of them used one time, "Ah, I don't believe this Adaspeak." In other words, they were quite happy that the LISP language model was hard-wired into the thing. They made claims that it was programming language independent, but . . . they weren't particularly interested in Ada. There were some issues there with just going to ask them questions.

In this case the prejudices of this group discouraged Dave from asking questions and therefore made it harder for him to work on this project.

DIALOGUE

The asking of questions is not always a preconceived activity. Sometimes they arise spontaneously in the nature of work. Although there are times when a programmer may work in isolation and assemble a list of questions to ask later, it is just as likely that opportunities can arise unexpectedly. For example, when I was interviewing Barbara for this study, I explained to her that I had been testing software whose output could serve as input to the billing programs she was working on. She inserted this information into her own work agenda, as the following dialogue shows:

MS: For the last month or so I've been setting up rating tests. I hadn't been aware you were working on this at all. You might in fact want to run [your programs] past my rating output at some point and see what you get from it.

BARBARA: That's wonderful. Do you have home, reseller, and roamers?

MS: They're small, but I do.

BARBARA: Oh, wow. What formatter are you using?

MS: I start with an unrated file. I don't go through the whole tape, and formatter, and things. It's whatever was there . . .

BARBARA: Is the formatter a piece of software that's specific to the market? Specific to the customer?

MS: I don't think so. I think it's something that takes a CIBER tape, which is standard, and reformats it. There may be a few varieties, but there aren't many. Have to talk to the guys downstairs about that, Jason and Burt.

BARBARA: What you're saying, well, 'cause according to Greg the formatter is used, in all the . . . you're saying it's only used for . . .

MS: I don't myself know where it's used, I've never had to deal with it. You can ask one of those guys.

BARBARA: Trevor recently changed rating to give us more information on the call-detail, roamer, all the call-detail records, so it would make the life of these reports easier. Now are you running those changes?

MS: The last time I ran a 1.6 rater—is it still a 1.6, or is this a 2.0?

BARBARA: Well, he was tying his changes to Minneapolis's switch upgrade that was happening in the middle of December. But I don't know.

MS: I'm not sure what [version] I'm running in. I'll have to check with Trevor.

BARBARA: What are you, are we changing rating, we're changing rating

MS: We're not supposed to.

BARBARA: You're like testing 1.6 rating?

MS: Not really. I'm assuming 1.6 rating works and I'm saving the results and running it against the 1.7 that the guys downstairs are doing. They've made some changes so that rating will be part of [the system] and run off menus. And I want to be able to run that on the same data and get the same results. And they've added one or two input files, tables or something. I haven't gotten to that piece, I've just been trying to get 1.6 working on their data.

BARBARA: How does that coordinate with what Trevor's doing?

MS: I'm not sure. We should all have a meeting and figure that out.

BARBARA: So people downstairs are changing rating, to drive it from a menu, and you're using . . .

MS: Yeah, what they're doing is building roamer rating as a sellable product. But it's the same rating that we use, pretty much. Oh [someone else is] working on rating too, by the way. He's studying it because [another client] wants changes to it.

BARBARA: Roamers like are outcollects, is that what you mean?

MS: And they're going to treat home as pretty much a subset of that.

BARBARA: OK.

SUMMARY

People use one another in a wide variety of ways. As *models*, people embody experience or serve as representations of what others can become. As *sources*, people explain difficult or unfamiliar material or put matters in context. As *foils*, people can allow one to recognize one's own knowledge by seeking it (*students*), refuting or enhancing it (*sages*), having less knowledge themselves (*fools*), or just being there and saying nothing at all (*dogs*). Through dialogue people incorporate one another into their respective frames of reference.

Also, people ask questions in a variety of settings and for a variety of reasons. People differ on how much and when to ask. Some only ask questions when they have exhausted other resources, while others, like Bill, ask "at the drop of a hat." They may ask questions to save time or to fill in gaps in their overall understanding. The people whom they ask, like other resources (such as documentation, as described in chapter 6), are likely to be the most conveniently situated and (as in Dave's case) those not averse to being asked or hostile to the questioner. Even the most knowledgeable people on a subject will not be asked many questions if they are hard to find or unfriendly. Questioning and dialogue are, after all, social activities, and it makes perfect sense that who asks whom, how much, and how often is as much a matter of personality and style as any other aspect of learning.

8

Working at the Computer

What do programmers do when they sit at their terminals? What sorts of activities do they perform, and how do they learn from them? How do these activities relate to the conventional models of programmers' work?

In contrast to the ideals of structured programming and systems analysis, which advance the importance of top-down thinking, of conceiving a problem broadly and then gradually breaking it down into ever smaller and more manageable pieces, the daily life of programmers (like that of most people) is lived and experienced sequentially. Consider that a program itself is a *sequence* of instructions, executed one at a time, and it should not be surprising that the work of generating, understanding, and interpreting programs is also a sequential activity. The steps that a programmer uses to learn a program, to solve a problem, or to explain the operation of a system are often not analyzed beforehand. They come about from the nature of the work and of the problems to be solved and can be viewed by sitting with (or being) a programmer conscious of his or her work.

Another important aspect of learning at the computer is the use of the *scientific method*. Arno Penzias (1989, p. 174) pointed out that "while most people aren't employed as professional scientists, we all need the ability to demystify the world through the creation and testing of hypotheses." Programmers, who may or may not be trained in scientific disciplines, are constantly guessing how things work and revising their guesses in light of what the computer tells them. A computer provides continual feedback and constant identification of errors, but the programmers still need to figure out which errors are being identified. A working program is like a scientific hypothesis in the sense that it may always possess errors no one has yet found, and there is no definitive "proof" that it works correctly, no matter how much it is tested.

In this chapter I present two detailed illustrations of programmers at work. These illustrations, from the CAD group described in chapter 4, demonstrate respectively the use of play and of multiple media to learn about systems, and the sequential nature of identifying and solving software problems. I shall also describe two specific types of on-line activities: using the debugger and referring to on-line help.

"DECBURGER":   LEARNING BY PLAYING

Robert, the CAD manager who was trained in electrical engineering, described his learning style this way: "I learn by doing. And I've always learned by doing. I'm still a fix-it man, a handyman around the house, and the way I learned to do that is take things apart, and when I was a kid my parents would glare at me and say, 'You better get that back together 'cause we want it!' And so I would struggle along sometimes, and got it back together."

In his current job, although he is not required to program, he continues to do so out of a combination of fun and a desire to learn. When I interviewed him, he was teaching himself DECWindows, a windowing system for Digital's VMS operating system, modeled after X Windows. To teach himself, he said, "I'm busy doing a DECWindows user interface on a game, which is a kaleidoscope, you know, toy, demonstration, so that I can learn how that [works] and have intelligent conversations with people who are doing it for real."

Robert learned this by using a common technique, that of reducing the problem to the small piece he wanted to learn. Essentially he combined two techniques we have seen elsewhere, namely, prototyping and copying from a preexisting template, to build a controlled experiment. Starting by taking a program he found by communicating with other window developers through electronic mail, Robert, holding everything else constant, changed one variable at a time and saw what happened.

> Since I want to learn how to do the user interface, I want the computational part of the problem to be simplistic, so I don't have to work hard on that. So I've picked up off the network a kaleidoscope that was written at MIT, [that] puts pretty patterns on the display, and then I said, "What I'd really like to do is change the speed, change the color mix, and whatnot; let me build a user interface to do that, and that will teach me how to do a lot of user interface."

When I asked him how it was going, he replied,

> Currently, it's broken because I just tried to adjust process priority and I've broken it badly. But in fact, it was operational. A week ago, as long as you didn't touch process priority, I could change burst

rates, probability of color percentages, changes, pattern shifts, all sorts of things, so I had probably about a dozen controls that I had programmed and I tried to make them a variety of different control objects so that I'd learn about each type.

Robert also found another program to work on:

There's been an example floated about by the DECWindows developers called Decburger, which was provided on all DECWindows systems, which illustrated how to order at McDonald's using a DECWindows user interface. And it was a synthetic example, you know, Big Macs and whatnot. And you could click, or twist, or slide, or push, or whatever, all sorts of different objects, and they gave you both the executable code and the user interface definition.

Note that here Robert was using both his workstation and printed code. Next he added on-line documentation, an entire set of on-line manuals called the *book reader*, described in more detail toward the end of this chapter:

So I printed that out, I studied that, I said, Oh, OK, I see the order of things I have to do here, sat with that in hardcopy, had the DECWindows book reader up so I could read the reference manual for the routine calls, and had my source code in another editor.

Robert used the book reader to learn more about Windows:

I have a library of goodies, and I can roll down here, to, let's see, DECWindows programming, just click on that, it turns out I'm going off to a book. . . . I happen to have a different set of ROMs on here so I'm going off across the building to another style guide that tells you how to design the interface.

(When he said "going off across the building," he did not really leave his chair; he simply meant that the computer storing this particular manual was located elsewhere and that he had access to it through a network.)

So if I want to know about menus, I just click on the table of contents, look at the picture; if I want to see the figure I just click on the figure.

This use of on-line documentation, called *hypertext*, allows one to go from one reference to another through an automated system of cross-references. However, its usefulness here was limited:

As a matter of fact, this version only highlights when you point at it, so you're gonna have to guess what you can point at. Any time there's a cross-reference I would think that [the] next version out in fact will allow you to highlight all hot spots so you know what you can point at. But essentially I sit here and browse through the documentation without too much effort.

So Robert had a printed copy of the program and a workstation with two windows, of which one contained the on-line documentation and the other contained the program, which he could edit.

And so I'd be referring to this to get the reference material, looking at the example to see how they were doing it, and then synthesizing that into mine. And then running it, and saying, Oh! Didn't work?

At this point Robert continued to work by trial and error, guessing what to do next as he integrated documented examples into his own program, but he viewed this as the nature of programming: "I mean, any program takes some debugging."

Sometimes you get some unexpected results. In particular I found object positioning within windows to be non-intuitive. I don't seem to have a good sense for how big ten pixels are. So there was a lot of trial and error in positioning items and getting it to look aesthetically pleasing. Most of the interface stuff worked pretty well. You know, it's always the trivial stuff that gets you, like not doing the right level of indirection in C, you know, not throwing enough ampersands in at the right time.

In addition to learning to program DECWindows, Robert was using this project to teach himself the C programming language as well. "I had looked at C programs, but this was really the first real programming that produced a result that I had ever done." He was motivated by "personal interest, and needing to be able to talk with some authority about using this stuff." He said, once again demonstrating the experiential, non-theoretical bent of many programmers, that the best way to "be able to talk with some authority" is to "have done it yourself. I know you can do that, I know you can't do that, I know this confused me, [and so on]." This is another example of someone acting in the role of sage to other programmers, in this case his subordinates.

SEQUENTIAL PROBLEM SOLVING

Anne, a programmer in her thirties who works for Robert in the CAD group, demonstrated her approach to problem solving with an example she was debugging at the time I interviewed her. Unlike all the other people interviewed in this study, Anne did not articulate her approach to learning but simply demonstrated it by working on a real problem and explaining it as she went along. By following her I was able to identify a sequence of activities in the apparent disorder of actual work.

The problem was an error in a drawing presented by an engineer who worked upstairs from Anne. The CAD group's job is to provide software support for a group of electrical engineers who design microchips that go into computers, terminals, and other hardware. Anne's group plays a role for these people analogous to Cellsoft's role for cellular carriers, except that in this case both organizations are within the same company. This makes the interaction between programmers and users, and the software-development process, less formal than at Cellsoft. Robert described the contrast between these types of organization this way:

Actually it's a very different space. One of the things we can do being a local group with a small user base is be pretty responsive. And so we probably do less planning and more reaction than a typical software-development group does. As soon as you get into doing products [here] you probably know there's this huge bureaucracy you have to satisfy, product management, and . . . planners and all sorts of things which are, you know, necessary components to have a commercial product where your users are essentially remote folks you never meet, unless you happen to show up at [a user-group conference] and one of them walks up to you, and you have very infrequent releases so you have to have an exceptional [sic] high quality or you should at least strive for that, solid documentation, you know, and once a year you let a piece of software go.

When I spoke with Anne, she was dealing with a problem furnished by one of her users. The problem as Anne described it concerned the program's treating two different types of electrical connections the same way. "There are two different kinds of connections in here and the code is supposed to know that. And it's supposed to generate the right thing for either one of them, but in fact it doesn't know the difference, so it only generates one of them, and it generates it for all cases."

This is actually a common situation with computer programs. They are built to handle a particular situation and later have to be generalized to deal with other cases; this is how Henry worked with talkers. This may happen either because no one thinks of more general cases when the program is first conceived, or more commonly because it doesn't matter at the time and there is pressure to solve an immediate problem quickly. Generalization is left for a later date and forgotten until a problem comes up. Anne believed that the former was the reason in this case.

> You had the normal case. . . . That stuff works fine. And then there's stuff that's totally abnormal, like this little area right in here is totally abnormal. And then there are places where the normal stuff and the unusual stuff come together. And the way we said we were gonna handle them, although in fact we didn't ever actually do it anyway, was that we weren't going to handle the interface case between the two areas, because at the time . . . the person who decided what we should do didn't think anyone would ever do something where there was an interface case. But in fact there was a very sensible reason for doing that, and this guy did it. So that's going to have to have special handling. But the case where everything is of the unusual case ought to work right. [But it] work[s] the same as the normal case right now, and so does the transitional case between them, which has to be special case completely, and which we had said we weren't going to handle anyway, but we had to do something for it in the meantime.

The program Anne was working on processes CAD diagrams and prepares them for input to another program called a *logic simulator*, which takes a diagram representing the wiring on a microchip and simulates what it would actually do. Anne identified two problems with her user's example: that the logic in the diagram was itself wrong, and that the code that prepared the input for the simulator also did not work. So there was a compound problem, that incorrect data was being incorrectly processed. The first program should have identified ("flagged") the unusual data so that the second could deal with it properly and thus pass manageable input to the simulator. However, there were a number of pieces missing from this process.

> Even if this code got it right, that code which I did write most of is gonna do the wrong thing because it doesn't know where to find the information that isn't being created correctly anyway, because this code isn't creating it. But . . . if this code did the right stuff, which was code not written yet, what it would do would be that it would flag the places where the unusual connections occur, and then the code that prepares the simulator input would notice this flag and prepare the correct stuff instead of the wrong stuff that it's making now. But that code wasn't written either.

However, Anne did not see this as the user's basic problem, because he could flag the unusual cases himself. All of this activity was carried out on a diagram that appeared on Anne's workstation as she described it. She pointed to two green lines that crossed one another and identified them as the problematic case. She said that she could manually (at her workstation) *edit* the diagram, called a *schematic*, and enter text identifying the unusual case, "except I don't want to mess up the original of his schematic." She continued to describe the lines and symbols on the drawing: "Well, all the things starting with dots are commands to the simulator, but see, he's already got three things in here that he has to define. This is [simulator] input but with symbolic names. See, he already has to define three things and, sure enough, guess what one of them is. That's the nonstandard connection."

Anne had now broken the problem into two parts. She had dealt with the first of these—the nonstandard input—basically by not dealing with it, by manually changing it so the second program, which was really her area of expertise, could process it properly.

> Anyway, he'll have to add a couple of lines in here, but this'll enable him to go do his work while I solve the other half of his problem. 'Cause the calculations are actually correct, that's what I was checking with that bunch of stuff I was playing with with the other schematic that I had out, the test case one. The calculations are correct. It's just, what they're connected to is wrong, because it thinks they're always connected to the same thing and that's not true here. So, if I put that part in, then I can get him going in a day or two.

Anne's style consistently involves reducing a problem to increasingly manageable smaller pieces. So far she had lopped off half the code. Next she initiated a sequence of activities to pinpoint the problem further.

1. The first step was to run a program called GENIE that made a list of connections and devices from the schematic. This list is called a *wirelist*. As Anne explained,

> It's not just a list of wires, though, it's also a list of which things the wires are connected to. It's actually a list of the things, and the wires are in there by name. So it'll find somebody, like here's an inverter, so you'll see that a wire named IN goes into the inverter and a wire named A comes out. OK? And the rest of it's all transparent. And here's some resistors here. So that stuff is now sitting in memory as a wirelist and we can write that stuff out.

2. After generating the wirelist, Anne ran it through another program, a part of the logic simulator called the *wirelist utility*. This program figures out

> what's connected to what. Like, here's this capacitor, whose name is P7. And he's a thirty-picofarrad capacitor, so here he is and he's got VSS on one side and CAD on the other. This wire here is called CAD, and this one's called VSS. And so, everybody's in here, this is not a very, especially big thing. There's the inverter. I presume that's the first inverter. IN is coming in, and A is coming out. That's it. The names got, that's the name of the device and he didn't name them, so, when the schematics editor did this it went and named them P1 through N, however many devices he had in here.

Here Anne digressed to stress the importance of using recognizable, meaningful names in designing the solution to her problem; this is also important when one is debugging programs. The names are not important to users because users do not break their drawing down into such detail, except when problems arise:

> I usually give the things explicit names 'cause then I know what they're gonna be called before I have to go look for them. But most users wouldn't normally give things explicit names 'cause they don't care what they're gonna be called 'cause they're never gonna look at this thing unless it comes out wrong.

3. Once she had run the wirelist utility to get the data into their proper format, Anne's next step was to find the focus of the problem. She identified what the program did right in order to limit further exploration to what it did wrong.

> Now this is gonna perform several operations, most of which are gonna do the right thing, though it takes a while to do it. It's gonna find things like these inverters and turn 'em into transistors. And it's gonna go and compute the parasitic connections and that's what it's gonna do wrong, and then it's gonna write out a simulator input file, which is gonna be wrong, because it's gonna have all the wrong connections in it.

Having recognized that the input to the simulator was incorrect, Anne did not bother to run the simulator. She stopped the process where the problem emerged. "Well, the thing is, garbage in, garbage out, we've already got garbage so there's no point in running the simulator on it, it's already trash."

She identified a particular element, number 10 on the wirelist, as the problem case. Again she commented on the meaningless of the element name:

> See, the reason it's a pain for this guy to have to create this thing by hand, the reason you do it from a program like this is that the input uses all these numbers instead of names. This is a pain in the neck. It's error-prone, it's not user-friendly, it has many bad attributes like that. So there's thing number 5, now lemme see. Number 10, I mean. We gotta find the right guy [types]. Unless it's the last one. There he is, anyways. See all these zeroes down here? Well, those should've been 10's. See, this is the stuff that's coming out wrong. It's got all those things connected to the wrong thing. This is stuff that it's sucked in from elsewhere.

Anne demonstrated the purpose of the wirelist utility by contrasting the input with the output:

> See, here's his input file coming through again, see, that was his control file? There's all the commands that were in it, except they've been translated so they're numbers instead of names.

4. At this point, by identifying the problem Anne was halfway to solving it. She could now begin to change the properties of the wires so the simulator could process them properly. In order to do this, she needed to make sure that the names she gave the variables were not being used elsewhere in the system. To do this, she referred to a printed document, a *list of property names*. This was the first occasion when Anne referred to anything other than her workstation screen and a copy of the program. Anne leafed through a thick binder to find the properties she needed. She did not like this document, but it was all she had.

> Unfortunately, I am the baby-sitter of this list, it ought to be an official manual done by an official technical writer who speaks decent English and writes better than I do and knows how to run the crazy program that produces these manuals. But we only have 25 percent of a writer, so this is mine. We share her with three other projects. So, I do this, because otherwise there wouldn't be enough cycles around here to do it.

(As a digression, note Anne's use of "cycles." She took the computer concept of "CPU cycle," a unit of processing time, and used it as a metaphor for human time. It is quite common for serious systems programmers or "hackers" to model themselves after computers in their speech and imagery, while end users, on the other hand, are more likely to ascribe humanlike qualities to the machines. Anne did this as well, as when she referred to data elements as "guys." See Turkle, 1983, for more discussion of this.)

When Anne finally found what she was looking for, she discovered a cross-reference to another document: "Well, it says to see the functional specification written by the guy in the next office." This is a frustration many programmers find with written manuals: that it is very seldom possible to find everything in one place, or even in one book. Still, rather than looking for the functional specification, she continued searching through the same binder, and eventually an insight emerged through the cloud of documentation, which she courteously accompanied with narrative as she skimmed:

> Let's see if the other one says the same thing [turns pages in binder].
> No, it's gonna say the same thing except with P's. This is the case
> this guy actually has, this would be the normal case because of, well,
> because of the way chips are made around here this would be the
> normal way. If you're gonna run into this problem at all this is the
> side of it that you'd see, you wouldn't see the other side of it, you'd
> have to be doing something really highly weird rather than just
> unusual . . . input . . . AHA!

Anne's "AHA!" came from a blending of two sources: the problem in front of her and another manual that she had recently been reviewing. Something she had come upon in the latter appeared to be incorrect, and the problem she was now working on elucidated what was wrong with the manual:

> Because [of] the way she had described it in her manual I thought,
> boy, that can't be right, it must do something different than that,
> well sure enough it does do something different than that and this is
> why. So I'll have to tell her about that if someone else hasn't
> already. John, the guy in the next office, has already reviewed that
> other manual so he probably already fixed that anyway, but I'll have
> to make sure.

5. Once she had identified the problematic area in the schematic, Anne made her own copy of the drawing so she could play with it without disturbing the original. First she tried it in its original form. "I'm gonna try the obvious technique first [types]. I'm gonna copy the file, and I'm gonna read in the copy and see whether it likes that, it may have some information internal to it that tells it what it is, in which case I'm not gonna be able to do it this way." She ran the copy through the schematics editor and then reported that it "hasn't complained yet."

6. In order to simplify the problem, Anne found a smaller example that could serve as a prototype. She leafed through some papers and eventually discovered what she was looking for:

> Simple parcam logical is what it's called. [This is a] much smaller
> case of the same thing, should be anyway. That's much smaller,

6sixtransistors [a variable name]. This, I guarantee you, does no useful things. . . . This has the highly unusual case as well as the [merely] unusual case 'cause I put both of them in here. This is what he's got, up here, the top half of this drawing is what the user has and then, any user that's gonna find this is gonna have the top half, but there's a symmetrical set of problems on the bottom, so, you know . . . and here, see D? D is the interface between, this side is normal. This is what people would normally have over here. And from here over is abnormal. This thing here is the abnormal thing here, . . . ssx for the symmetrical case on the bottom. Which, chances are real good nobody's gonna see for many years to come, probably. Might as well fix it now, at any rate it's probably harder to fix only half of the problem than the whole problem. The code is totally symmetrical for it.

Anne reduced the complex figure of the original problem to a smaller case by eliminating details extraneous to the matter to be solved. Although she said that "this . . . does no useful things," it is important, much like a classroom example or a textbook exercise, in restricting work to the essential. For all the complexity of computer software, it can all be reduced to simple modularity. Here we have returned to the top-down, "divide-and-conquer" methodology of academic programming, but it comes at the end of the problem, not at the beginning. The difficult work of this example was precisely in identifying and duplicating the conditions of the problem. Once she arrived at this stage, Anne had no trouble continuing. Ultimately, however, she stopped short of a programming solution. Her job at that moment was to help a user, not to fix bugs in the code. Having analyzed his problem and having changed his input data to make it acceptable to the simulator, Anne considered her task done for the moment.

This thing the guy is still gonna have to do by hand, because it's, see, this is connected to this wire. This is all one connection here. So, this side of it's normal and this side of it's abnormal. So he's gonna have to do that part by hand, but he knows that and that's OK with him, it's just that he'd be much happier if he doesn't have to do the whole thing by hand, which is what he's gotta do now. And also he probably wasted some amount of time figuring out why it was that his simulation was so bizarre in the first place, since he thought of course, since we thought so too, that we had actually done this stuff already. Luckily, this is not the kind of guy who gets mad.

This example illustrates the sequential nature of problem solving when one uses the computer itself as a tool. Analytic methods—systematic design, spec writing, and note taking—are carried out separately from using a terminal or a workstation, though one may be available to provide answers through querying or through on-line help. But the act of using a computer to solve problems enforces the computer's own way of "thinking"—single small steps, taken one at a time—on the programmer, necessitating serialistic rather than holistic learning. Again, the system comes from the details.

USING THE ON-LINE DEBUGGER

The on-line debugger is a programming tool, actually a metaprogram, that allows one to run another program and stop wherever one wishes in order to see what that program is doing at any point. Typically, a debugger allows a programmer to examine the contents of the computer's memory at various points during a program's execution, to change the contents of memory in order to simulate running the program with different inputs, and to keep track of how the program reached its current point (that is, to track all the subroutine calls that led it to where the programmer has chosen to stop it). A debugger, then, is a powerful tool for programmers seeking to find and correct problems ("bugs") in programs.

However, it also has other uses. Using a debugger to execute one instruction at a time and to stop after each one (*single-stepping*) teaches the structure of the program in great detail. For inexperienced programmers it also provides direct illustrations of the meaning of commands in the programming language. Ultimately, using the debugger on a number of related programs can teach a great deal about the way an entire software system is constructed, and programmers at Cellsoft and elsewhere have employed the debugger in these ways as a learning tool.

One way to appreciate the importance of the debugger is to encounter it for the first time after programming without it. When Barbara began working with the VMS operating system, which has an on-line debugger, she said, "I would look at [a] program for four hours, because that was my technique at [my first job], we didn't have DEBUG, you use a series of displays, so you have to put displays in your program, recompile, and run it." By "display" she meant a COBOL statement requesting the program to type the value of a variable into an output record of the program run, called a log file. Then "you print out the screen, you print out your log file," and read the results. Once she found the values of certain displayed variables, she could begin to find the bugs. Then she would put displays in other parts of the program, run the whole thing again, and gradually narrow down the source of the problem.

With the debugger, on the other hand, it is not necessary to run the entire program. All Barbara needs to do now is to run the program under DEBUG, set *breakpoints* at lines of code where she wants to stop the program, tell the debugger to execute up to the first breakpoint, examine any variables (that is, the contents of named memory locations) set at that point, and then either continue to the next breakpoint or single-step through the program, examining the output after each line of code. In time, using the debugger has become a habit for Barbara: "Now I'm down to looking at the program, seeing if [the error] hits me in the face, and if not I'll go on DEBUG right away, whereas [when I started] I would look at that program a longer time because I wasn't that comfortable with how I could use DEBUG."

Barbara said that in order to use the debugger effectively, it is necessary to be familiar with the flow of the program first. This is consistent with the holistic strategy we have seen Barbara employing elsewhere: to study a problem as much as possible before attempting a solution. Characteristically, this means that she does not actually try things out on the computer until she has spent time reading a program and any accompanying specifications or other documents and asking questions. Therefore, Barbara comes to the debugger late in her learning cycle and does not spend much time with it. In explaining a particular problem, she said that "I had a general idea where in the program or in what subroutine they [the bugs] were occurring. The bugs that I had to deal with just were not occurring every time that subroutine was executed, only under certain data conditions, so I would set a break at that subroutine and I would set a break when a phone number equalled a certain number and would find out what was happening."

Bill, by contrast, takes a more serialistic approach to learning and to problem solving. A detail-oriented programmer, Bill is enthusiastic about the debugger and uses it as much as possible. "Debugger is beautiful! You can just pop in, go step by step, examine values, and see what's going wrong. Or see what's going right, as the case may be." Bill, unlike Barbara, begins with the debugger rather than just ending with it. "I like stepping through the debugger on the code the first time through, because I find that if you let it run in batch, you see where you blew up and everything, but you still never got to see the value it blew up on, so you may as well go through the first time and find out where you screw up."

This does not mean that Bill does no analytic work beforehand. For him the important thing is knowing what the program is supposed to do, or else it is impossible to say whether it is working as it should be. This means that before running a program with the debugger, Bill ascertains what the results of the program ought to be. He carries on a process very similar to quality assurance by defining test conditions and expected results and then using the debugger to demonstrate whether or not the program performs as it should.

> Find what you're expecting first. Run a bat[ch job], run either in Datatrieve, or, I haven't used it here, but I used it elsewhere, Focus— run something that's a third, a fourth GL [-generation language], that doesn't—real quick and easy for you to code, is a hog. Run it overnight, let it get your figures, then run your good code.

That is, write a prototype program to produce the data that the real program should produce, then run the real program and see if the results match. Or, if a prototype is not feasible,

> sometimes you just go in and fudge the data. Change it. And then see what happens. I try to figure every permutation out possible before, and then I try to go in, Oh, it didn't do this, why didn't it do it? Then I go back into the code and figure out where it screwed up. Frequently using the debugger, 'cause you can stop it and instantly see where something changed, and why it changed, how it changed. What condition didn't I trap for? What happened, but, pretty much that's the fun part.

Bill does not use the debugger only to understand or to fix other people's programs; he also uses it as a testing tool for his own programs as he writes them. "I consider it a challenge to write a program with as few bugs as possible. But I still always walk through it, and I always—before I test, I figure out how many different permutations do I have to do, what type of data do I have to come up with? And I'll construct the data for every damn single type of condition that can be met."

In addition to the obvious uses for fixing or learning individual programs, the debugger serves other functions for programmers. For Arthur it provided assistance with learning the COBOL language. Arthur referred to examples frequently; much of his early work at Cellsoft, when he did not know COBOL and had minimal programming experience, consisted of making new programs by copying old ones and making minor changes to them. The debugger gave him insight into how the COBOL programs worked, because he could see how data changed after each line of code was executed. When he was learning Cellsoft's application, he also used the Digital ACMS debugger to work his way through various tasks. Arthur never had the formal "Cellular 101" training, but instead "I was stepping through it using DEBUG and just looking at the task and stuff."

Of course, the debugger, like any individual tool, has its problems. Because it deals with one program (and its associated subroutines) at a time, learning a large system via DEBUG can be a very slow, tedious process, and, as we have seen with Newton, people who learn at the detail level may fail to understand the system as a whole. Thus Arthur said that after working with individual programs with the debugger and with pieces of the whole system, "I didn't understand, still don't, the whole big picture and how it all works."

Also, even with individual programs, the debugger does not necessarily find the problems. When the nature of the problem and the conditions under which it occurs are clear, then programmers find the debugger an extremely powerful tool in isolating precisely where in the program the difficulty occurs. On the other hand, often in identifying and testing problems the difficulty is re-creating the problem. Sometimes the error occurs rarely, and it is hard to define the conditions under which it occurs. Bill put the matter this way:

> Sometimes you have a problem, and you cannot re-create a bug. . . . That can happen due to a number of reasons. Could happen because you're in one environment, the production environment [where the software runs for clients] and yet when you try to re-create the bug you're in another environment, the development environment [where the programmers work], and it's just not acting the same. I have heard about it, I have never seen it, and, because most of the time you didn't actually do everything explicitly the same, you made some difference and that's why you didn't get the bug. [On the other hand,] once you've re-created the bug, again it's you set your breakpoints, and you home in on it. . . . [Even then] it might not be easy because sometimes you've got a long path to follow. Sometimes you can get a bug within a street block worth of code and sometimes you get it within a mile's worth of code.

Gary, on the other hand, doesn't even bother with conditions that are hard to reproduce. "I refuse to work on bugs that are unpredictable. If I can't make it happen every time, I know it's a bug that I'm not gonna be able to fix because I won't be able to slowly track it down." The debugger, then, in a sense is only helpful in solving a problem when one already knows what the problem is; but in conjunction with other basic tools, such as printed programs, reference materials, and other people, programmers can learn a great deal about their programs and their systems by using it.

ON-LINE DOCUMENTATION

As Guy pointed out (see chapter 6), a leading difficulty with manuals at Cellsoft is keeping access to them. People spend more time talking with one another, reading code, and trying one thing after another when documentation is unavailable, but the habits persist. Since I conducted these interviews, Cellsoft has placed copies of all its own and the computer manufacturers' reference manuals in a central library area, from which programmers can sign out materials as they need them. However, use of documentation does not appear to be any greater than it was before.

Even when manuals are available, however, it is not always easy to find anything in them. There may be many manuals for a particular application, and it is difficult to determine which one has what one needs. The Digital VMS operating system does have an on-line HELP facility that provides basic information about each command, and VMS carries this fairly consistently through its applications. At various levels one can type "HELP" followed by a command name to see what the command does and how to use it. One can also refer to subtopics within a command. For example, from the system prompt in VMS, if one types "HELP DIRECTORY" a description of the DIRECTORY command appears on the screen, followed by a list of subtopics one can type to get more information, including examples of how to use the command. It is also possible to print the output of a HELP command. One programmer at Cellsoft kept notebooks full of HELP text. (Evidently, this was not sufficiently helpful for him, as he was fired after less than six months with the company.) Curiously, while most programmers use the on-line HELP facility occasionally, no one at Cellsoft claimed to rely on it as an important method of learning.

Outside of Cellsoft, however, on-line documentation is used more extensively. Programmers working on the Unix operating system make extensive use of its on-line facility, called **man** (short for manual). Unix on-line documentation (known to users as *man pages*) has a standard format for all commands. It is not easy to read and can be somewhat daunting for the uninitiated, but Unix programmers are very fond of it. For example, Ed used it at Cornell but never actually printed anything from it: "Any time I needed it I just typed 'man' and looked at it on the screen." One of the virtues of **man** for Ed was that he could refer to it even when he was working at home on his personal computer, while all the printed documentation was in the school computer center.

Gary, who began his programming career in Unix, described both the difficulty and the value of **man**. Although it is not easy to master, it serves as a model that software developers use in documenting Unix-based products, such as the X Windows system, and therefore serves as a standard for people in the Unix world. Although **man** pages are cryptic,

> you somehow learn how to understand it. They're not tutorial, they're stating the facts, and you have to know enough context to put it in action, and over the course of years of writing Unix code you learn how to read them. . . . But once I've got that under my belt, for example, learning X Windows was easier because it follows the Unix pattern pretty much. It's a different thing, but really, the information is stored . . . right there in a book, full of pages that look just like Unix **man** pages.

Another way of storing documentation on line is with compact disk technology. Robert, the manager of the CAD group, has the entire VMS documentation set available to him on CD-ROM, accessible through one window of his workstation while he does his actual work at another window. This version of VMS documentation, enabling a programmer to view the equivalent of fifty or more manuals from a computer screen, saves a great deal of space and is vastly more informative than the on-line help available to the programmers at Cellsoft. The program for referring to this on-line library is called a *book reader*. Robert said that manuals work poorly for him, that he prefers the book reader "because I can get to things quicker." In addition to being faster and more readily available than printed documentation, the computerized version also contains a master index, accessible by typing keywords from the screen.

After this study was completed, Cellsoft bought the Digital book reader. The workstation and CD player were kept in a small room used as a corporate library, and the training department provided classes on how to use the book reader. However, while a number of people used it in the first few weeks after its installation, most found it difficult to use and did not like leaving their desks to work in isolation in the library. If the book reader were more easily accessible, programmers might make more extensive use of it.

SUMMARY

On-line work at the computer takes shape from the sequential nature of CPU processing. The programmers interviewed here use the computer, in some respects, as they would use a person (see chapter 7). They carry on a dialogue with it, asking it questions by typing commands, and use the feedback as answers that they use to build and test hypotheses concerning how things work. At the terminal they copy programs to provide templates for new programs and build prototypes to model parts of a problem before attempting to solve the whole. In contrast to the analytic, top-down methods of structured programming, actual work at the computer is synthetic, bottom-up, best used in conjunction with, or as a supplement to, analysis. Analysis poses the major questions that the computer must answer, but the answers themselves provide springboards to additional questions and to further, often incidental, learning.

Play at the computer can be used for learning multiple subjects, as when Robert uses it to learn DECWindows and the C language at the same time. Most of these programmers do not work at their terminals in isolation from each other and from other media: On-line work is often accompanied by reference to notes, manuals, and printed copies of programs and is frequently interrupted by conversations with other programmers. When programmers, such as Robert and Anne, have workstations with multiple windows, they are more likely to make use of on-line help than programmers with single-screen terminals like those used at Cellsoft; this may be one reason why Cellsoft programmers make little use of this facility.

Finally, the on-line debugger, though primarily (as its name implies) a tool for finding problems in programs, is itself a powerful technique for learning. These programmers use it for finding out more about programming languages. Also, since it is a means for going through a program very slowly, it provides them with insight into the data structures of, and by inference the business decisions encapsulated in, the system as a whole. Thus it is a powerful educational tool as well as a diagnostic one.

9

Building the System

We have now seen the major activities programmers carry out during their work. Chapters 4 through 8 have discussed the ways in which computer workers approach problems, and how they use documentation, the computer, and each other to solve them. In these chapters I have allowed the participants to speak for themselves as much as possible. The work of the discussion has been much like programmers' own, and that work is generally defined on a piecemeal, task-by-task basis.

However, just as a computer executes one operation, one line of code, at a time but in so doing solves a complex problem, so the programmers themselves, in executing one task at a time, are in fact engaged in a greater task—that of learning the *system* in which all their tasks are embedded; and even though they may often appear to be as oblivious to that system as the computer itself is to the work that it performs, in fact, learning the system is a key factor in the programmers' effectiveness. However, as Barbara said, that learning is very largely *incidental*. Management does not allocate time for it (except in formal training programs); it is just supposed to happen, and, by and large, it does. If we examine the programmers' tasks, as we have done in the preceding chapters, we can see the building of the system in them.

LEARNING BY ITERATION

To the extent that these programmers and other computer workers are conscious of a system as a thing to be learned, and of themselves as learners—and I believe that few of them were very conscious of this until I began discussing the subject with them—they speak of the process almost mystically, in terms of *osmosis*, of something that "just happens." As Bill put it, "You're so close to it, it comes up your fingers and goes in your head." Or they use images of *immersion*. Thus Joyce spoke of "being thrown into some of the situations. But it's not like it's really negative . . . it happens in a lot of cases when people are learning anything. You're not going to get everything in the steps that you should, or get all the training that you need up front." Leslie likened starting her job to "going into the war," adding that "it's the best kind of training there is." Colleen, not at Cellsoft, used similar language in learning the style of another programmer's work:

> Very often you're inheriting something from someone else or you're
> having to interface with someone else's work, and I find that there's a
> style, and sometimes you have to—it's like learning a language.
> You know, total immersion works. You have to get the flavor of
> how they do their thing, and how they code it. And now, having
> worked with several other people's stuff, I almost know just by, you
> know, tell me the name of who wrote this [and I know] how to
> approach it.

When I pressed respondents to elaborate further on what happens when they are immersed in the system, they spoke of iteration, repetition, and practice. For example, Barbara said, "I think learning is an incremental process; I think you sort of build on prior blocks of what you know. And it's an iterative process; you have to keep doing it, until you own it."

Iteration is not quite the same as repetition: each time one goes through something, one gains a bit more knowledge, and that knowledge feeds back into the process. It is a continual feedback loop. Barbara took notes one day, and the next, "my notes were Greek." Arthur, similarly, said of the material in his notes that "I thought every day I'd go home and know it, and then I'd come in the next day and look at it and say that's ridiculous, it doesn't make sense, and I'd ask, and people would say I told you that yesterday. It was like this one block, I had a mental block about it."

People constantly forget and have to go over the same material a second or third time, but each time more sinks in and the review takes less time. Sometimes it is necessary to wait for something to make sense, or the material only gradually takes shape in the mind. For example, Doug spoke of his question-and-answer sessions with Ahmed: "It wasn't necessarily like a one-session-type question. Sometimes he would give me an answer that described the interaction and I might [come back] two hours later to ask for further details about a certain aspect or 'What about this case?' So it was a discussion that took place over a period of a couple days." Bill described this iterative process more elaborately in talking about understanding a particular program:

> It bothers me that I don't know it in any more detail, and every
> couple weeks or so I ask another question to someone else on it and I
> think I understand it well enough, but I'm always like, this seems

too simple, there's gotta be something I'm missing. And that's another way I do it: Sometimes I say, well, I've learned this, I'm not gonna learn any more detail today, I'm not absorbing it and I take a step back and I open up that can of questions in a couple weeks again, when I feel, OK, I'm ready to absorb more.

The other thing is, what you're working on, you will absorb obviously, you're working on the programs, what you've learned from reading, or someone telling you, or understanding it from a meeting, or going to a presentation, or whatever, and then [when] you start working on it, you retain it. It's right there, you're more familiar with it, you're working on it every day. And it's a combination of everything that helps you.

What actually happens during the repetitive practice of a programmer's work? There seems to be a snowball effect. A bit of knowledge the programmer acquires through working on a small part of a large system gradually expands as more bits are added to it. The programmer undergoes a continual but not necessarily conscious process of relating each new piece to those learned so far. He or she weaves this information into a matrix of bits, categorizing each in relation to what has come before. He or she may derive the categories from an intellectual schema that comes from formal training or may simply figure one out for himself or herself based on the data presented by his or her experience. Over time the programmer modifies the conceptual schema as the data increase, adapting the "system" to fit the ever-increasing repertoire of activities and the growing mass of technical, social, and experiential data, perhaps supplementing the data with reading reference material as well. Thus programmers learn, or actually *create*, "systems" by constantly relating new material to what is already known. They then, in their interactions with each other, with clients or management, and with the computer and its software, intersubjectively validate their understanding, and in fact the existence, of those systems.

To some extent, all of the programmers and other computer workers in this study learn in this way. Individual differences are apparent in the following areas:

- *Consciousness of the process*: Programmers differ in their awareness of the methodologies that they pursue and in their active involvement in learning.

- *Extent of iteration:* Some programmers, such as Barbara and Jack, go through very extensive iterative loops while learning, while others, such as Dave, carry out (or at least describe themselves carrying out) learning activities more in a single sequence.

- *Degree to which they seek overview:* For some of these programmers, such as Jack (who reads introductory sections of manuals) or Leslie (who likes to learn from lecture courses), study or analysis at an early stage is an important component of learning, while for others, such as Henry, who starts with small pieces of knowledge and then develops and expands prototypes, an early overview of the whole process is less significant. Programmers of this sort may (as Joyce did) even disparage too much emphasis on overview as a distraction from experience.

- *Amount of background research and incidental learning:* The distinction here is between those programmers who learn enough to do their work and those who spend time investigating problems further or merely following their own interests. In the former category are people like Newton, who solves each problem separately without tracking down more detail than is needed to get the job done, while the latter includes people like Barbara, who devoted six hours to learning a subsystem not immediately useful to her, or Robert, who spends at least two hours a week just playing or experimenting with something new, and who encourages his staff to do the same.

The method outlined here, as tempered by the individual differences just described, produces a discrete mental system in each person who works on the software. "The system," as an *intersubjective* product, comes about as the *team* of persons involved with it at various levels (Kling and Gerson's "computing world," as described in chapter 2), express and resolve *disagreements* about various aspects of it, such as the following:

- How the product works (based on different inputs)

- How the product should work (design issues)

- How fast the product works (performance issues)

- How the product looks (user-interface issues)

- How the pieces of the product fit together (component-interface issues)

- Whether the product does what it is supposed to do (error reporting)

- Whether the product does what the users want it to do (client-support issues)

Of course, in the midst of the disagreement and the intersubjective understanding, there is a real product to be created, modified, tested, and sold; and this product is, in fact, more or less a system. Cellsoft's cellular-management and billing product has a number of characteristics that make it easier to see the system within it.

HOW SYSTEMATIC IS THE SYSTEM?

People can find a system even in chaos. Harold Garfinkel (1967, pp. 79-103) described an experiment in which subjects were told that behind a screen there was a counselor who would provide help with personal problems. The counselor, however, would only answer "yes" or "no." In fact, the "yes" or "no" answers were generated randomly, but subjects often were able to discern meaning inherent in the actually meaningless nonpattern of responses.

Once we recognize that human beings are creators and finders of patterns, we still need to determine the nature of what they are looking into to find them. Garfinkel's subjects found meaning in meaningless responses because they could identify the entire dialogue as a structure in which meaning inheres. Harvey Sacks and others have developed the discipline of conversation analysis as a means to elucidate this structure (see, for example, Sacks, Schegloff, and Jefferson [1978], McLaughlin [1984]); similarly, Roger Schank (1984), working from an artificial-intelligence perspective, has derived the concept of *scripts* as a model for explaining how people know what to do, for example, when ordering in restaurants, and by contrast for demonstrating how much computers do *not* know, and must be taught, about the simplest and most mundane settings.

In the case of a computer "system," however, we are not dealing with a chimera that exists only in the minds of its creators and users and whose existence is validated by mutual consent among the members of a particular social world. Rather, there is a *reality* to a computer system. The system can clearly be seen to do certain things and not to do others; to match written specifications or not to match them; and to exhibit or to fail to exhibit internal consistency. To the extent that it can be seen to obey certain internally derivable or externally imposed rules, the system is indeed a system and deserves to be called one; and learning that system is by far an easier matter, for those who must work with it, than generating one's own order upon apparent chaos. So it is not enough, in seeking to understand how programmers learn a system, to analyze their thought processes and their repertoires of resources, but we must also know how systematic the system itself is.

The cellular-information system (the set of programs most of the Cellsoft programmers work on) has three main components: customer information, billing, and rating. The first of these itself has a number of components:

- *Lead tracking,* the ability to enter marketing leads who are not yet customers

- *The Customer Information System (CIS),* the core of customer tracking, including the abilities to activate, cancel, suspend, and restore service; to inquire on subscribers; and to change a subscriber's cellular telephone number, electronic serial number (that is, to assign the cellular number to a new phone), or account number

- *Accounts Receivable (AR),* which includes cash receipts, adjustments, and collections

- *Phone Number Inventory (PNI),* which alllows the carrier to keep track of which phone numbers have been allocated, and to whom

- *The Equipment Inventory System (EIS),* which keeps track of physical equipment owned or leased by the carrier

These elements, with billing and, to some extent, rating (a piece not fully integrated into the overall product, and the element that requires the most specialized knowledge), are joined, from the point of view of both programmers and developers, into a system because of consistencies maintained in a number of areas.

Consistent Directory and Structures

From the point of view of a programmer or system manager, all of the functions look alike because of a directory hierarchy linking the facilities identified previously (Billing, AR, EIS, and so on). Under a main library directory for each facility (called BILLING_LIB for Billing, AR_LIB for Accounts Receivable, and so on) is a group of subdirectories, identified by logical names consistent throughout the hierarchy. Thus, source programs for billing are in a directory called BILLING_SRC, while executable programs are in BILLING_EXE. Similarly, corresponding programs in AR are in AR_SRC and AR_EXE, respectively, and so on for the other facilities. Likewise, data elements in the Common Data Dictionary (CDD) are similarly grouped; so there are CDD nodes called BILLING_FORMS, BILLING_MENUS, BILLING_RECORDS, AR_FORMS, AR_MENUS, AR_RECORDS, and so on.

Programmers working on the Cellsoft development computer can access all of these logical names by executing a command procedure called ASSIGN.COM and passing it a version number. Thus each version of the system (and there may be two or three versions available at any given time: one for new development, one to maintain current customers, and perhaps one older one as well) has its own library structure as described earlier.

Consistent User Interface

Users of the system, on the other hand, identify it through a series of *menus*, all reachable from a main menu. The main menu contains one entry for each facility (billing, AR, and so on). Within each menu under the main menu is a list of options, each of which points to another menu (for example, each facility has a reports menu under it) or to the actual *task*, that is, the program or procedure that executes the user requests. Users can find nearly everything they want to do simply from reading the titles of menu entries. Once users are in a task, they also have access to on-line help at two levels: *field-level* help (what to do when the cursor is positioned at any field on a screen) and *form-level* help (what are all the commands a user can execute from this screen to get to another screen or to return to a menu). Because all of the forms the user sees are written in Digital Equipment's transaction-processing system TDMS, and all of the tasks are linked through the menus by the related application-management program ACMS, the large number of discrete programs, command procedures, forms, and data elements that make up the system appear to end users as a coherent whole.

Standards

Although Cellsoft has never succeeded in enforcing a formal set of programming, testing, or user-interface standards, informal methods have preserved a certain cohesiveness in the system. Coding standards are enforced to some degree by the (never officially defined) methodology that almost every program in the system starts out as a modification to an existing program. Thus, although certain deviations from the norm are inevitable since the norm is never articulated, identities or similarities of structure are also inevitable, given the template of the original program. For example, each program is likely to include a title, a copyright notice, and comments at the beginning listing the purpose of the program, input and output parameters, if any, and modification history. Also, programming languages used at Cellsoft, primarily COBOL but others as well, enforce a certain structure of their own, so all programs written in a given language look alike to some extent. In this sense programs take on the characteristics of a *genre* (Yates and Orlikowski, 1992).

There are other elements that enforce similarity across programs besides those inherent in the structure of any given programming language. For example, record layouts are stored in libraries and are copied into each program as needed. Therefore, when the contents of a record change from one program version to the next, a programmer needs only to recompile and relink any module that references that record, and the changed fields are automatically included in the new version. This maintains consistency between versions and also eliminates the possibility of spelling errors in any given module (though not in multiple modules, so whoever makes the original change must be very careful). Commands to access the database are standardized across programs and copied from templates. Every program has standard error-handling and failure routines. ACMS tasks also have a common structure. Thus programmers do not have to familiarize themselves with a large number of unique formats; once they have seen one or two examples of a few formats, they are in a position to master much of the system. This is why a programmer's first task, almost whatever it turns out to be, can become a vehicle for learning a great deal about the system (for we can now say, because of these perceived and real consistencies, that it indeed is a system) as a whole.

Business Needs

Another way in which the product can be seen as a system is in its relationship to the end users, Cellsoft's clients. Here again, we can see consistencies in the user base: a limited number of customers, all in one industry, generally not in competition with one another. Because all are engaged in basically the same activities, differences in how they carry on those activities are less important than the similarities between them. Thus the product can be modified in many ways to accommodate users' varied ways of doing business, but their overarching similarities allow the differences to be handled within a generally (if only very broadly) coherent and unified system. Cellsoft handles this by establishing a *personality* for each customer, a data record encapsulating such specific attributes as how the customer's bill will look, whether certain categories of calls will be charged or free to all clients, or even whether the customer is using certain broad subsections of the system, such as the Phone Number Inventory. Also, the menu structure can be tailored to client specifications, so many clients can have what look like unique versions of the same system with minimal change to the user interface and generally with minimal programming effort.

Learning the system, then, is an interaction between system and learner. The learners can apply their repertoire of methods and resources as their individual styles and the requirements of their work dictate, but only in their interaction with a genuine thing called a system can their application make sense and produce a sensible result. On the other hand, the constant changes and enhancements the Cellsoft programmers make to the product continually re-create and redefine the system, stretching its structure to accommodate an ever-wider variety of user requests, so in reality the system and the programmers "learn" from one another and constantly affect one another.

In the preceding chapters I have described the many ways in which members of this group of computer professionals have gone about learning the pieces of a computer system and combining them into a meaningful whole. I have let the programmers speak for themselves as much as possible, allowing them to reveal their own understanding, and I have tried not to let my own theoretical bias or perspective obstruct their world. However, the starting point of my research was in learning-style and cognitive-style theory, and many of the questions raised in chapter 1 concern the relationship between individual learning styles and programmers' learning on the job. In order to attempt to answer these questions, it is necessary to turn now to a number of models of style, as described in the theoretical literature, and to relate these models as best I can to the experience of the programmers and others whom I interviewed for this study.

10

Models of Learning

In chapters 3 through 9 we have examined the ways that programmers at Cellsoft and elsewhere learn their jobs and the software systems for which they are responsible. In describing these individuals and their learning modes, I have relied on their own words as much as possible and have, for the most part, carefully avoided either fitting them into a theoretical framework or creating a new one to accommodate them. Indeed, it has been my operational contention that theory must grow from reality rather than the other way around.

As I stated in chapter 1, while I was conducting my interviews, working, and observing and absorbing life at Cellsoft, I tried to forget my explorations in the literature of learning styles, although this study began as a project in learning-style research. The categories of learning and of experience, the resources described, must be the workers' own, not those of other theorists. But now that I have elaborated their perspective, from orientation to learning a complex system, it is necessary to tackle the relationship of the programmers' learning to the constructs of learning-style theorists.

One would think that bodies of research and developed models of learning dating back two decades or more would shed a great deal of light on the real work of learning, but surprisingly enough this has not been the case. Detailed reading of numerous books and articles on cognitive styles, learning styles, and learning strategies unearths few findings directly relevant to the work of the Cellsoft programmers. At the conclusion of this chapter I shall discuss the reasons for this.

This chapter summarizes the theoretical models I expected to find most germane to the learning styles of adult professionals. After exploring a number of models, definitions, and concepts, I have settled on David Kolb's experiential-learning theory as the most logical starting point for examining learning style in a work environment. On the way, I encountered a number of interesting theories that, though not ultimately germane to my topic, provided stimulus for thought and important additional components that must ultimately be worked into a broader theory.

In addition to Kolb's model, I was primarily interested in two others. The first, the concept of *field independence/field dependence*, developed by Herman Witkin, is primarily a construct from physiological psychology that researchers have shown to apply to many dimensions of personality. It is really an aspect of "cognitive style," a more inclusive term than "learning style." The second is the idea of *depth of processing*, referring to how deeply a student absorbs material. This concept, deriving from the work of Fergus Craik and others, led to Ronald Schmeck's development of the Inventory of Learning Processes (ILP).

I thought that these two models would be useful in understanding my original topic, the learning styles of computer professionals. From field-independence/dependence theory I came to understand how people of a certain type develop psychological characteristics suited to the computing world, and I thought that I could use Schmeck's ILP as a tool to assess the learning styles of both student and professional programmers. However, I decided that both of these models were too limited: field independence/dependence because of its fixity as a psychological trait, and the ILP because it really assesses study skills when what I am after is a broader concept of learning, encompassing work and life as much as formal study. Ultimately, experiential-learning theory gave me the conceptual framework I needed, and Kolb's Learning Style Inventory (LSI) is a starting point for measuring and explaining it. I shall elaborate on all of this in describing the three models.

Of course, these models are only a subset of the vast number of learning-style theories available. L. A. Bonham's recent dissertation (1988) provided a comprehensive review of a great deal more of the literature than I can cover in this chapter, including many theories with no special relevance to on-the-job learning. The very breadth and inclusiveness of Bonham's dissertation inadvertently shows up the vast gulf between nearly all academic models of learning and the daily work that adults in technical fields perform when they are learning their jobs. I shall discuss this further toward the end of this chapter, but for the sake of brevity I shall confine the bulk of my discussion to the three models described here.

FIELD INDEPENDENCE/DEPENDENCE

The earliest major body of research on cognitive style stems from the work of Witkin and others on field independence and field dependence (Witkin and Goodenough, 1977, 1981; Witkin, 1976; Bonham, 1988; Shipman and Shipman, 1985). The earliest studies merely described whether people oriented themselves to a vertical position by relating to their own bodies (field independence) or to their surroundings (field dependence). The original tests, the Rod-and-Frame Test (RFT), the Body-Adjustment Test (BAT), and the Rotating-Room Test (RRT), tilted the subject's visual framework so that he or she could find the upright (correctly) with respect to his or her own body or (incorrectly) with respect to the altered surroundings. Orientation to body cues was labeled field independence, while orientation to external cues was defined as field dependence.

More generally, field independence came to refer to the ability to separate an item from its surrounding field. Thus the results were soon extended to people's ability to abstract pictures embedded in a context, as measured by the Embedded-Figures Test (EFT).   It was discovered that field-dependent people had more difficulty disembedding pictures from their contexts and restructuring them by putting them into different contexts. This was related to the general cognitive trait of structuring: Field-dependent people tend to accept a context as given, while field-independent people are more likely to try to restructure it. Field independence and dependence were further linked to *articulation*, or the experiencing of discrete items; Witkin and Goodenough referred to field-independent people as having an "articulated field approach" as opposed to the "global field approach" of field-dependent people. Ultimately, researchers demonstrated a broader link to personality, relating field independence to a superior differentiation between self and nonself and the ability to differentiate psychological activities from one another, such as thinking versus acting or feeling versus perceiving.

The apparent superiority of field independence is limited to spatial domains. For example, though they are better at disambiguation on visual tests, field-independent people are not distinguished from field-dependent people at distinguishing auditory stimuli. Similarly, verbal embedding contexts such as letters and words are not very highly related to spatial contexts, and sentence disambiguation is correlated with performance on the EFT where the ambiguity is syntactic, but not where it is lexical. In children, researchers have found a relationship between EFT performance and the ability to restructure sentences (for example, changing from active to passive voice).

Subsequent research found a wide variety of traits correlated with field dependence or independence across many cultures. Several studies involved vocational preferences and academic skills of field-independent versus field-dependent people. Studies have found field-independent people more likely than field-dependent people to go into occupations requiring analytical skills, personal autonomy, and comparative isolation from peers (for example, mathematics or engineering), while field-dependent people are more drawn to professions where involvement with and sensitivity to others are important.

One of the most interesting aspects of this research, as modified since the 1970s, is that neither field dependence nor field independence is considered intrinsically better than the other, but that each is adaptive in some ways and maladaptive in others, while some important contributors to academic success such as verbal ability do not correlate with field dependence or independence at all. While field-independent people may be generally more skilled at or drawn to logical thinking, their relative insensitivity to others makes them hard to deal with in social settings. Witkin and Goodenough (1981, p. 44) described the feeling aroused by field-dependent people in others as

> warm, affectionate, tactful, accommodating, nonevaluative and accepting of others, not likely to express hostility directly against others when such feelings are aroused in an interpersonal context. They contrast with those [reactions] reported for people who are field independent and do well on the EFT: demanding, inconsiderate, manipulating others as a means of achieving personal ends, cold and distant in relations with others.

This difficulty field-independent people have with social relations may be one of the bases in reality for the stereotype of the "engineering nerd": It is not that he (and it is usually he; from adolescence on, males are more generally field-independent than females) is too busy studying to learn how to make friends or to go on dates, but rather that the very independence from his environment that encourages his strong analytic skills isolates him from his peers, except as they can relate to him intellectually.

There is a vast literature on field independence/dependence. According to Goodenough (1986; cited in Bonham, 1988, p. 47), there are over three thousand published references. Obviously, it would be an impossible task to review all of them. Bonham (1988) provided the most recent comprehensive review of the field. I shall describe only a few recent works dealing with educational and learning-style implications of the theory.

Barbara Ash (1982) compared two groups of female students at Bunker Hill Community College, near Boston: secretarial versus business majors. She was trying to determine significant personality or cognitive-style differences between the two groups. She selected samples of over eighty students from each of the two groups and administered the Group Embedded-Figures Test (a version of the EFT modified for groups), the Bem Sex-Role Inventory, and the Myers-Briggs Type Indicator to measure field independence/dependence, masculinity/femininity, and Jungian personality type, respectively, and a personal data questionnaire. She developed ten hypotheses concerning relationships between the two groups on various test measures and concerning correlations among various test scores. With a few exceptions, differences were not sufficiently significant to reject the null hypotheses; that is, there were no significant differences between business and secretarial students in the characteristics Ash studied. The largest percentage of students in both programs were field dependent.

Though she did not discuss this in her 1982 dissertation, Ash said to me (1988, telephone conversation) that because of difficulties with scoring the GEFT, she would not use it now. According to Ash, the GEFT has a range of possible scores. A subject scoring in one end of the range is classified as field dependent and someone scoring in the other end is classified as field independent, while people scoring toward the middle are classified as neither. This results in a considerable waste of data, affecting the value and the accuracy of the results.

More recently, D. K. Garlinger (1987) attempted to discover a relationship between field independence/dependence, the learning strategy subjects used on a memory task, and their actual performance on the task. Using the Hidden Figures Test as the determinant of field independence, Garlinger gave 227 college students, both field dependent and independent, memorization tasks using two word lists, one more and the other less organized. For each list, some subjects were given instruction in a categorization strategy and some practice examples, while others were not. For each group, two dependent variables were measured: total recall score, and the number of categories generated.

The study found that field-independent students tended to perform better on these tasks than the field-dependent students regardless of the degree of organization of the word lists, but there was no statistically significant evidence indicating that performance differences were due to differences in information-processing strategies between the two groups. Further, while both groups benefited from pretest instruction, the instruction did not reduce the gap in performance between the two groups. This bears out Witkin and Goodenough's findings (1981) that although people can be trained in the specific skills measured in tests of field independence/dependence, the basic differences in the two cognitive styles are innate and tend to remain constant over time.

Although field independence and field dependence lead to different cognitive styles, implications for educational practice are uncertain. For example, Halpin and Peterson (1986) assigned college students study materials randomly matched or mismatched to the students' cognitive styles as measured by the GEFT. They prepared materials aimed at people who conformed to Witkin's descriptions of field-independent or field-dependent individuals. They found that while cognitive style led to differences in achievement and attitudes, attempting to match or mismatch instruction to field dependence and field independence did not result in significant differences in learning. Perhaps using other criteria for determining cognitive style, such as those described in Messick (1976), would yield other educational implications.

Threadgill (1979) performed a similar study, using two methods of mathematics instruction on seventh-grade students. Her hypothesis was that field-dependent students would respond better to a didactic presentation with rules, examples, and feedback, while field-independent students would learn better from a "guided discovery" presentation allowing them to learn inductively. As demonstrated by other studies, such as Halpin and Peterson's, field-independent students' performance was superior to that of field-dependent students regardless of instructional method chosen. Also, as in Garlinger (1987), there was no statistically significant difference in learning attributable to one instructional method over the other. Thus, once again, it would be hard to derive useful educational implications from field independence as a cognitive-style attribute.

The following example illustrates the positive value of field dependence. Quinlan and Blatt (1972), testing the relation of field dependence to the processing of social cues, studied twenty-six student nurses randomly assigned to rotations in surgical nursing or psychiatric nursing. The hypothesis was that moderately field-dependent nursing students would perform better and experience less anxiety in the psychiatric setting, which the authors defined as "a loosely structured interpersonal task," while the field-independent group would perform better and experience less anxiety in the surgical setting, described as "a highly structured nonpersonal task" (p. 517).

The authors found field dependence, as measured by the Rod-and-Frame Test, to correlate positively and significantly ($r = .55$, $p < .05$) with grades in psychiatry and negatively but not significantly ($r = -.27$) with grades in surgery, and the differences in the grades were significant ($p < .05$). They also reported that the RFT error score (the measure of field dependence) correlated positively with reported anxiety in psychiatry ($r = .63$, $p < .05$) and negatively with reported anxiety in surgery ($r = -.47$, $p < .10$), and the difference between these scores was also significant ($p < .01$). If these data seem paradoxical, the authors also found a positive correlation between anxiety and grades. Quinlan and Blatt concluded from the results that field dependence may be linked to a capacity for empathy that helped students to deal with the high anxiety of dealing with a group of psychiatric patients; this seems somewhat conjectural, however, and follow-up studies are needed.

There are a number of limitations to the idea of field independence/dependence that led me to reject it as a useful model for studying programmers and their learning style. The first of these lies in the fact that field-independence or dependence is truly a *cognitive* style, not a learning style at all. Shipman and Shipman (1985, pp. 229-230) discussed this term as follows:

> Broadly, a cognitive response tendency is conceived of as a relatively stable tendency to respond in a certain cognitive manner to a specified stimulus situation. Stable individual differences in these response tendencies are believed to reflect stable differences in information processing among individuals responding to similar stimuli. These behavioral response tendencies, and the characteristic processing presumed to underlie them, are referred to as cognitive styles to indicate that this stability extends over a variety of tasks with similar task demands and/or stimulus properties. Thus cognitive styles are generally considered to be information-processing habits:

individually characteristic ways of interpreting and responding to the environment.

This definition provides the important distinguishing features of anything that can be called a cognitive style. We may break down these features as follows:

- A cognitive style is stable within an individual over time.

- It represents a difference between individuals.

- It is stable only with respect to specific types of stimuli.

As a result of these aspects, cognitive style, however it is measured, is considered an aspect of personality and difficult to change. Therefore, educational implications of cognitive style focus on adapting to individual differences rather than on training people to change their styles; and even here, evidence is murky concerning whether matching any sort of activity to field-dependent or field-independent persons leads to any useful result.

Bonham (1988, pp. 29-30) offered the following contrasting uses for "cognitive style" and "learning style":

> The term "cognitive style" is used somewhat arbitrarily now. It most often identifies a particular list of theories that were formulated in the 1950s and 1960s, were tied closely to laboratory research (as opposed to classroom-based research, for instance), and had their foundations in psychology rather than in learning theory. If used consistently, the term could be said to include some newer theories that operate in the larger realm of cognition and arise from the field of psychology. That would leave the term "learning styles" to apply to (1) theories focusing on learning as one aspect of cognition, or (2) the application of cognitive style theories to learning contexts.

This pair of definitions views learning style, in effect, as a subset of cognitive style, that is, that aspect of cognitive style that deals specifically with learning. However, if I take Bonham's second definition, using field independence/dependence as the relevant "cognitive style theory," I am left no farther along the path of understanding.

Further, in viewing field independence/dependence as an example of cognitive style, I am confronted with its limited value within the concept of "cognitive style" itself, and this concept has within it a great many attributes that differ in ability to be measured, scope of applicability, and theoretical justification. Shipman and Shipman (1985) pointed out that the numerous measures and constructs that compose the broader concept "cognitive style" did not grow out of a unified theory but rather evolved from a number of areas of research such as ego psychology, research into individual differences, and cognitive psychology. As a result, the various terms used to delineate aspects of cognitive style, such as field independence/dependence, conceptual tempo, reflection-impulsivity, or conceptualizing style (they cited Messick [1976], who drew up a list consisting of nineteen distinct and unrelated cognitive-style constructs), differ from each other in a number of important ways. For example, some (such as field independence/dependence) are now closely linked to broader aspects of personality, while others (such as reflection-impulsivity) really only measure specific results of specific tests and are hard to apply to other situations. Thus even within the term "cognitive style" are many aspects that have yet to be integrated into a systematic theory, if indeed they can be.

A second limitation of field dependence or independence is that it is a fixed personality trait with limited ability to guide anyone involved in training people or in designing products for people to use. The construct views people as unable to change and is therefore based on a view of human nature as severely limited, a view making meaningful growth highly unlikely, at least in what appears to be a significant dimension of personality.

In addition, there is confusion in the literature (Bonham, 1988; Shipman and Shipman, 1985) about the extent to which field independence/dependence refers to an *ability* or to a *style*. That is, is field independence superior to field dependence, or merely different from it? This was a question that Witkin himself answered both ways at different times. It was only in the late 1970s that he came around to the view that field dependence is itself a positive trait, but much of the research is still based on the view that it is an ability (such as orientation to vertical or ability to disembed) that is being measured, and therefore that field dependence should be defined as a deficiency. This confusion makes the construct even more difficult to use in a setting such as a corporate environment, in which all people should be valued positively and appreciated rather than disparaged because of their differences.

Most important--and this is a drawback to almost all cognitive-style research—the theory of field independence/dependence is based entirely in laboratories, not in the reality of people's life and work situations. Even if it can be determined by testing that most programmers are field independent (and this makes sense from the kinds of work that they do), the information tells nothing about their actual learning and is therefore useless in understanding their world. Also, there is no information on what it would mean for a field-dependent person to succeed as a programmer or an engineer: Would it indicate a flaw in the theory or point to compensating mechanisms that need to be discovered? All of these difficulties and limitations, then, led me to reject field independence/dependence as the basic model to explain how programmers and other computer professionals learn complex systems.

DEPTH OF PROCESSING AND THE INVENTORY OF LEARNING PROCESSES

Another interesting avenue in learning-style research led me to R. R. Schmeck's Inventory of Learning Processes (Schmeck, Ribich, and Ramanaiah, 1977; Schmeck, 1983). This questionnaire, an assessment of learning strategies as applied to studying, grew out of research conducted in the 1970s concerning how students process information when they study for exams. In this context Schmeck (1983, p. 93) defined learning style as

a predisposition on the part of some students to adopt a particular learning strategy regardless of the specific demands of the learning task. Thus, a style is simply a strategy that is used with some cross-situational consistency. In turn, I define a learning strategy as a pattern of information-processing activities used to prepare for an anticipated test of memory.

It is learning strategies, then, that the Inventory of Learning Processes (ILP) actually measures.

The work of Schmeck and his colleagues grew out of several studies of learning strategy during the 1970s, among them the work of Fergus Craik (Craik, 1977; Craik and Lockhart, 1972; Craik and Tulving, 1975) and of researchers at the University of Gothenburg, Sweden (Marton and Saljö, 1976a, 1976b; Svensson, 1977; Fransson, 1977). Craik developed the concept of *depth of processing* as an indicator of subjects' ability to retain information during memory tests, both short- and long-term. Craik and Lockhart (1972) postulated a hierarchy of processing strategies, starting with a simple response to sensory stimuli and moving toward pattern recognition, comparing new data with previously stored material, and extracting meaning. They stated (p. 675):

This conception of a series or hierarchy of processing stages is often referred to as "depth of processing" where greater "depth" implies a greater degree of semantic or cognitive analysis. After the stimulus has been recognized, it may undergo further processing by enrichment or elaboration. For example, after a word is recognized, it may trigger associations, images or stores on the basis of the subject's past experience with the word.

Craik and Lockhart labeled these two levels as "Level I" and "Level II," respectively.

In 1977 Craik expanded on the notion of depth of processing. Arguing that it was correct but inadequate as an explanation, he modified the theory to stress the importance of elaboration as well as depth. Finding that some experiments revealed differences in retention without showing different depths of analysis, he said that the problem could be

> resolved if it is postulated that retention is enhanced by greater degrees of trace elaboration. It is not so much the depth of processing that is important for memory, perhaps, as the richness and complexity of cognitive operations carried out on the stimulus. As a further speculation, trace elaboration may depend on the context as much as on the item to be remembered, and on the extent to which the item and the context can be integrated to form a coherent unit. (Craik, 1977, p. 690)

As a result of his researches, Craik finally arrived at the following definitions of depth and elaboration (p. 695):

> *Depth* of processing refers to qualitatively different perceptual/cognitive analyses, possibly organized in an hierarchical fashion . . . ; it is postulated that deeper encodings are associated with higher levels of retention. . . . *Elaboration* of encoding refers to further, richer processing within one qualitative domain.

Schmeck later used these concepts of deep and elaborative processing to develop two of the scales of his Inventory of Learning Processes.

The Swedish studies used interviews to determine what students do in reading an article when they will have to answer questions about it. Thus they dealt with learning strategies, as defined by Schmeck at the beginning of this section. The first two, though not citing Craik, worked with similar concepts of deep and elaborative processing. In the first study (Marton and Saljö, 1976a), analysis of interview data revealed that students approached material at one of two levels of processing, labeled *deep-level* and *surface-level* and described as follows (p. 7):

> In the case of *surface-level* processing, the student directs his attention toward learning the text itself (*the sign*), i.e., he has a "reproductive" conception of learning which means that he is more or less forced to keep to a rote-learning strategy. In the case of *deep-level* processing, on the other hand, the student is directed towards the intentional content of the learning material (*what is signified*).

Thus, though they are not derived from Craik and Lockhart (1972), the concepts of deep-level and surface-level processing correspond closely to their levels I and II.

The second study (Marton and Saljö, 1976b) demonstrated the flexibility of learning strategies in response to situations. In this study, students were again asked to respond to questions about an article, but the students were divided into two groups. One group was told that the questions would be about factual content, while the other was told that the questions would deal with understanding the meaning of the whole passage; then both groups were given a mixture of questions of both types. The two sets of demands were associated with surface and deep processing, respectively. The results indicated that students did in fact read the passage differently in response to different expectations, demonstrating that "learning seems to be defined differently depending on, for instance, anticipated task demands" (p. 124).

The third Gothenburg study (Svensson, 1977) evaluated learning strategies according to another dimension. Descriptive data from this study distinguished between *holistic* and *atomistic* learning strategies. A group of thirty students was given a passage and had to answer questions on it, as in the other studies. In addition, the students were interviewed and asked to describe how they studied the material; this was an attempt to relate study skill to understanding. Atomistic learners (corresponding to surface processors) focus on parts and details, whereas holistic learners (corresponding to deep processors) focus on the overall meaning of a passage and relate it to wider contexts (Craik's elaborative processing). Holistic learners were found to be decidedly superior to atomistic learners in understanding the meaning of a passage. In terms of study techniques, atomists stress memorization and overlearning, while holists relate new material to their own knowledge or experience, "stressing the importance of reorganizing new information in terms of existing knowledge structures" (Svensson, 1977, p. 240).

The final study (Fransson, 1977) dealt with motivation and anxiety and their relation to test performance. In this study, it was found that lack of interest in the subject matter, efforts to adapt to test demands, and increased anxiety all had detrimental effects on retention and test scores.

Drawing on these and other studies, Schmeck, Ribich, and Ramanaiah (1977) developed a self-report inventory, called the Inventory of Learning Processes (ILP), to assess the strategies students employ when they study. Thus the ILP deals essentially with learning strategies in terms of information processing rather than cognitive style and personality and is concerned with verbal and prose learning. The authors started from a three-part model of information processing, viewing this activity as consisting of encoding, storage, and retrieval (following Melton and Martin, 1972). Their concern was with what happens to the information between presentation and recall. Especially important are the ways in which and the degrees to which students elaborate on what they learn: their use of imagery (after Paivio, 1971) and their depth of processing (building on the model developed by Craik and his associates), on a scale from shallow to deep processing.

The authors reported five studies used in developing the ILP. In the first, they gave 503 undergraduates at Southern Illinois University a set of 121 true-false questions identifying specific behaviors students may or may not use when they are learning. After subjecting the students' responses to factor analysis, the authors found four prevailing factors. Factor I, which they called "Synthesis-Analysis" (subsequently changed to "Deep Processing"—see Schmeck, 1983), entails comparison of different concepts and attempts to derive general principles from the material studied. Factor II, "Study Methods" (later called "Methodical Study"), measures students' reliance on study techniques, such as outlining, amount of reading, and use of the library. Factor III, "Fact Retention," concerns students' abilities to deal with facts and remember details, and Factor IV, "Elaborative Processing," involves students' abilities to make connections with other bodies of information, to discover practical applications for what they learn, and to elaborate beyond the surface of the material.

In the second study, the authors reworded a number of statements to reduce the imbalance of true and false answers in the factor loadings. Then they compared the stability of responses by giving both versions to one group of students and giving another group the new version twice. They found no significant differences in scores between the original ILP and the one with reversed questions.

The third study investigated sex differences and measured the inventory for internal consistency, test-retest reliability, and scale intercorrelations. Multivariate analysis of variance revealed no significant sex differences in the test as a whole, and univariate F-tests showed no significant sex differences on individual scales; therefore, scores for males and females were combined in subsequent studies. Intercorrelations showed the scores on the four scales to be relatively independent, and test-retest reliabilities were considered acceptable (Schmeck, Ribich, and Ramanaiah, 1977, p. 421).

The last two studies provided experimental validation of ILP results. The fourth study explored the relationship between the ILP and performance in class. In this experiment students viewed a televised lecture and then were given an exam for which they had no warning. The exam combined questions eliciting high- and low-level cognitive skills, based on Bloom's (1956) taxonomy. As there was no preparation for the exam, this experiment was not designed to reflect study methods, but rather hypothesized a positive correlation between Synthesis-Analysis and Elaborative Processing scores, on the one hand, and test performance on the high-level cognitive questions, on the other. As expected, there was no correlation with Study Methods, but it was the total test score that related to the deep-processing scales, with no significant differences in correlation coefficient based on the types of questions. Of course, even here, the researchers attempted to relate ILP scores to classroom performance, not to on-the-job or other real-world learning situations where a variety of materials and motivations would exist. As with other strategies for studying learning, what their method gains in control it loses in its distance from reality.

The fifth study required students to learn a word list and then tested them on retention. Unlike the fourth study, which measured incidental learning (that is, students did not know that they would be tested on the material), this one measured learning in both incidental and intentional conditions; in the latter, students were told to study and to remember items on the list. For the intentional-learning group, the authors expected a correlation between learning and the ILP scores for fact retention and study methods but no relationship with elaborative processing. The test consisted of equal numbers of concrete and abstract nouns, on the theory that the latter are supposed to be harder to remember (Paivio and Csapo, 1973). The test included both recall and retrieval questions. Also, in order to relate the ILP to measures of cognitive style and personality, the researchers gave the students three other tests: the Pittsburgh Social Extraversion-Introversion Scale, on the theory that extraverted subjects learn better; the Hidden-Figures Test, on the theory that since field-independent subjects rely more on internal organizing schemas, there may be a correlation between field independence/dependence and the ILP Synthesis-Analysis and Elaborative Processing scales; and the Category Width Scale, to determine a correlation between the use of narrow categories and the ILP Fact Retention scale.

The experiment found higher scores on both abstract and concrete words in the incidental-learning group than in the intentional group, indicating the superiority of more elaborative methods of information processing over simple rote learning and memorization. In both groups the success rate was higher for concrete than for abstract words, supporting Paivio's theory that people more easily remember what they can visualize. As expected, the ILP Study Methods scale correlated only with intentional learning, while Synthesis-Analysis and Elaborative Processing correlated with incidental learning. When "false alarms" (words mistakenly identified as having been present on a list) and corrections were taken into account, neither group had a significantly higher "false-alarm" rate than the other, but there was a significant ($r = .44$) correlation between Synthesis-Analysis and the corrected recognition score. There was also a significant negative correlation ($r = -.35$) between Synthesis-Analysis and false alarms; people with high Synthesis-Analysis scores were better at recognizing incorrect words but not necessarily at spotting correct ones. Fact Retention correlations were higher for intentional than for incidental learning, showing that the scale in fact indicates a general memory for details. Of the other tests used, only the Hidden Figures Test correlated with the number of concrete hits; the authors could not explain the correlation and thought that the result might be spurious. From the general lack of correlations with the other tests, the authors inferred the independence of the ILP.

In general, Schmeck, Ribich, and Ramanaiah found the Synthesis-Analysis scale related to the three highest categories of Bloom's (1956) taxonomy of cognitive activities: synthesis, analysis, and evaluation. The Study Methods scale, measuring techniques used by the typical "good student," only applies when a student is explicitly instructed to "learn" the material, while Fact Retention indicates a generalized good memory used even when one is not deliberately "studying." Elaborative Processing measures the degree to which a student encodes information. A combination of high Synthesis-Analysis and Elaborative Processing scores suggests that a student plays an active role in learning, using deep information-processing strategies. As contrasted with Elaborative Processing, Synthesis-Analysis correlates with note-taking style, performance on objective tests, and free recall of idea units.

In their concluding section the authors stated that students may not always know which study habits are conducive to learning and that most techniques are probably effective for some students under some conditions. In this study, how students processed the information and which study skills they used were partly a function of what they were told to do. This points to the importance of teachers' knowing what makes for successful learning and also ties in to the view that people's learning styles are malleable by direct teaching.

In a further validation study of the ILP, Schmeck and Ribich (1978) correlated ILP scores with the Watson-Glaser Critical Thinking Appraisal. They found significant correlations between the Synthesis-Analysis score and the Watson-Glaser scores for deduction ($r = .34$) and interpretation ($r = .39$) and for the total score ($r = .33$, $p < .01$), demonstrating the connection between learning and deep and elaborative processing. On the other hand, Study Methods correlated negatively with deduction ($r = -.25$, $p < .05$), interpretation ($r = -.27$, $p < .01$), and the total score ($r = -.34$, $r < .01$), thus demonstrating that conventional study methods (representing surface processing modes in the Swedish studies, or Level I in Craik and Lockhart's schema) are detrimental rather than conducive to true learning.

Ribich and Schmeck (1979) related the ILP to two other learning-style instruments: the Study Behavior Questionnaire and Kolb's Learning Style Inventory. There was little relationship among them, and what correlation was found was in a factor related to depth of processing. Schmeck (1980) related the scale scores to reading comprehension as measured by the Vocabulary, Comprehension, and Reading Rate scores of the Nelson-Denny Reading Test and found the Synthesis-Analysis scale significantly correlated with Vocabulary ($r = .27$, $p < .001$) and Comprehension ($r = .37$, $p < .001$) and not significantly related to Reading Rate ($r = .07$).

Gadzella, Ginther, and Williamson (1986), investigating intercorrelations among the four ILP scales, found a significant correlation between Deep Processing and Elaborative Processing, indicating overlap but not identity between the two scales. They also found significant differences between academic high and low achievers (defined as students with grade-point averages above and below median, respectively) on the Deep Processing and Fact Retention scales, though not on the other two, indicating at least some predictive validity for the ILP. Once all of these studies demonstrated the reliability and validity of the ILP, Bartling (1987) developed a shortened form of the instrument and validated that as well. Other research projects involving the ILP have found that students who perceive themselves to be competent learners take more time on a problem-solving task and make fewer mistakes

(Armstrong and McDaniel, 1986), that attempts to teach elaborative and deep processing skills have mixed results (Reid, 1981), and that the ILP is valid cross-culturally, as demonstrated in a study of Australian and Filipino children (Watkins and Hattie, 1981a, 1981b).

Though the ILP is clearly useful in assessing study skills and depth of processing, it is not useful beyond conventional learning situations. In assessing adult learning, there seems to be little connection between the types of activities measured by the ILP and the tasks adult professionals are called upon to do in most jobs, although one could posit a correspondence between degree of elaboration and synthesis, as defined by Schmeck and his colleagues, and the Cellsoft and other programmers' relative degree of understanding: Because few programmers learn their systems formally, they must draw on synthetic and analytic skills to "create" the systems in their own minds (see chapter 5). That said, however, the ILP is not very useful in understanding learning among professionals, such as programmers or engineers, whose work is tied to practical action more than to mastery of a body of theory. Therefore, for all its theoretical interest, the work of Schmeck and his colleagues does not appear to provide useful direction for this study.

THE EXPERIENTIAL-LEARNING MODEL

By far the most fruitful model I found for evaluating adult learning styles as applied in much broader settings than Schmeck's "anticipated task of memory" is the experiential-learning model of David Kolb (1974, 1981, 1984; Kolb and Wolfe, 1981). Kolb's view is essentially that all of life is a learning opportunity, that the workplace should be seen as a learning environment, that "learning is the major process of human adaptation" (Kolb, 1984, p. 32), and that learning itself is best defined as "the process whereby knowledge is created through the transformation of experience" (p. 38).

Kolb derived his theory from three main sources: John Dewey's idea of education as a process linking work, formal education, and personal development; Kurt Lewin's work in social psychology and group dynamics, as developed in laboratory methods and T-groups through the 1960s; and Jean Piaget's theories of cognitive development in children. From each of these sources Kolb drew the notion of a cyclical learning process in which basic life experience is tempered by observation and reflection, leading to hypotheses about how the world works, and these hypotheses are tested in experimentation and lead in turn to new experiences. Kolb saw these stages in many aspects of the world, including the scientific method, Piaget's theories of child development, and problem solving techniques in general. Kolb referred to the four stages in this feedback loop as concrete experience (CE), reflective observation (RO), abstract conceptualization (AC), and active experimentation (AE) (see Figure 1).

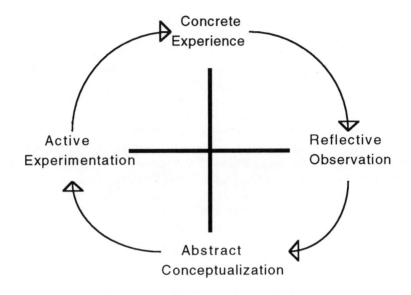

Figure 1. Kolb's Experiential-Learning Model

Where Kolb differed from Piaget was in his valuation of these stages. To Piaget, children grow in the direction of increased abstraction, but for Kolb, each of these realms is important and must be valued. An adult must integrate all four stages to accomplish the fullest learning and interaction with the world. This is difficult, however, because these four aspects of the learning cycle draw on two pairs of opposing dimensions (abstract-concrete and active-reflective). In fact, individuals tend to favor one of each pair more than the other. One of the most important aspects of Kolb's model is that it views each learning orientation as a strength:

> An orientation toward *concrete experience* focuses on being involved in experiences and dealing with immediate human situations in a personal way. It emphasizes feeling as opposed to thinking; a concern with the uniqueness and complexity of present reality as opposed to theories and generalization; an intuitive, "artistic" approach as opposed to the systematic, scientific approach to problems. People with concrete-experience orientation enjoy and are good at relating to others. They are often good intuitive decision makers and function well in unstructured situations. . . .

An orientation toward *reflective observation* focuses on understanding the meaning of ideas and situations by carefully observing and impartially describing them. It emphasizes understanding as opposed to practical application. . . . People with a reflective orientation enjoy intuiting the meaning of situations and ideas and are good at seeing their implications. They are good at looking at things from different perspectives and at appreciating different points of view. . . .

An orientation toward *abstract conceptualization* focuses on using logic, ideas, and concepts. It emphasizes thinking as opposed to feeling. . . . A person with an abstract-conceptual orientation enjoys and is good at systematic planning, manipulation of abstract symbols, and quantitative analysis. . . .

An orientation toward *active experimentation* focuses on actively influencing people and changing situations. . . . People with an active-experimentation orientation enjoy and are good at getting things accomplished. They are willing to take some risk in order to achieve their objectives. (Kolb, 1984, pp. 68-69)

Individuals' learning styles are based on their dominant mode of what Kolb calls "prehending" reality and on their primary method of transforming that reality. Thus people may grasp the world primarily by raw *apprehension* (concrete experience) or by *comprehension* of experience in a theoretical framework (abstract conceptualization); and the experience, once grasped, may be transformed primarily by *intention* (turning inward, or reflective observation) or by *extension* (developing outward, or active experimentation). Thus there are four combinations of prehension and transformation, and these combinations are Kolb's four learning styles, defined as follows:

The *convergent* learning style relies primarily on the dominant learning abilities of abstract conceptualization and active experimentation. The greatest strength of this approach lies in problem solving, decision making, and the practical application of ideas. We have called this learning style the *converger* because a person with this style seems to do best in situations like conventional intelligence tests, where there is a single correct answer or solution to a question or problem. . . . Convergent people are controlled in their expression of emotion. They prefer dealing with technical tasks and problems rather than social and interpersonal issues.

The *divergent* learning style has the opposite learning strengths from convergence, emphasizing concrete experience and reflective observation. The greatest strength of this orientation lies in imaginative ability and awareness of meaning and values. The primary adaptive ability of divergence is to view concrete situations from many perspectives and to organize many relationships into a meaningful "gestalt." . . . This style is called *diverger* because a person of this type performs better in situations that call for generation of alternative ideas and implications. . . . Those oriented toward divergence are interested in people and tend to be imaginative and feeling-oriented.

In *assimilation*, the dominant learning abilities are abstract conceptualization and reflective observation. The greatest strength of this orientation lies in inductive reasoning and the ability to create theoretical models, in assimilating disparate observations into an integrated explanation. . . . As in convergence, this orientation is less focused on people and more concerned with ideas and abstract concepts. Ideas, however, are judged less in this orientation by their practical value. Here, it is more important that the theory be logically sound and precise.

The *accommodative* learning style has the opposite strengths from assimilation, emphasizing concrete experience and active experimentation. The greatest strength of this orientation lies in doing things, in carrying out plans and tasks and getting involved in new experiences. . . . This style is called *accommodation* because it is best suited for those situations where one must adapt oneself to changing immediate circumstances. . . . People with an accommodative orientation tend to solve problems in an intuitive trial-and-error manner, relying heavily on other people for information rather than on their own analytic ability. . . . Those with accommodative learning styles are at ease with people but are sometimes seen as impatient and "pushy." (Kolb, 1984, pp. 77-78)

The Learning Style Inventory (LSI) was developed to evaluate people's awareness of their learning styles within the experiential-learning model. The latest version of the LSI (Kolb, 1985) is a twelve question multiple-choice instrument. Each question comprises an incomplete statement about how a person learns, followed by four choices. One takes the LSI by numbering each choice (from 4 down to 1) in descending order of relation to one's own learning style. The first column of choices forms the concrete experience (CE) score, the second reflective observation (RO), the third abstract conceptualization (AC), and the fourth active experimentation (AE); thus the test is automatically skewed if subjects understand it before taking it. (A sample question is "I learn by: _____ feeling. _____ watching. _____ thinking. _____ doing." [Kolb, 1985, p. 3]) The subject (the test is meant to be self-scoring) computes CE, RO, AC, and AE scores by totaling the numbers in the columns and then computes composite scores for the abstract-concrete dimension (AC minus CE) and the active-reflective dimension (AE minus RO). The four single-trait scores are marked on a grid to form a rectangle, indicating a learning-style profile, and the two composite scores are used to compute a point on a coordinate system. This point, based on the intersection of (AC-CE) and (AE-RO) on an axis pair, will fall into one of the four learning-style quadrants previously described (Converger, Diverger, Assimilator, or Accommodator), giving the testtaker a sense of himself or herself as belonging to one of these categories.

Kolb and others have been using one or another form of the LSI since the early 1970s. It is a deceptively simple survey, easy to administer and score, and quite simplistic in appearance. However, it has been found useful in a wide variety of settings. It has been widely used as a tool in vocational counseling, because a very strong association has been found between learning style as measured on the LSI and college major and vocational preference. For example, an extensive study of engineers and social workers at Case Western Reserve University (Kolb and Wolfe, 1981) showed them to be very largely convergers and accommodators, respectively; and this was true both of students in the professional schools and of professionals up to twenty-five years after graduation. A study of MIT seniors (Kolb and Goldman, 1973) found engineering and management students in the accommodator quadrant, humanities majors in the diverger quadrant, and assimilators largely among mathematicians and theoretical physicists. Kolb commented on this study that

> humanities, architecture, and management are the most concrete departments in the university, and our observations would indicate that these are all quite scholarly in comparison with more concrete programs in other, less "academic" schools such as fine arts, drafting, or business administration. . . . With the exception of electrical engineering, the engineering departments are the most active in the university. With the exception of chemistry, the basic sciences and mathematics are more reflective. (Kolb, 1984, p. 167)

Despite the reliance of Kolb and his colleagues on the LSI as an evaluative tool (Kolb and Wolfe, 1981; Gypen, 1980; Sims, 1981; Griggs, 1980), there have been questions as to its reliability and validity. Merritt and Marshall (1984; Marshall and Merritt, 1985) considered the test generally reliable and supported the construct validity of two forms (ipsative and normative) of the LSI. They subsequently (Marshall and Merritt, 1986) suggested a variant of their own, which they called the Learning Style Questionnaire.

On the other hand, in a study assessing the usefulness of the LSI in designing educational programs, Fox (1984) accepted the reliability of the LSI but questioned its validity as applied to educational decision making and for problem solving. Asserting that no one has ever studied the relevance of the LSI to actual educational programs and activities, Fox and colleagues designed a continuing-education seminar for health professionals, basing the format of the seminar on principles derived from Kolb's writings. Material was presented to participants in a mixture of didactic lectures and small-group workshops and discussions. The assumption was that "if gathered using a valid and reliable technique, information on learning styles and instructional preferences allows continuing education planners to develop programs according to the characteristics of learners rather than the characteristics of subject matter only" (Fox, 1984, p. 73).

Fox used two instruments to assess participants' learning preferences: The LSI itself was administered before the conference, and afterwards participants filled out a questionnaire in which they responded to evaluative statements derived from Kolb's descriptions of characteristics of specific learning styles. For example, Kolb's comment (1984, p. 78) that divergers perform "better in situations that call for generation of alternative ideas and implications such as a 'brainstorming' idea session" became the evaluative statement "The conference allowed me the opportunity to brainstorm" (Fox, 1984, p. 79).

The evaluation tested two hypotheses: that responses to evaluative statements derived from Kolb's descriptors would vary according to learning styles determined by the LSI, and that there would be a relationship between learning style and lecture or small-group format. Neither of the hypotheses was confirmed. Analysis of variance revealed that at alpha = .05, learning style as determined by the LSI was not related to the evaluative statements. The only statistically significant difference among learning styles was between accommodators on one hand and convergers and divergers on the other. This is inconsistent with Kolb's theory, which would have accommodators differing primarily from assimilators, their opposite type.

Thus Fox questioned the construct validity of the LSI even when it was compared with statements closely patterned after the precise attributes the learning styles are supposed to represent. He concluded (p. 84) that "without further validation of the relationship between the LSI and either learning preferences or learning performance, one must question the usefulness of the LSI as a guide to educational design decisions."

In yet another use of Kolb's theory, Stice (1987) suggested that one could improve mathematics training for engineers by incorporating more concrete examples into calculus courses. Drawing on the experiential-learning model, Stice argued that because engineers are primarily convergers while mathematicians are mainly assimilators, mathematics courses are too abstract in their orientations, and therefore engineering students do not see the connections between the material being taught and their own needs. Stice demonstrated this by showing an illustration of how a math textbook explains first-order differential equations (without any example), and then by showing how a concrete example (involving the volume of water in a tank) would increase engineers' understanding of the purpose of the equations and therefore give them more motivation to learn them than would an abstract presentation of mathematical theory. The latter, however, would be easier for an assimilative student of pure mathematics. Thus Stice argued for a mixture of approaches to accommodate people with a mixture of learning styles.

Dorsey and Pierson (1984) administered the LSI to 513 adult students enrolled in a nontraditional program in occupational education at Southwest Texas State University. They found the dominant learning style to be abstract conceptualization for males and active experimentation for females; they also attempted to sort data by ethnic and occupational background, but sample size made this difficult.

Dorsey and Pierson's most interesting finding concerns the relationship between mean LSI scores and age. They traced changes on the abstract-concrete (AC-CE) and active-reflective (AE-RO) continua, reporting the following results (p. 9):

> The abstract/concrete dimension indicates that from age 18-33 the tendency toward abstractness increased; from age 34-49 the tendency toward concreteness increased, and then from age 60-65 abstractness increased again. The active/reflective dimension indicated that from age 18-49 respondents preferred an active role and then moved to a more reflective role in later life.

The authors also attempted to generalize about age and learning-style type. They said that the accommodator learning style becomes prevalent at about the age of thirty-three: "The adult, especially after age thirty-three, learns better by doing" (Dorsey and Pierson, 1984, p. 10). Also, adults move from simply assimilating information to relating it more to things already learned and to previous work and life experience, and to associating material learned with personal needs for self-actualization and career development. Dorsey and Pierson recommended that anyone teaching adult learners in nontraditional programs use an experientially based, active method of instruction.

Ash (1986) surveyed some of the literature on cognitive and learning styles to assess its implications for educational practice. She concentrated on three models: Joseph Hill's Cognitive Style Mapping, Kolb's experiential-learning approach, and Witkin's work on field independence/dependence. After describing each model briefly, she discussed the importance of matching teaching style with learning style and the relationship of learning or cognitive style (she tended to use the terms interchangeably) with career choice. For Kolb's model, she attempted, though she cited no research, to match his four learning types with instructional methodologies, recommending laboratory-style learning for convergers because of their emphasis on experimentation, group problem-solving techniques for divergers because of their proclivity to view problems from multiple perspectives, and inductive approaches for assimilators because of their tendency to construct theoretical models. For accommodators she was even less specific, advocating only that they not be given a passive role in their own education, because of their active-concrete orientation. Even as she said all this, however, she recognized that everyone should have to develop all the learning styles as much as possible since the real world requires people to work in a variety of ways.

All of these studies, and many others as well, indicate that although the LSI itself may not be perfect as a tool, experiential learning theory has a great deal to offer in a study of adult learning. Kolb's concern was with learning as a broad, absorbing area of life, not with cognitive style as a fixed dimension of personality (as in field independence/dependence) or with learning strategy as a way to study for memory tests (as in depth of processing). Rather, learning is an important part of adult development and life, encompassing creativity, problem solving, and decision making, and therefore experiential-learning theory is the most applicable model to my further research into learning as an aspect of the work environment. In the concluding section of this chapter I shall demonstrate its applicability to programmers in this study.

MODELS AND REALITY: INADEQUACIES OF THE RESEARCH

In the concluding section of her dissertation, Bonham provided thirty-two recommendations concerning cognitive and learning styles. She divided these into three categories: recommendations affecting literature, recommendations affecting practice, and recommendations affecting research and theory. As Bonham's dissertation provides one of the most comprehensive overviews of this literature, her recommendations are worth noting as much for the world they portray as for their intrinsic value to the field; in fact, in themselves they help to illustrate what "the field" of learning-style research is and why, despite my interest in it, the literature has seemed as remote as it has from the world of programmers and their techniques for learning complex systems.

For example, under "Recommendations Affecting Literature," Bonham (1988, p. 621) advocated that

3. Writers use phrases such as "a learning style" or "learning styles" as opposed to conveying the idea that the one theory they write about is the total of learning style theory. When cited authors do not represent compatible theories, writers should make that fact clear and not cite them as contributing to a unified viewpoint.

As examples of her "Recommendations Affecting Practice," Bonham recommended that

> 10.   Institutions refrain from adopting as policy a single implementation approach or adopting exclusively one instrument or battery for measuring styles. Institutions may need to be involved, however, in coordinating use of instruments if a number of teachers plan to use them. . . .

> 12.   Instrument developers offer a range of implementation approaches, not just suggestions for matching style with an instructional method or other learning component. At the same time, developers should refrain from offering approaches not substantiated by research. (p. 623)

Under "Recommendations Affecting Research and Theory," Bonham provides, among others, the suggestions that

> 17.   Instruments for theory building be of different kinds than those for consumer use. . . .

> 18.   Production be delayed on consumer-oriented instruments until theory has been formulated to a reasonable degree. (p. 624)

In addition, but as a minor part of these recommendations, Bonham advocated that

> 21.   New and revised theory focus on the whole range of adult years and on life-span issues.

> 22.   New and revised theory not be limited to classroom learning but consider the wide range of contexts in which adults learn. (p. 625, my emphasis)

My point in quoting at length from Bonham's recommendations is not to find fault with any or all of them. Rather, I am using them to illustrate two weaknesses of learning theorists in general. The first is that, for those whom Bonham surveys, learning is something that occurs primarily, if not exclusively, in school. School constitutes the "reality" of learning. Thus Bonham referred to learning-style tests and experiments carried out in schools as more "realistic" than those, such as Witkin's Rod-and-Frame Test, carried out in laboratories. Of course, she was right, but this seems to be the limit of "reality" in these studies.

The second weakness of these sorts of studies is simply a limitation of any sort of quantitative research, namely that the constituents of learning are those that can be, and have been, measured. For example, to derive the questions used in the Inventory of Learning Processes, Schmeck, Ribich, and Ramanaiah

> consulted advanced information-processing and verbal- and prose-learning texts in order to list the major processes which have been uncovered by research or advocated by various theoretical points of view. Each of the authors then attempted to write items to assess these processes by phrasing behavioral descriptions in terms of the environment and activities of the typical college student. In addition, the authors prepared a variety of items which were related to academic activities but which had no obvious preconceived relationship to any established learning processes. These items were included in the hope that some of them would cluster with the information-processing items or form separate clusters revealing unanticipated learning processes. These latter items were concerned with behaviours which students engage in while attending lectures and films, taking notes, writing papers, making plans, interacting with other students, and generally preparing for academic examinations. (1977, p. 414)

Examples of "Study Methods" items include "I cram for exams" and "I increase my vocabulary by building lists of new terms"; "Fact Retention" includes such items as "I do well on tests requiring definitions" and "For exams, I memorize the material as given in the text or class notes"; "Elaborative Processing" comprises statements like "I learn new words or ideas by visualizing a situation in which they occur" or "When learning a unit of material I usually summarize it in my own words"; and "Synthesis-Analysis," later changed to "Deep Processing," is scaled from responses to statements like "I have difficulty learning how to study for a course" or "I can usually state the underlying message of films and readings" (Schmeck, Ribich, and Ramanaiah, 1977, pp. 416-417).

All of these and many other statements were constructed by the authors from the research literature rather than derived directly from interviews with students; thus subjects are asked to evaluate themselves according to criteria not their own. Once developed, the statements were subjected to factor analysis to ascertain the categories, and the results of giving the tests to 434 subjects are amenable to a variety of statistical tests. All that is missing here is to capture what it is that students actually do (though the statements in the ILP do in fact describe a variety of activities and media, more so than the Swedish studies, which are geared to learning one specific, limited task), and of course to acknowledge that "studying" is not all there is to learning.

THE VALUE OF THE EXPERIENTIAL-LEARNING MODEL

Of the various models analyzed here, David Kolb's experiential-learning model is the most closely tied to a professional world, not merely to an academic one. Kolb and others have used the LSI on professionals in a wide variety of settings, and he and his associates have correlated LSI scores with different professions and fields of study. Kolb has also applied his experiential-learning model to a longitudinal study comparing learning styles of engineers and social workers, tracking changes in learning modes over twenty-five years' work experience (Kolb and Wolfe, 1981). In this study the authors found that engineers in particular, predominantly convergers in Kolb's typology and not generally people-oriented, needed to develop nondominant (chiefly divergent) learning modes as they progressed in their careers and moved into management, and that little in their training or personal style prepared them for dealing with people.

Although the way the LSI categorizes learning modes is simplistic (basically feeling-doing-watching-thinking), the loop—or at least *a* loop—does in fact describe the learning of many of the programmers in this study. As I described in chapter 9, system learning, for these programmers, is iterative learning. Several programmers have described their work as a repetitive process of one kind or another. Barbara oscillates among reading, asking questions, taking notes, and looking for feedback. Henry learns a bit about how something works, builds a prototype, modifies and expands his knowledge based on how the prototype works, and then gradually adds more pieces to the prototype. Guy constantly builds on and expands what he knows. Bill asks questions, uses the answers, in conjunction with testing on the computer, to attempt a problem solution, and then uses his mistakes to derive a theory of what is going on inside the program.

These loops are not quite Kolb's, but they are structurally similar. The programmers' learning tasks can be matched up with Kolb's four poles roughly as follows:

- *Reflective observation:* Watching programs run; consulting manuals; reading code; asking questions; soliciting feedback

- *Abstract conceptualization:* Taking and reviewing notes; developing mental models of problems and systems

- *Active experimentation:* Building prototypes; running programs with different combinations of test data

- *Concrete experience:* Dealing with day-to-day problems on the job; relating new problems to those encountered previously; integrating conceptual and experimental knowledge into the product

Kolb's theory goes further into describing individual differences in learning styles on the basis of which pair of poles (AE + AC = Converger, and so on) is dominant. While we can characterize the programmers in this study according to his schema, listing the number of convergers, assimilators, and so on (and it would be useful to do this both on the basis of interviews and by administering Kolb's LSI, and then comparing the results), it seems more valuable to point out that all of the programmers who successfully come to grasp the systems on which they work use a variety of these methods, use them iteratively, and use them, unless prompted by a researcher, with little conscious awareness of how they go about their work. In short, for these programmers, the learning of systems is not systematic. This may help to explain why, for many of them, formal education and training have not been helpful in their work lives: The work of learning systems only occurs in real experience, and there is little time in the classroom (even when lectures are coupled with exercises—that is, when all learning modes are drawn upon) for the iterative work involved in the learning of complex systems.

11

Conclusions and Recommendations

In chapter 1 I listed a number of questions, assumptions, and expectations governing this study. In this chapter I revisit them and attempt to answer the questions and to see if the assumptions and expectations were borne out. As there was no experimental research plan, this section does not provide a formal evaluation of hypotheses; my point was never to confirm or to disconfirm, merely to understand what computer professionals at Cellsoft and similar places do when they learn systems. Understanding of this sort is never complete and is not really amenable to a final theoretical construct, but the purpose of this chapter is to evaluate the knowledge gained from my interviews, analysis, and work experience at Cellsoft.

As part of this review, I have included a critique of conventional learning-style research. I have indicated that it addresses on-the-job learning poorly or not at all. Instead, I suggest that researchers in this field adopt a method similar to what I have done here, building an ethnomethodological, experience-based framework and drawing on detailed observation and interviews rather than on predetermined theories of learning, in order to elucidate the learners' understanding rather than superimpose their own upon the learners.

I also shall provide, as is the custom in works of this type, a set of recommendations for two distinct audiences. The first set regards the use that researchers in organizations or in learning theory can make of studies of this kind. The second set points out the implications of this type of research for anyone interested in improving the climate for learning in the workplace.

THE ORIGINAL RESEARCH QUESTIONS REVISITED

Having described the world of the Cellsoft programmers, their understanding (and mine) of their learning processes, and the relationship of these processes to several cognitive-style and learning-style theories, I can pose answers to the questions I raised in chapter 1.

1. What are the techniques programmers use in learning systems? Are those techniques employed systematically or randomly? How wide a range of activities do individuals engage in when they are learning systems on the job?

As I stated at the end of chapter 10, the programmers and other computer professionals I interviewed do not learn systems in a systematic way. Although formal training provides an overview, most Cellsoft employees do not seek to learn systems as a whole. On the other hand, the systems programmers I interviewed in other companies have a more holistic approach and are more interested in the totality of the software they work with. The latter are also more likely to relate their current software to other projects and jobs they worked on in the past, or simply to systems known from reading, from conversations with other programmers, or from experimentation on their own. Among the Cellsoft programmers, however, system learning is incidental rather than deliberate, and in some cases (for example, Newton's) it appears to happen minimally if at all.

The techniques these programmers use when they are learning systems are the same as those they use to solve problems (reading, working with the computer, and the other activities described in chapters 4 through 9), but the systems knowledge grows out of a combination of solved problems. The design of the software itself—the commonalities of language, directory structure, programming conventions across modules and facilities, and consistent user interface—is a prime contributor to programmers' ability to grasp the system as a whole.

2. Are some techniques more useful than others? If so, are those techniques more commonly employed? Does usefulness vary with the individual?

At Cellsoft the most important repository of system knowledge is the more experienced programmers. Documentation oriented to programmers is minimal. On-line help within the system itself is useless. The programmers themselves are often too busy coding to write down their knowledge. The computer does not keep track of its own interconnections. Therefore, programmers who want to learn about the system as a whole must derive this knowledge from long, fragmentary practice on their own or must go to other people, using them as teachers, mentors, or confirmers of individually gained knowledge (see chapter 7). Other than through formal presentations or training, there are no techniques for acquiring knowledge of this sort.

3. What are the variables that determine which techniques are used, in what order, and in what organizations?

The programmers in this study use formal training when it is available, when time permits, and when their managers encourage them to do so. They speak with one another on an informal basis many times each day and learn a great deal about their systems from these conversations.

One place where individual differences in learning style are apparent is in people's readiness to ask questions and to discuss their problems with others. As we have seen in chapter 7, some people bring questions to others immediately, while others work on their own for as long as possible. Curiously, there is little discussion of this aspect of learning style in the literature, possibly because so much research is based on students, who are expected to work alone (none of the Swedish depth-of-processing studies, for example, allowed for cooperative studying), or is limited (like field-independence/dependence research) to isolated individuals observed in laboratory settings.

When individuals are sitting at their desks, they engage in a variety of activities—reading code, specifications, and reference materials; "conversing" with their terminals; writing down notes; occasionally drawing diagrams—that help to build the system knowledge, but this knowledge is almost always incidental to a specific problem at hand and is often lost until work in another part of the system may alert the programmer to the relevance of a previous problem. Which of these activities a programmer performs, and in what order, is a function of the problem and of the individual, but I have not found any clear link between use of specific techniques and any other way of categorizing learning style. Programmers are pragmatists, using whatever materials come to hand in order to do their work. Again, because their work is not defined in terms of learning activities, or in terms of the software system as a whole, almost none of the programmers I interviewed (Barbara is a rare exception; Arthur, with his extensive note taking, may count as another) think in terms of systematizing their knowledge or of building models for themselves of the system as a whole.

To some extent, this is a function of the organization, but it is more a matter of the type of work to be performed and of the value placed on one or another aspect of the work. That is, Cellsoft is a business dedicated to making and selling a software product. The company's interest is in building software systems that are both properly functioning and commercially viable. It is much less concerned with developing and promulgating knowledge. Therefore, although it would be valuable to Cellsoft if its employees, and perhaps its customers as well, possessed broad understanding of the product and of the world in which it is used, providing something that works for the customers is the primary task. Knowledge is secondary.

In other environments this is less true. At MIT, where Stuart has been working on the X Windows project, the commercial value of X is a spinoff from basic research into windowing systems. Here, while recognizing potential industrial applications of the software is valuable, certainly in gaining corporate support and funding for research projects and joint ventures, the primary goal is the system itself and its applications and implications; the potential "customer base" is secondary. Therefore, Stuart and his colleagues can devote themselves more to individual research interests.

Horace works in a third type of environment. His company manufactures computers to be used mainly in artificial-intelligence applications. The company's clients are more likely themselves to be research oriented. Horace is an instructor rather than a professional programmer, and therefore he is more likely to set himself projects whose purpose is instructive rather than practical. As a result, learning can be a primary goal for him. In fact, the demands of his students require that he be as knowledgeable as possible in all aspects of his company's products, not just those for which he has immediate use. This is in sharp contrast to Cellsoft, where programmers have no time to learn what is not immediately relevant to the problem at hand, including the system as a whole.

Robert and Anne's environment provides yet another picture. There the end users are peers in the same company rather than external customers, so demands on their time, again by contrast with Cellsoft, are not directly tied to profitability. This leaves them time to pursue knowledge and to delve into details of their products. Also, Robert himself believes in the importance of this activity, allocating time for himself to work on projects just for the sake of learning and encouraging his employees to do the same (so long as they do not turn into pure "hackers" and fail to get any work done).

These various environments are also different from one another with respect to the educational resources available to their members. At Cellsoft, as we have seen, documentation is hard to come by, and on-line help for the software is very poor. In Robert and Anne's company, on-line documentation includes the company's entire set of product manuals, accessible through the CD-ROM "book reader" and readable at a developer's workstation that at the same time has another window displaying the problem at hand. Unix manuals are available on-line through the **man** commands to programmers on that system, and documentation to software developed in Unix is designed to be compatible with that of the computer system itself, making system-level learning easier through a common user interface. Manuals developed for Unix have features such as the permuted index that make them easier to use than more conventional reference materials.

Thus the most important variables in determining both the techniques of system learning and the extent to which it occurs are the following:

- The organization itself—its mandate, its values, and its willingness to commit time and money to its employees' learning

- The resources available for system learning, including the quality and quantity of reference materials and the quality of on-line help built into the system and available either through the operating system itself or through peripheral devices such as CD-ROM

- The particular job that an individual is called upon to perform

- The interest and support of management, whether individual supervisors or corporate management as a whole, in fostering, requiring, or rewarding learning

The similarities in learning modes of the Cellsoft programmers, when contrasted with those of the system programmers employed elsewhere, reveal that these external variables are far more significant indicators of how, and how much, these programmers learn their systems than any individual learning styles are. The differences are greater between organizations and occupations than between individuals doing the same kind of work in the same company.

4. Is there any relation between learning style and organizational culture?

The answer to this question follows from the previous one. If an organization encourages learning, it will take place. If an organization's priorities are elsewhere, learning will only happen so that employees can further those priorities, or it will happen in spite of them, to the extent that employees can control their own time and choose to use it in increasing their knowledge. The "learning style" formed by the type of work, the available resources, management support, and the "theories-in-use" of the organization (to use Chris Argyris's term, distinguished from the "espoused theories" that nearly always include a commitment to employee learning) play a more significant role than individual style as described in interviews or as measured by self-report inventories such as Schmeck's ILP or Kolb's LSI.

5. Is there any relation between learning style and workplace design?

I did not have sufficient information to answer this question. Certainly the porosity of the Cellsoft environment, the lack of private offices, and the placement of cubicles along corridors after the company's relocation in 1990 increased the number of encounters employees had with one another and the number of people to which any individual had easy access, and this had an impact on the degree to which people used one another as resources. However, this could have as much to do with the lack of documentation or with people's inclination to socialize as with workplace design. Also, in my interviews with computer professionals outside of Cellsoft, design and other environmental factors did not emerge as meaningful topics. Therefore, the issue must lie beyond the scope of this book.

The assumptions I stated in chapter 1 were largely borne out by the study. The people I interviewed did use a variety of activities, whose usefulness varied with the individual. The major exception was that most of the variables I thought to be important determinants of how these people approached learning—college major, amount of programming experience, training in programming and formal exposure to systems thinking—were not. It does appear from my interviews that the nature of the work and the culture of the organization are the most important variables in determining learning strategies and learning styles.

The most important conclusion of this study concerns not the particular schemes and resources that programmers use in learning systems, but the method used in deriving this knowledge. Like their knowledge, my own is tentative, iterative, forever growing, but never conclusive. Like theirs, mine grew from a number of resources: an often inadequate body of literature; a computer to be used as a plaything, a scribe, and a learning tool; my own prior training in education and research methods; my experience as a computer professional. Most important to me, of course, was the people from whom I learned; both as subjects and as coworkers, they were immensely valuable to me.

The knowledge I gained from this project was not, finally, tied to Kolb's, Witkin's, Schmeck's, or anyone else's conceptual scheme. It grew from the material itself and must forever remain situated in that material. In this respect I followed Garfinkel's ethnomethodological approach. The important concern of ethnomethodology is the meaning of activities and experiences for those who participate in them, not for someone seeking to observe or to study them. I have studied the process of making sense; the programmers strive to make sense of the world, and I strove to make sense of the programmers. Ethnomethodology is simply the study of that process.

Anyone who seeks to understand learning within an organization must become rooted in the organization and must come to know it as its members know it. Though this does not have to mean actually being a member, as I have been an employee at Cellsoft, it entails immersing oneself in the actual experiences of members through talking with them and if possible through participating in their experience. It most emphatically does not mean deriving theoretical pictures of experience from the outside, creating formal hypotheses, and then testing them through statistically validated instruments.

I am not saying, of course, that measurements have no value in the study of organizations or of learning within organizations. As Crompton and Jones (1988, p. 72), for example, pointed out, "In organizational research it is not a mutually exclusive decision between quantitative and qualitative methodology. In reality it is very difficult to study organizations without using both sorts of methods. In any event quantitative data always rests on qualitative distinctions." They elaborated as follows:

For example, . . . the mechanisms of the internal labour market have organizational specificities . . . which can best be researched using qualitative methods. The often confusing world of organizational titles can be penetrated, and the extent of real mobility more accurately assessed. However, if you wish to present evidence about the operation of internal labour markets you will have to collect some quantitative data. For example, you will need to know the average number of job moves made before becoming a bank manager, or the aggregate effects of post-entry qualifications on promotion. Such questions require quantitative methods. The issue turns on the appropriateness of methods, not with taking sides in the debate between qualitative and quantitative methodologies. (Crompton and Jones, 1988, pp. 72-73)

Similarly, in studying learning one can gather quantitative data as well—number of years of training, grade-point average, or number of computer courses taken. However, these types of measures are useless for getting at the experience of learning, or of any other kind of experience, for that matter. Experience is in the details, in the minutiae of work. The daily work life of computer professionals is the basis of this study. The job of understanding and explicating their knowledge, as Garfinkel described his own work, "seek[s] to treat practical activities, practical circumstances, and practical sociological reasoning as topics of empirical study, and by paying to the most commonplace activities of daily life the attention usually accorded extraordinary events, seek[s] to learn about them as phenomena in their own right" (Garfinkel, 1967, p. 1). There is no quantitative method of capturing experience.

The way computer professionals go about learning their environment and their jobs is far less a function of their "deep processing" skills, their "convergence" or "divergence," or their "field independence" than it is of the world around them and of how they perceive it. In this respect those who work together build and maintain that world jointly as they "grow older together" (Schutz, 1962, p. 220). In Schutz's thought, as Jehenson described it, "The social world is from the outset experienced as intersubjective. As an actor on the social scene, I can recognize my fellow-man not as a 'something,' but as a 'someone,' a 'someone like me' " (Jehenson, 1973, p. 221).

Schutz and Luckmann spoke of a "life-world" (*Lebenswelt*) underlying all experience:

The everyday reality of the life-world includes . . . not only the "nature" experienced by me but also the social (and therefore the cultural) world in which I find myself; the life-world is not created out of the merely material objects and events which I encounter in

> my environment. Certainly these are together one component of my
> surrounding world; nevertheless, there also belong to this all the
> meaning-strata which transform natural things into cultural objects,
> human bodies into fellow-men, and the movements of fellow-men
> into acts, gestures, and communications. (Schutz and Luckmann,
> 1973, p. 5)

This life-world is the product of all of a person's experiences over time, not
easily blended into stock attributes amenable to statistical correlation:

> Each step of my explication and understanding of the world is based
> at any given time on a stock of previous experience, my own
> immediate experiences as well as such experiences as are transmitted
> to me from my fellow-men and above all from my parents, teachers,
> and so on. All of these communicated and immediate experiences are
> included in a certain unity having the form of my stock of
> knowledge, which serves me as the reference schema for the actual
> step of my explication of the world. All of my experiences in the
> life-world are brought into relation to this schema, so that the objects
> and events in the life-world confront me from the outset in their
> typical character—in general as mountains and stones, trees and
> animals, more specifically as a ridge, as oaks, birds, fish, and so on.
> (Schutz and Luckmann, 1973, p. 7)

The learning I have described in this book takes place within the segment
of the life-world artificially blocked off and given the name "work," but this
does not mean that that segment is so detached from the rest of life that it does
not partake of normal experience. The process of learning a software system
must be studied as a part of the learner's experience, and the system itself is a
part of the life-world and must be grasped as such.

The "system" with which software professionals work can serve as an
account of the world within which it is embedded. Computer systems, to use
Garfinkel's term, are *reflexive*, referring back to themselves as documents of the
people and the work that produced them. The reality of a system lies in its use
and in its creators' and users' shared understanding of it, not in some external,
objective property, which does not in fact exist. Handel (1982, p. 36) said that
accounts

> do not more or less accurately describe things. Instead, they establish
> what is accountable in the setting in which they occur. Whether they
> are accurate or inaccurate by some other standard, accounts define
> reality for a situation in the sense that people act on the basis of what
> is accountable in the situation of their action. . . . The account
> provides a basis for action, a definition of what is real, and it is acted
> upon so long as it remains accountable. *If men define things as real,*

the definitions are real in their consequences. Whatever the content of an account, whatever it seems to be about, the effect of accounts is to provide a definition upon which action can be based. Accounts establish what people in a situation will believe, accept as sound, accept as proper—that is, they establish what is accountable.

Thus, if the "system" is a loose, porous, "accountable" thing—rather like the cubicle walls at Cellsoft—then the process of learning it is simultaneously the processes of interacting with it, changing it, and defining it. Because the system is reflexive, it is also, to use another key concept of Garfinkel's, *indexical*; that is, its meaning is dependent on the time and place of its use. There are different versions of Cellsoft's system for different customers. Programmers view it in different aspects, and their understanding of it is a function of their location as well as of any intrinsic properties it possesses.

The proper method for studying what members do as they come to understand a system of this kind is to follow them as they do it: to immerse oneself in the life-world of the computer professionals and to see it as they do, but even more to reconstruct how they came to see it that way, or better still to be present as their understanding grows. Learning-style theories can at best provide a superficial typology, a set of glosses on the situation that must be fleshed out by observation and if possible by participation in the actual work if one is to grasp the process of learning the system in its full complexity; for the learning and the process are part of one another. Here is where the iterative nature of learning "the system" becomes clear: System (including its human members, as well as its artifacts such as software and documentation) and learner (the relative novice in the community) each grow and have impacts upon the other; for the system, ultimately, is the account of its many learners. The learner of the process (the researcher), in leading his subjects (the members) to explicate their own understanding, affects the system as well.

RECOMMENDATIONS

Recommendations derived from this research fall into two general categories. The first is directed at researchers in education and business who would like to learn more about the application of learning-style theory to the workplace or who are interested in organizational learning. The second category of recommendations is directed to those who train programmers, whether in universities or in industry, and to professionals in the software industry concerned with improving their employees' learning and training.

Recommendations for Researchers

1. The most salient criticism of learning-style research, as described in Chapter 10, is its distance from the work lives of adults. Therefore, I begin my research recommendations by advocating more studies like this one, grounded in ethnomethodology or a phenomenological approach to understanding learning as an artifact of the learner's life-world. I have focused on a small group of programmers and other computing professionals, mainly employed by one small company. It would be useful if more studies of this kind could be conducted in order to find out whether people doing similar work in similar places learn systems in roughly the same way. Such studies should address both the unique lives and worlds of the individuals involved and the unique conditions of each organization in which they work. Perhaps researchers can graph the interactions of individual life experiences with a common organizational culture in order to distinguish individual from environmental influences more fully than I have been able to do. From a number of studies like this, it would be possible either to develop more general theories of how computer professionals learn systems or to analyze more fully the organizational variables that produce differences in corporate learning styles.

2. In order to reconcile qualitative studies like this one with the more familiar, quantitatively oriented learning-style research described in chapter 10 and more fully summarized in Bonham's (1988) dissertation, researchers in this area should expand the individual biographies in this study and others like it in order to derive new typologies of resources and their use (as I have done in chapters 5 through 8) and to connect individuals' styles in using resources with other aspects of their lives, as well as with their specific jobs or organizations.

3. Laboratory-based research into learning styles should include experiments in which students can learn their assigned materials from a variety of media rather than simply, as in the Gothenburg studies, from a printed text. Also, studies should allow students to use one another as resources rather than only evaluate students' work in isolation, because the use of people as resources is an important component of real-world learning.

4. A limit of the current study is that it dwells on *activities* of its subjects and neglects their inner world. Future research should attempt to construct the programmer's inner world and to discover the meaning of the activities described here to those who participate in them.

Recommendations for Professionals Who Deal with Programmers

The first two recommendations are for instructors in academic programs geared to computer professionals:

1. Academic courses geared to programmers, in addition to focusing on specific elements of the craft, such as programming languages, and general structures, such as algorithms, should also pay attention to the understanding and maintenance of large systems, because this activity constitutes much, if not all, of many programmers' professional lives.

2. Academic courses preparing programmers for actual jobs (as opposed to courses dealing with theory or techniques) should simulate actual programming environments as much as possible and offer students an opportunity to learn by using a variety of methods (copying templates, experimentation, reading and debugging source programs) similar to those encountered in actual jobs. Students should be encouraged to collaborate as much as possible in building and maintaining large systems and in reviewing one another's work.

Recommendations 3-7 apply to corporate training, whether in-house or offered for students from many companies:

3. Corporate training should focus on programmers' jobs, not just on disembodied skills. Jobs should be carefully modeled, based on organizational research like this study. Training should be as specific and as situated in the workers' exact environment as possible.

4. Training classes should be staggered so that students are not separated from their work for long. Students should be encouraged to integrate new skills with their work as soon as possible and only return for more training when they have reached the limits of that integration.

5. Instructors and course developers should create materials that double as references. Student guides should be easy to consult after training is completed.

6. Training should include on-line examples that remain available to students after courses are completed. That is, the examples should be packaged with the products the students are learning so that students can consult them easily from their terminals or workstations when they return to work.

7. Where possible, computer-based training should be embedded directly into the software, so that programmers can use their own work as a training exercise.

The next group of recommendations pertains to making software documentation more suitable for facilitating learning:

8. Documentation should be accessible on line as much as possible, both in simple format, such as Unix **man** pages, or in more complex format, such as the Digital book reader, in which an entire set of manuals is available in CD-ROM.

9. Product documentation should look as similar as possible to that of the operating system under which the product is written. Documentation of

software written for the Macintosh strives to achieve this; similarly, X Windows documentation is written to resemble that of Unix.

10. Reference manuals should use the same examples as training materials, and these should be placed on line and bundled in with the product. A good example of this is Digital's VAX Layered Architecture products, which provide a set of examples that are uniform throughout the product line and that are used with documentation, training materials, and the product itself as illustrations.

The next group of recommendations is for workplace designers interested in constructing learning environments:

11. To create a learning environment, it is essential to consolidate the resources described in this book. That is, all learning materials must be near to hand. Printed documentation or on-line references should be convenient for all programmers, with little or no contention.

12. Workers should be placed such that more experienced people are accessible to serve as mentors for less experienced people.

13. Training should be readily accessible in computer-based formats (both standalone and embedded into products and the environment), formal courses staggered through the work cycle and convenient to the work site, and examples programmed into the standard software.

The final recommendations are for management concerned with fostering system learning by employees:

14. Mentors should be assigned to new and inexperienced programmers. Mentoring should be a formal part of senior programmers' and managers' responsibilities.

15. People should be given time to learn. Time for experiment and play as well as for formal learning must be factored into project schedules.

16. Software systems should be designed to look like systems, with consistent user interfaces, directory structures, and programming styles within and across products.

17. Most important, managers at all levels must examine their genuine commitment to creating a learning environment. If learning truly matters, then resources, including time, must be allocated. If management finds it more important to meet deadlines and to reduce costs by keeping staffing down and increasing each individual's workload, it must deal with the consequences that are bound to occur when programmers, in fact, do not learn the systems on which they must work.

References

Andres, C. (1980). *CPU wars.* Westford, MA: Chthon Press.

Argyris, C. and Schon, D. (1980). *Theory in practice: Increasing professional effectiveness.* San Francisco: Jossey-Bass.

Armstrong, P., and McDaniel, E. (1986). Relationships between learning styles and performance on problem-solving tasks. *Psychological Reports, 59,* 1135-1138.

Ash, B. L. F. (1982). An investigation of the relationship between field-dependent/field-independent cognitive style, sex-role identity, and personality type among young adult female community college office occupations and business administration majors. Doctoral dissertation, Boston University.

Ash, B. L. F. (1986). Identifying learning styles and matching strategies for teaching and learning. (ERIC Document Reproduction Service No. ED 270 142, JC 860 277)

Bartling, C. A. (1987). Reliability and validity of a shortened form of the Inventory of Learning Processes. *Educational and Psychological Measurement, 47,* 253-260.

Bernard, J. (1990). *The cellular connection: A guide to cellular telephones.* 4th ed. Mendocino, CA: Quantum Publishing.

Bloom, B. S. (Ed.) (1956). *Taxonomy of educational objectives: Handbook 1: Cognitive domain.* New York: David McKay.

Bogdan, R. C., and Biklen, S. K. (1982). *Qualitative research for education: An introduction to theory and methods.* Boston: Allyn and Bacon.

Bonham, L. A. (1988). *Theoretical and practical differences and similarities among selected cognitive and learning styles of adults: An analysis of the literature.* Doctoral dissertation, University of Georgia. *Dissertation Abstracts International, 48,* 2788A. (University Microfilms No. 88-00,255)

Braverman, H. (1974). *Labor and monopoly capital.* New York: Monthly Review Press.

Buchanan, D., Boddy, D., and McCalman, J. (1988). Getting in, getting on, getting out, and getting back. In A. Bryman (Ed.), *Doing research in organizations* (pp. 53-67). London: Routledge.

Button, G., and Sharrock, W. (1994). The mundane work of writing and reading computer programs. In P. ten Have and G. Psathas (Eds.), *Situated order*. Washington, DC: University Press of America (in press).

Charmaz, K. The grounded theory method: An explication and interpretation. In R. M. Emerson (Ed.), *Contemporary field research: A collection of readings* (pp. 109-126). Prospect Heights, IL: Waveland Press.

Clapes, A. L. (1993). *Softwars: The legal battles for control of the global software industry*. Westport, CT: Quorum Books.

Cook, D., and Roach, C. (1991). *Roaming . . . cellular on the the go*. Monroe, LA: Century Cellunet, Inc.

Craik, F. I. M. (1977). Depth of processing in recall and recognition. In S. Dornic (Ed.), *Attention and performance* (Vol. 6, pp. 679-697). Hillsdale, NJ: Lawrence Erlbaum Associates.

Craik, F. I. M., and Lockhart, R. S. (1972). Levels of processing: A framework for memory research. *Journal of Verbal Learning and Verbal Behavior, 11*, 671-684.

Craik, F. I. M., and Tulving, E. (1975). Depth of processing and retention of words in episodic memory. *Journal of Experimental Psychology: General, 104*, 268-294.

Crompton, R., and Jones, G. (1988). Researching white collar organizations: Why sociologists should not stop doing case studies. In A. Bryman (Ed.), *Doing research in organizations* (pp. 68-81). London: Routledge.

Dorsey, O. L., and Pierson, M. J. (1984). A descriptive study of adult learning styles in a nontraditional education program. *Lifelong Learning, 7* (8), 8-11.

Emerson, R. M. (Ed.). (1983). *Contemporary field research: A collection of readings*. Prospect Heights, IL: Waveland Press.

Entwistle, N. (1983). *Styles of learning and teaching*. New York: John Wiley and Sons.

Etzioni, A. (Ed.). (1969). *The semi-professions and their organization: Teachers, nurses, social workers*. New York: Free Press.

Fox, R. D. (1984). Learning styles and instructional preferences in continuing education for health professionals: A validity study of the LSI. *Adult Education Quarterly, 35*, 72-85.

Fransson, A. (1977). On qualitative differences in learning: IV—Effects of intrinsic motivation and extrinsic test anxiety on process and outcome. *British Journal of Educational Psychology, 47*, 244-257.

Gadzella, B. M., Ginther, D. W., and Williamson, J. D. (1986). Differences in learning processes and academic achievement. *Perceptual and Motor Skills, 62* , 151-156.

Garfinkel, H. (1967). *Studies in ethnomethodology*. Cambridge, England: Polity Press.

Garfinkel, H. (Ed.). (1986). *Ethnomethodological studies of work.* London: Routledge and Kegan Paul.

Garlinger, D. K. (1987). *Field-independence and free recall memory performance and strategy use: The effect of strategy instructions and inherent list organization.* Doctoral dissertation, Kansas State University. *Dissertation Abstracts International, 48,* 2833A.

Glaser, B. (1978). *Theoretical sensitivity: Advances in the methodology of grounded theory.* Mill Valley, CA: Sociology Press.

Glaser, B., and Strauss, A. L. (1967). *The discovery of grounded theory: Strategies for qualitative research.* Chicago: Aldine.

Goetz, J. P., and LeCompte, M. D. (1981). Ethnographic research and the problem of data reduction. *Anthropology and Education Quarterly, 12*(1), 51-70.

Goffman, E. (1959). *The presentation of self in everyday life.* New York: Doubleday Anchor.

Goffman, E. (1967). *Interaction ritual.* New York: Doubleday Anchor.

Goffman, E. (1969). *Strategic interaction.* Philadelphia: University of Pennsylvania Press.

Goffman, E. (1974). *Frame analysis.* New York: Harper Colophon.

Goodenough, D. R. (1986). History of the field dependence construct. In M. Bertini, L. Pizzimiglio, and S. Wapner (Eds.), *Field dependence in psychological theory, research, and application: Two symposia in memory of Herman A. Witkin* (pp. 5-13). Hillsdale, NJ: Lawrence Erlbaum Associates.

Griggs, W. H. (1980). *On the measurement of the learning press of technical work environments.* Doctoral dissertation, Case Western Reserve University.

Gypen, J. (1980). *Learning style adaptation in professional careers: The case of engineers and social workers.* Doctoral dissertation, Case Western Reserve University.

Halpin, G., and Peterson, H. (1986). Accommodating instruction to learners' field independence/dependence: A study of effects on achievement and attitudes. *Perceptual and Motor Skills, 62,* 967-974.

Handel, W. (1982). *Ethnomethodology: How people make sense.* Englewood Cliffs, NJ: Prentice-Hall.

Jehanson, R. (1973). A phenomenological approach to the study of the formal organization. In G. Psathas (Ed.), *Phenomenological sociology: Issues and applications* (pp. 219-247). New York: John Wiley and Sons.

Joffe, C. (1977). *Friendly intruders: Childcare professionals and family life.* Berkeley: University of California Press.

Kelley, R. E. (1985). *The gold-collar worker: Harnessing the brainpower of the new work force.* Reading, MA: Addison-Wesley.

Kernighan, B. W., and Pike, R. (1984). *The Unix programming environment.* Englewood Cliffs, NJ: Prentice-Hall.

Kling, R., and Gerson E. M. (1977). The social dynamics of innovation in the computing world. *Symbolic Interaction, 1*, 132-146.

Kolb, D. A. (1974). On management and the learning process. In D.A.Kolb, I.M.Rubin, and J.M.McIntyre (Eds.), *Organizational psychology: A book of readings*. Englewood Cliffs, NJ: Prentice-Hall.

Kolb, D. A. (1981). Disciplinary inquiry norms and student learning styles: Diverse pathways for growth. In A. Chickering (Ed.), *The Modern American College* (pp. 232-253. San Francisco: Jossey-Bass.

Kolb, D. A. (1984). *Experiential learning: Experience as the source of learning and development*. Englewood Cliffs, NJ: Prentice-Hall.

Kolb, D. A. (1985). *Learning-Style Inventory: Self-scoring inventory and interpretation booklet*. Boston: McBer and Company.

Kolb, D. A., and Goldman, M. (1973). *Toward a typology of learning styles and learning environments: An investigation of the impact of learning styles and discipline demands on the academic performance, social adaptation, and career choices of M.I.T. seniors*. M.I.T. Sloan School Working Paper No. 688-73.

Kolb, D. A., and Wolfe, D. (1981). *Professional education and career development: A cross-sectional study of adaptive competencies in experiential learning*. Final report NIE grant no. NIE-G-77-0053. (ERIC ED 209 493 CE 030 519)

Kraft, P. (1977). *Programmers and managers: The routinization of computer programming in the United States*. New York: Springer-Verlag.

Kraft, P., and Dubnoff, S. (1986). Job content, fragmentation, and control in computer software work. *Industrial Relations, 25*, 184-196.

Leibowitz, D., Gross, J., and Buck, E. (1991). *The cellular communications industry*. New York: Donaldson, Lufkin, and Jenrette Securities Corporation.

Marshall, J. C., and Merritt, S. L. (1985). Reliability and construct validity of alternate forms of the Learning Style Inventory. *Educational and Psychological Measurement, 45*, 931-937.

Marshall, J. C., and Merritt, S. L. (1986). Reliability and construct validity of the Learning Style Questionnaire. *Educational and Psychological Measurement, 46*, 257-262.

Marton, F., and Saljö, R. (1976a). On qualitative differences in learning: I— Outcome and process. *British Journal of Educational Psychology, 46*, 4-11.

Marton, F., and Saljö, R. (1976b). On qualitative differences in learning: II—Outcome as a function of the learner's conception of the task. *British Journal of Educational Psychology, 46*, 115-127.

McLaughlin, M.L. (1984). *Conversation: How talk is organized*. Santa Barbara: Sage Publications.

Melton, A. W., and Martin, E. (Eds.). (1972). *Coding processes in human memory*. Washington, DC: Winston and Sons.

Merritt, S. L., and Marshall, J. C. (1984). Reliability and construct validity of ipsative and normative forms of the Learning Style Inventory. *Educational and Psychological Measurement, 44*, 463-471.

Messick, S. (1976). Personality consistencies in cognition and creativity. In S. Messick (Ed.), *Individuality in learning* (pp. 4-22). San Francisco: Jossey-Bass.

Nash, J. E. (1990). Working at and working: Computer fritters. *Journal of Contemporary Ethnography, 19*, 207-225.

Paivio, A. (1971). *Imagery and verbal processes.* New York: Holt, Rinehart, and Winston.

Paivio, A., and Csapo, K. (1973). Picture superiority in free recall: Imagery or dual coding. *Cognitive Psychology, 5*, 176-206.

Parnas, D. L. (1984). Software engineering principles. *Infor, 22(4),* 303-316.

Parnas, D. L, and Clements, P. C. (1985). *A rational design process: How and why to fake it.* Software Engineering/Education Cooperative Project, Publication No. 3. University of Victoria, BC, and IBM Canada Ltd.

Penzias, A. (1989). *Ideas and information: Managing in a high-tech world.* New York: W. W. Norton.

Quinlan, D. M., and Blatt, S. J. (1972). Field articulation and performance under stress: Differential predictions in surgical and psychiatric nursing training. *Journal of Consulting and Clinical Psychology, 39*, 517.

Reid, E. (1981). *Training higher-level cognitive skills.* Doctoral dissertation, Southern Illinois University, Carbondale.

Ribich, F. D., and Schmeck, R. R. (1979). Multivariate relationships between measures of learning style and memory. *Journal of Research in Personality, 13*, 515-529.

Ross, M. (1989, February). The remarkable growth of mobile cellular communications. *Spectrum: Telecommunications industry—Equipment and networking.* Burlington, MA: Arthur D. Little Decision Resources. 2-1 to 2-10.

Sacks, H., Schegloff, E. A., and Jefferson, G. (1978). A simplest systematics for the organization of turn taking for conversation. In J. Schenkein (Ed.), *Studies in the organization of conversational interaction.* New York: Academic Press.

Schank, R. (1984). *The cognitive computer: On language, learning, and artificial intelligence.* Reading, MA: Addison-Wesley.

Schein, E. (1985). *Organizational culture and leadership.* San Francisco: Jossey-Bass.

Schmeck, R. R. (1980). Relationships between measures of learning style and reading comprehension. *Perceptual and Motor Skills, 50*, 461-462.

Schmeck, R. R. (1983). Learning styles of college students. In R. F. Dillon and R. R. Schmeck (Eds.), *Individual differences in cognition* (Vol. 1, pp. 233-279). New York: Academic Press.

Schmeck, R. R., and Ribich, F. D. (1978). Construct validation of the Inventory of Learning Processes. *Applied Psychological Measurement, 2,* 551-562.

Schmeck, R. R., Ribich, F. D., and Ramanaiah, N. (1977). Development of a self-report inventory for assessing individual differences in learning processes. *Applied Psychological Measurement, 1,* 413-431.

Schoenfeld, A. H. (1983). Beyond the purely cognitive: Belief systems, social cognitions, and metacognitions as driving forces in intellectual performance. *Cognitive Science, 7,* 329-363.

Schoenfeld, A. H. (1987). Cognitive science and mathematics education: An overview. In A. H. Schoenfeld (Ed.), *Cognitive science and mathematics education.* Hillsdale, NJ: Lawrence Erlbaum Associates.

Schutz, A. (1962). *Collected papers I: The problem of social reality.* The Hague: Martinus Nijhoff.

Schutz, A., and Luckmann, T. (1973). *The structures of the life-world.* Evanston, IL: Northwestern University Press.

Senge, P. (1990). *The fifth discipline: The art and practice of the learning organization.* New York: Doubleday.

Shipman, S., and Shipman, V. C. (1985). Cognitive styles: Some conceptual, methodological, and applied issues. In E. W. Gordon (Ed.), *Review of research in education* (Vol. 12, pp. 229-291). Washington, DC: American Educational Research Associates.

Sims, R. R. (1981). Assessing competencies in experiential learning theory: A person-job congruence model of effectiveness in professional careers. *Dissertation Abstracts International, 42,* 1219B-1220B.

Stice, J. E. (1987). Using Kolb's learning cycle to improve student learning. *Engineering Education, 77,* 291-296.

Suchman, L. (1987). *Plans and situated actions.* Cambridge, England: Cambridge University Press.

Svensson, L. (1977). On qualitative differences in learning: III—Study skills and learning. *British Journal of Educational Psychology, 47,* 233-243.

Threadgill, J. A. (1979). The relationship of field-independent/dependent cognitive style and two methods of instruction in mathematics learning. *Journal for Research in Mathematics Education, 5,* 219-222.

Toffler, A. (1971). *Future shock.* New York: Bantam.

Turkle, S. (1983). *The second self: Computers and the human spirit.* New York: Touchstone Books/Simon and Schuster.

Watkins, D., and Hattie, J. (1981a). The internal structure and predictive validity of the Inventory of Learning Processes: Some Australian and Filipino data. *Educational and Psychological Measurement, 41,* 511-514.

Watkins, D., and Hattie, J. (1981b). The learning processes of Australian university students: Investigations of contextual and personological factors. *British Journal of Educational Psychology, 51,* 384-393.

Weinberg, G. M. (1971). *The psychology of computer programming.* New York: Van Nostrand Reinhold.

Weinberg, G. M. (1975). *An introduction to general systems thinking*. New York: John Wiley and Sons.

Weizenbaum, J. (1976). *Computer power and human reason*. San Francisco: W. H. Freeman.

Witkin, H. (1976). Cognitive styles in academic performance and in teacher-student relations. In S. Messick (Ed.), *Individuality in learning* (pp. 38-72). San Francisco: Jossey-Bass.

Witkin, H., and Goodenough, D. R. (1977). Field dependence and interpersonal behavior. *Psychological Bulletin, 84*, 661-689.

Witkin, H., and Goodenough, D. R. (1981). *Cognitive styles: Essence and origins. Psychological Issues*, Monograph 51. New York: International Universities Press.

Yates, J., and Orlikowski, W. J. (1992). Genres of organizational communication: A structurational approach to studying communication and media. *Academy of Management Review, 17*, 299-326.

Index

About the Author

MARC SACKS is an Advanced Systems Engineer with Electronic Data Systems. His areas of expertise include software development, training, documentation, and quality. His research interests include on-the-job learning, organizational behavior, and qualitative methodologies. He is involved in a variety of professional and community activities relating to education, computers, and research.